GOD OF MY VICTORY
The Ancient Hymn in Habakkuk 3

HARVARD SEMITIC MUSEUM

HARVARD SEMITIC MONOGRAPHS

edited by
Frank Moore Cross

Number 38
GOD OF MY VICTORY
The Ancient Hymn in Habakkuk 3
by
Theodore Hiebert

Theodore Hiebert

GOD OF MY VICTORY
The Ancient Hymn in Habakkuk 3

Scholars Press
Atlanta, Georgia

GOD OF MY VICTORY:
The Ancient Hymn in Habakkuk 3

Theodore Hiebert

Library of Congress Cataloging in Publication Data

Hiebert, Theodore.
God of my victory.

(Harvard Semitic monographs ; no. 38)
Bibliography: p.
1. Bible. O.T. Habakkuk III--Theology.
2. Theophanies in the Bible. I. Bible. O.T.
Habakkuk. II. Title. III. Series.
BS1635.5.H54 1986 244'.9506 86-24807
ISBN 1-55540-077-9

Printed in the United States of America
on acid-free paper

To Paula

PREFACE

The most lively issue in Habakkuk studies is the meaning of Chapter 3 and its relationship to the prophetic corpus as a whole. The vivid and, in its canonical context, unusual imagery of this theophanic hymn has intrigued and puzzled exegetes. The study which follows is an effort to address this issue in a synthetic fashion—employing insights from textual, poetic, linguistic, historical, archaeological, and theological investigations based on the most recent data available in these areas. The intention is to clarify, as far as possible, the source of this poem in Israelite life and the reason for its position in the canon in order to contribute to the developing understanding of this brief but complex prophetic book.

The results of this study were presented to Harvard University as a doctoral thesis in 1984. The thesis was directed by Frank Moore Cross, to whom I am deeply indebted. His scholarship, in particular on the history of the religion of Israel and on Israel's early poetry, has provided the basic orientation for my research and thought. His personal suggestions were seminal in the development of the thesis presented here.

The guidance and encouragement of the other members of my thesis committee, Paul D. Hanson and Michael David Coogan, also deserve special acknowledgement. The work by Paul Hanson on the development of apocalyptic thought in Israel was foundational for the understanding of the canonical position of Habakkuk 3 presented in this study. Michael Coogan's careful critiques in conceptual matters and in the smallest details from the earliest drafts to the completion of the work contributed a rigor the study would otherwise have lacked.

My interest in the study of Habakkuk actually began at Princeton Theological Seminary as a student of Bernhard W. Anderson. His suggestion that I examine Habakkuk in a senior thesis, as well as his literary and theological sensitivity, continue to influence my work.

Many of the results of Chapter 2 of this study have appeared in "The Use of Inclusion in Habakkuk 3" in *Directions in Biblical Hebrew Poetry*, edited by Elaine R. Follis. I am grateful to JSOT Press for permission to use that material in this volume.

Thanks are due to Janine Genelin, at Gustavus Adolphus College, for the typing of the original manuscript, and to Diane D. LeNoir and Joyce Miller-Grant at Louisiana State University, who prepared the manuscript for this monograph series. I am particularly grateful to Neal Stoltzfus who solved all the computer glitches necessary to produce the fine quality print of this volume. The TEX system developed by Donald Knuth at Stanford University was used in the production of the final copy.

Finally, I wish to thank my wife, Paula, with whom I have discussed this work from beginning to end and who has offered assistance throughout the preparation of this study.

Theodore Hiebert
Baton Rouge, Louisiana
May 1986

TABLE OF CONTENTS

ABBREVIATIONS

AASOR	Annual of the American Schools of Oriental Research
AB	Anchor Bible
AJSL	*American Journal of Semitic Languages and Literature*
ANEP	J. B. Pritchard (ed.), *Ancient Near East in Pictures*
ANET	J. B. Pritchard (ed.), *Ancient Near Eastern Texts*
Aq	Aquila
BA	*Biblical Archaeologist*
BAR	*Biblical Archaeology Review*
Barb	Barberini Codex; the Barberini Greek version of Habakkuk 3
BASOR	*Bulletin of the American Schools of Oriental Research*
BDB	F. Brown, S. R. Driver, and C. A. Briggs, *Hebrew and English Lexicon of the Old Testament*
BHH	B. Reicke and L. Rost (eds.), *Biblisch-Historisches Handwörbuch*
BHS	*Biblia hebraica stuttgartensia*
Bib	*Biblica*
BKAT	Biblischer Kommentar: Altes Testament
BZ	*Biblische Zeitschrift*
CAD	*The Assyrian Dictionary of the Oriental Institute of the University of Chicago*
CAH	*Cambridge Ancient History*
CAT	Commentaire de l'Ancien Testament
CBQ	*Catholic Biblical Quarterly*
CTA	A. Herdner, *Corpus des table ttes en cunéiformes alphabétiques*
EA	J. A. Knudtzon (ed.), *Die El-Amarna-Tafeln*
GKC	Gesenius' Hebrew Grammar, ed. E. Kautzsch, tr. A. E. Cowley
HTR	*Harvard Theological Review*
HUCA	*Hebrew Union College Annual*
ICC	International Critical Commentary
IDB	G. A. Buttrick (ed.), *Interpreter's Dictionary of the Bible*
IDBSup	Supplementary volume to *IDB*
IEJ	*Israel Exploration Journal*

JAOS	*Journal of the American Oriental Society*
JB	A. Jones (ed.), *Jerusalem Bible*
JBC	R. E. Brown et al. (eds.), *The Jerome Biblical Commentary*
JBL	*Journal of Biblical Literature*
JE	The Yahwist and the Elohist: epic tradition
JEA	*Journal of Egyptian Archaeology*
JNES	*Journal of Near Eastern Studies*
JPOS	*Journal of the Palestine Oriental Society*
JQR	*Jewish Quarterly Review*
JSS	*Journal of Semitic Studies*
JTS	*Journal of Theological Studies*
KAI	H. Donner and W. Röllig, *Kanaanäische und aramäische Inschriften*
KAT	E. Sellin (ed.), Kommentar zum A. T.
LSJ	Liddell-Scott-Jones, *Greek-English Lexicon*
LXX	Septuagint
MT	Masoretic Text
NAB	*New American Bible*
NEB	*New English Bible*
OG	Old Greek
OL	Old Latin
Or	*Orientalia* (Rome)
PEQ	*Palestine Exploration Quarterly*
PRU	*Le Palais royal d'Ugarit*
R	The scroll of the Minor Prophets from Naḥal Ḥeber
RB	*Revue biblique*
RSV	*Revised Standard Version*
Sem	*Semitica*
Sym	Symmachus
Tg	Targum
Th	Theodotion
TZ	*Theologische Zeitschrift*
UF	*Ugaritische Forschungen*
Vg	Vulgate
VT	*Vetus Testamentum*
VTSup	*Vetus Testamentum, Supplements*
ZAW	*Zeitschrift für die alttestamentliche Wissenschaft*

INTRODUCTION

The unique character of Habakkuk 3 has led to much debate about its form, setting, and interpretation and about its relationship to the prophetic corpus within which it is located. The recent trend has been to interpret this poem as a prayer of the prophet Habakkuk within which his vision is described. Thus it represents an integral element of the Habakkuk corpus and reflects the thought of late seventh century prophecy. An earlier generation of scholars, however, widely suspected that Chapter 3, because of its peculiarities, originated from a source other than the prophet Habakkuk and was appended to the corpus bearing his name.

The purpose of this study is to reexamine this poem and the issues it raises in order to clarify the nature of the poem itself as well as its relationship to the prophecy of Habakkuk. The initial chapter includes a study of the text of Habakkuk 3 and a new translation. Chapter 2 is an analysis of the literary structure of the poem which focuses on inclusion as the basic technique used in the construction of the poem. Chapter 3 presents an interpretation of the poem, with conclusions about its original form, setting, and place within Israelite religion. The final chapter examines the relationship between Habakkuk 3 and the first two chapters of Habakkuk.

The conclusion of this inquiry is that the suspicions of older scholars were in fact sound. Offered here, though, is a new proposal for the origin and the history of the transmission of Habakkuk 3. The thesis presented in the following pages is that Habakkuk 3 is an ancient Hymn of Triumph, comprised of a theophany in two stanzas (vv 3–7, 8–15) enclosed within a literary framework (vv 2, 16–19). The original text, linguistic features, literary form, historical allusions, and religious motifs all suggest that this poem was composed in the premonarchic era as a recitation of the victory of the divine warrior over cosmic and earthly enemies.

Preserved in a collection of psalms and eventually reinterpreted as a prophecy of God's eschatological victory, the old hymn was added to the Habakkuk corpus by postexilic editors of the prophets who were caught up in the apocalyptic fervor of their era. Once included in the corpus of Habakkuk, the hymn was understood as a prophetic vision described within the prophet's prayer for God's salvation. Habakkuk 3 is therefore not to be understood as representing the thought of Habakkuk or the prophetic conceptions of the late seventh century B.C.E. It is rather a witness, in its original form, to Israel's earliest religious thought and, in its canonical position, to the apocalyptic expectations of the postexilic era.

CHAPTER 1

The Text of Habakkuk 3

No study of Habakkuk 3 can proceed far without a thorough examination of its text. Certain key points in the poem have suffered disruption in one or more versions, and careful textual judgments are an essential part of the interpretive process. Furthermore, variants in the versions provide clues to the oldest interpretations of Habakkuk 3 and thereby provide assistance in recovering the original meaning of the poem.

In this chapter, the text of the poem itself is examined. The title (v 1) and the musical notations (*selâ*, vv 3, 9, 13; and the subscription, v 19b) which accompany Habakkuk 3 will be dealt with in Chapter 4. The numbers in the Hebrew text which follows refer to numbered sections of Chapter 1 in which the Hebrew text preceding these numbers is discussed. Notes within these numbered sections of Chapter 1 appear as endnotes at the end of the work. Notations regarding poetic structure have been included with the text for easy reference. These notations will be discussed in detail in Chapter 2.

Translation

Yahweh, I heard the account of you.
I am in awe, Yahweh, of your work.

Through the years you sustained life.
Through the years you made yourself known.
In turmoil you remembered to have compassion.

'Eloah from Teman came,
The Holy One from Mount Paran.

His majesty covered heaven,
His praise filled earth,
He shone like a destroying fire.

Horns ...
He rejoiced in the day of his strength.

Before him marched Deber.
Resheph advanced at his feet.

He stood and shook earth,
He looked and startled nations.

Ancient mountains were shattered,
Eternal hills collapsed,
Eternal orbits were destroyed.

Tents of Kushan shook,
Tent curtains of the land of Midian.

Poetic Structure				Text	V
7	l:l		I	יהוה שמעתי שמעך	2
7				יראתי[1] יהוה פעלך	
6	l:l:l			בקרב[2] שנים חיית[3]	
7				בקרב שנים תודע[4]	
6				ברגז[5] רחם[6] תזכור	
7	l:l	A	II	אלוה מתימן[7] יבוא	3
6				()[8]קדוש מהר פארן[9]	
6	l:l:l	B		כסה שמים הודו	
8				()תהלתו מלאה[10] ()[11]ארץ	
6				()נגה[12] כאור[13] ()הוה[14]	4
	:l	C		קרנים . . .[15]	
6				ישמח ביום עזה[16]	
6	l:l	D		לפניו ילך דבר[17]	5
6				()יצא רשף[18] לרגליו	
7	l:l	C'		עמד וינדד[19] ארץ	6
7				ראה ויתר[20] גוים	
8	l:l:l	B'		()יתפצצו[21] הררי עד[22]	
7				שחו גבעות עולם	
9				הליכות[23] עולם ל()תחתאן[24]	7
8	l:l	A'		()[25]אהלי כושן ירגזון[26]	
6				יריעות ארץ מדין	

Translation

Against River did it burn, Yahweh,
Against River, your anger,
Against Sea, your rage;

When you mounted your horses,
Your chariot of victory?

You laid bare your bow,
You sated the shafts of your quiver.

Earth was split open with rivers,
Mountains saw you and heaved.

Clouds poured down water,
Deep uttered its voice.

Sun lifted its hands high,
Moon stood in its princely station.

Brightly, your arrows darted,
Brilliantly, your lightning spear.

In indignation you marched on earth,
In anger you trampled nations.

You advanced for the victory of your militia,
For the victory of the militia of your anointed one.

Poetic Structure				Text	V
9	1:1:1	A	III	הבנהר-ם[27] חרה[28] יהוה	8
7				הבנהר-ם[29] אפך	
6				אם בים עברתך[30]	
6	1:1			כי תרכב[31] על סוסיך[32]	
6				מרכבת[33] ישעתך[34]	
6	1:1			ערה תער[35] קשתך	9
7				שבעת[36] מטי[37] אשפתך[38]	
7	1:1	B		נהרות תבקע ארץ[39]	
7				ראוך יחילו[40] הרים[41]	10
6	1:1			זרמו[42] מים עבות[43]	
6				נתן תהום קולו	
7	1:1			רום ידיהו נשא שמש[44]	11
7				ירח עמד זבלה[45]	
8	1:1	B'		לאור חציך יהלכו[46]	
7				לנגה ברק חניתך[47]	
5	1:1			בזעם תצעד[48] ארץ	12
6				באף תדוש[49] גוים	
6	1:1			יצאת[50] לישע עמך[51]	13
6				לישע[52] עם[53] משיחך[54]	

Translation

You struck the back of the wicked one,
You laid him bare, tail-end to neck.

You pierced with your shafts his head.
. . .

You trod on Sea with your horses,
On the surge of Many Waters.

I heard, and my stomach churned,
At the account, my lips quivered.

Rottenness entered my bones,
Beneath me my steps trembled.

I groaned in the day of distress,
When the militia which attacked went up.

The fig tree did not bud,
No produce was on the vines.

The yield of the olive tree recoiled,
Terraces did not provide food.

The flock was cut off from the fold,
No cattle were in the stalls.

As for me, in Yahweh let me rejoice,
Let me be joyful in the God of my victory.

Yahweh, my lord, is my might,
He made my feet like the does'.
On backs he made me tread.

Poetic Structure				Text	V
6	l:l	A`		מחצת[55] ()במת[56] רשע[57]	13
7				ערית[58] יסוד[59] עד צואר	
6	l:			נקבת[60] במטיך[61] ראש[62]	14
				[63] . . .	
6	l:l			דרכת[64] בים[65] סוסיך	15
6				בחמר[66] מים רבים[67]	
8	l:l	A	IV	שמעתי[68] ותרגז בטני	16
8				לקול צללו[69] שפתי	
8	l:l			יבוא[70] רקב[71] בעצמי	
7				()תחתי[72] תרגז[73] אשרי[74]	
7	l:l			אאנח[75] ביום[76] צרה	
7				לעלות[77] עם[78] יגודך[79]	
6	l:l	B		()[80]תאנה לא תפרח[81]	17
7				()אין יבול בגפנים	
5	l:l			כחש[82] מעשה זית	
7				()שדמות[83] לא עשה אכל	
6	l:l			גזר[84] ממכלא[85] צאן	
7				()אין בקר ברפתים[86]	
9	l:l	C		ואני ביהוה אעלוזה	18
9				אגילה באלהי ישעי	
7	l:l:l			יהוה אדני[87] חילי[88]	19
8				()ישם רגלי כאילות[89]	
8				()על במותי[90] ידרכני	

Notes to the Text

The text of Habakkuk 3 is no longer in its original form, but it is not as corrupt as some textual critics have suggested.[1] Major sections of it have been preserved largely intact. There can be no doubt, however, that a number of passages have been rather severely disrupted during the history of transmission (e.g. vv 4, 9a, 13b, 16b, and especially 14). These disruptions of the text are usually signaled not only by awkwardness and obscurity in the Masoretic text but also by substantially divergent readings in the versions. In most of these cases, none of the extant witnesses appears to preserve the authentic text and recovering the original readings becomes truly the "art" of removing error.[2]

Overall, the Masoretic text (MT) is the best witness to the original text of Habakkuk 3. In many cases where it differs from the versions, it provides the better reading (see e.g. textual notes 9, 18, 22, 48, 59, 68, 79). The MT of Habakkuk 3 is already reflected in the Hebrew manuscript of the Minor Prophets from the era of the Second Jewish Revolt which has been recovered from the Wadi Murabbaʿat.[3] This manuscript, in which almost the entire text of Habakkuk 3 has been preserved, contains only three readings from Habakkuk 3 which are at variance with the MT, two of which are *plene* spellings. One variant, however, *zrmw mym ʿbwt* in v 10, represents a text different from the MT and in my judgment superior (see textual notes 42 and 43).

Among the Greek translations extant for Habakkuk 3 are the Old Greek (OG) and other Greek traditions; a scroll of the Minor Prophets from the Naḥal Ḥeber (R); occasional citations from the "three," Theodotion (Th), Symmachus (Sym), and Aquila (Aq); and a translation unique to Habakkuk 3 known as the Barberini version (Barb). Though usually inferior to the MT when differences occur—or equally problematic—these versions do occasionally carry better readings.

Of these Greek translations, the OG preserves the greatest number of variants which represent original readings (see textual notes 3, 4, 19, 33).[4] The Minor Prophets scroll from the Nahal Ḥeber, in which parts of vv 9, 10, 13, 14, and 15 of Habakkuk 3 have been preserved, is, as D. Barthélemy has shown, a recension of the OG which, like the translations of the three, represents an effort to bring the OG into harmony with proto-Rabbinic texts.[5]

This recension proves in fact to be closely related to the recension of Theodotion and to have provided the base for the recension of Aquila. When R departs from the OG it is "correcting" to a proto-Rabbinic text and thus provides little help for textual reconstruction, as the notes for the verses in which R is extant illustrate.

The Barberini version is an enigma. It is not a recension of the OG and contains many readings independent of the Masoretic and Septuagint traditions. It contains many double readings, and in Hab 3:2 represents a conflation with the OG (this same conflate text is also v 2 in the OG). M.L. Margolis has judged Barb a late translation based on its avoidance of *christos* in v 13, on constructions which Margolis characterizes as "free renderings or paraphrase of an interpretive character, often suggesting religious scruples in the manner of the Targums," and on its modern exegetical position (taking the Vulgate as a standard).[6] Others, such as H. St. J. Thackeray and E. M. Good, have taken the independence of Barb as evidence for its antiquity.[7] I am inclined to agree with Thackeray and Good but find the task of deciding whether alternate readings in Barb are free translations or witnesses to variant texts very difficult. In any case, independent readings in Barb certainly deserve serious consideration.

The Targum Jonathan to the Prophets (Tg) is in the Masoretic tradition and is thus of limited value, but it does appear to preserve some readings in Habakkuk 3 which are superior to the MT (see textual notes 3 and 19). Of the Latin versions, the Old Latin (OL) translation provides a witness to the OG and the Vulgate (Vg), like the Tg, presumes the MT.

1. *yārē'tî.* The witnesses offer two readings, *yr'ty/r'yty*, which because of their graphic similarity are certainly to be traced to a single original. Though most commentators emend the MT to *r'yty*, citing the Greek translation, *katenoēsa*, "I observed," and the use of *šāma'/rā'â* as a parallel pair in Hebrew poetry,[8] I still prefer the MT.

The Greek evidence as a whole lends more support to the MT than is generally recognized. Greek texts of Hab 3:2 reflect a conflation of the OG and Barb versions, as is clear from the double readings and identical rendering in both versions. The double reading *ephobēthēn*, "I was frightened,"[9] and *exestēn*, "I was astonished," in this conflate text suggests that each version originally carried a translation of *yr'ty*. The presence of a third verb, *katenoēsa*, suggests that in one of the Hebrew textual bases the double reading *yr'ty/r'yty* existed.

Though it may be impossible to tell in which of the texts the doublet *yr'ty/r'yty* was present, two facts point to the textual base of Barb as the source. In the first place, Barb is characterized by frequent doublets whereas the OG is almost entirely free of them. Furthermore, the translator of the OG version of the Minor Prophets never represents *rā'â* with *katanoeō*, preferring *horaō*, which is used twice elsewhere in Habakkuk 3 (vv 7, 10). The translator of Barb on the other hand prefers *katanoeō*, using it for two of the three instances of *rā'â* in the remainder of Habakkuk 3 (vv 6, 7).

The Greek evidence, thus, may actually support the reading of the MT. Both versions which contributed to the conflate text of Hab 3:2 apparently had the reading of the MT, *yr'ty*, in their textual bases, whereas only one, probably Barb, had also the reading *r'yty*. Two other factors lend support to the MT. First, the reading of the MT is the more difficult reading. *rā'â* occurs more frequently than *yārē'* in parallelism with *šāma'*, and this may have led the scribe to expect it here. Secondly, *rā'â* may reflect the bias in the Greek translations that Habakkuk 3 represents a temple vision observed (*rā'â*) by the author of the poem (see Chap. 4). It may have arisen on the basis of a specific interpretive bias which led the translator or copier to see *r'yty* rather than *yr'ty*.

Both *yr'ty* and *r'yty* are appropriate within this poem which focuses on a theophany. Either would be in place. In further defense of *yr'ty*, however, it may be noted, first, that *yr'ty* is not out of place in poetic parallelism with *šāma'* (e.g. Ps 76:9). Second, fear, awe, or terror is the normative response to a theophany, an event so powerful that the entire cosmos is shaken (vv 6–7, 9–10). The fear of the poet is in fact expressed elsewhere in the poem, by the term *rgz* in the tricolon which follows, and at length in the conclusion immediately following the theophany (v 16). Finally, the two themes of hearing and being in awe which are introduced here at the beginning of the poem provide the framework for the central part of the poem, the actual theophany (vv 3–15), by being resumed at the conclusion of the theophany in v 16: *šāma'tî watirgaz bitnî*.

2. *bĕqereb* is most easily understood as a ballast variant of *bĕ*, the preposition which introduces the final line of this tricolon.

The use of *bqrb* in parallelism with *b* occurs both in Ugaritic (*CTA* 4[51].5.75–76; 4[51].6.5–6; 17[2 Aqht].1.26) and in Hebrew poetry (Ps 82:1; Mic 5:7). The literal translation would be "in the years," but F. M. Cross has suggested to me the more idiomatic "through the years" or simply "in the past." This translation fits well with the interpretation of the verbs in this tricolon in the past tense, either perfect (see textual note 3) or prefix conjugation denoting the old preterit (see textual note 4). The poet is here introducing briefly the account which he has heard and which he mentions in the preceding bicolon.

3. *ḥiyyîtā*, the Piel perfect 2ms form of *ḥyh*.[10] The MT *ḥayyêhû* is suspicious because the pronominal suffix *-hû* lacks an antecedent. Though this suffix has been understood as referring to *p'lk* in the previous line,[11] the verb *ḥyh* in the Piel form elsewhere takes living things (e.g. *nepeš*, *'îš*, *zera'*, and *dāgān*) as direct objects.[12] Even more damaging to the reading of the MT (imperative with 3ms suffix) is the fact that it is supported among the versions only by the Vg, Jerome's translation carefully following the MT.

The Greek translation of this term certainly does not represent the original intent of the author of Habakkuk 3, but it does provide an indication of the original text. The Greek translation *zǭōn*, "living beings," interprets this term as a noun rather than a verb, treating the previous word, *šnym*, as the numeral "two" (*duo*) rather than as the plural noun "years." The most likely *Vorlage* for *zǭōn* is *ḥywt*.[13]

The Greek translation cannot be original. It destroys the poetic parallelism in this tricolon. But its text is likely closer to the original than the MT. The Greek *Vorlage ḥywt* likely reflects a corruption of *ḥyyt*, due to the common graphic confusion of *w/y*. The 2ms form of the verb parallels nicely the two 2ms verbs which complete this tricolon. The juxtaposition of perfect and imperfect verbs poses no difficulty since this convention is followed throughout the poem for past narrative. The Piel perfect 2ms form of *ḥyh* appears to be reflected in the Tg: *bgw šny' dyhbt lhwn ḥyy'*, "in the years (in) which you gave them life."

4. Read the Niphal imperfect 2ms, *tiwwadēa'*, with reflexive meaning. The MT understands this as a Hiphil form, the Greek translator as Niphal (*epignōsthēsē*). Since Niphal and Hiphil forms were spelled the same, *twd'*, in the preexilic era, scribes could eas-

ily have misinterpreted the conjugation and in the postexilic era added the *yod* marking the Hiphil form in the standard spelling of this period. The Hiphil form of *yd'* does occasionally appear without a direct object (e.g. Judg 8:16; Job 38:3; Prov 9:9), but this is rare. Furthermore, these occurrences are usually in wisdom literature, and they always carry the sense of "instruct, teach." Thus most textual critics who read the Hiphil with the MT try to supply an object, by suggesting either that the object of *ḥayyêhû* (likely a corruption itself) in the previous line is assumed here,[14] or by identifying the entire following line as the object.[15] The Tg adds its own object: *gbwrtk*, "your strength." It is more natural to read the Niphal form with the Greek translation and interpret it in a reflexive sense, the sense in which *yd'* is in fact frequently used with Yahweh as the subject (e.g. Isa 19:21; Ezek 20:5; Ps 9:17).[16]

This verb and the other verbs in the prefix conjugation in the remainder of the poem (except the cohortatives in v 18) are to be understood as old preterit forms rather than imperfect forms and translated in the simple past tense. In archaic Hebrew poetry as well as in Ugaritic poetry, the suffix and prefix conjugations of the verb are used interchangeably to express past narrative. D. A. Robertson has discussed in detail this way of reading the verbs in Hab 3:3–15.[17] A fuller discussion of Robertson's conclusions and an application of them to vv 2, 16, 17, and 19 as well can be found in Chapter 2.

5. *brgz* should be translated, with the MT, OG/Barb, and Tg, as a prepositional phrase, "in turmoil." This preserves the poetic parallelism of this tricolon in which the two previous lines begin with prepositional phrases. Less satisfactory is the attempt by some (Vg: *cum iratus fueris*; the double reading in the Greek translation: *en tǭ tarachthēnai*) to read a temporal clause (*birgoz*). This reading in the Greek translation has been influenced by the presence of *rwḥy* (*tēn psychēn mou*) rather than *rḥm* (*eleous*) in its *Vorlage*. The basic meaning of the root *rgz* is "to be in an agitated, disturbed, or unsettled state." The turmoil referred to here must be the general disruption caused by the theophany (note the uses of the root *rgz* in vv 7 and 16).

6. The two variants in the Greek translation, *tēn psychēn mou*, "my soul," and *eleous*, "mercy," are likely secondary. The former, which represents *rḥy* rather than *rḥm*, was probably given credence because of the focus on the inner distress of the poet in v

16 (note the use there also of *rgz*). The latter, a noun, is unlikely since the noun for compassion in Hebrew is *raḥămîm*.

7. This term should be understood with the OG (*thaiman*) as the proper name of a geographical location, rather than with Barb (*libos*), Th (*notiou*), and the Vg (*austro*) as the general designation "south." This is supported by its parallelism in this bicolon with another proper name, *har pā'rān*, and its association, through the literary device of inclusion, with two other specific geographical names at the end of this section of the poem in v 7. Furthermore, the location designated by the proper name Teman in biblical usage, a city or region of Edom (Amos 1:12; Jer 49:7, 20; Ezek 25:13; Obad 9), fits this context nicely: God's theophany in the south where it is depicted in other archaic poetry, Deut 33:2 (*sînay, śē'îr, har pā'rān*) and Judg 5:4 (*śē'îr, śĕdēh 'ĕdôm*), occurs in the area of Edom. But the best evidence for this reading is the recent discovery of the association of Yahweh with Teman in the inscriptions of Kuntillet ʿAjrud. There the phrases *yhwh tmn w'šrth*, "Yahweh of Teman and his Asherah," and *brktk lyhwh htmn*, "I have blessed you by Yahweh of Teman," occur. Taken together with the fact that Yahweh is associated in similar fashion in these inscriptions with another specific place, Samaria (*brkt 'tkm lyhwh šmrn wl'šrth*, "I have blessed you by Yahweh of Samaria and his Asherah"), Teman must certainly be understood as a place name.[18] The versions which render this term "south" no longer understand the old political and geographical significance of Teman in this context and have simply translated the term as a common noun. For further discussion on the identity and location of Teman, see Chapter 3.

8. Conjunctions are problematic in poetic texts. It is difficult to know in all cases whether they are original or not. The studies of F. M. Cross and D. N. Freedman have shown that conjunctions are infrequent in early Hebrew poetry and tend to be later prosaic additions.[19] The multiple addition of conjunctions which can be seen in the *Vorlage* of the OG translation of Hab 3:8–15 supports Cross and Freedman's findings and indicates that Habakkuk 3 was susceptible to this process. Sometimes the secondary status of conjunctions in the MT is indicated by their absence in the versions (vv 4a; 6a: *ytpṣṣw*; 16a: *tḥty*; 19a: *ʿl*). In other cases, their secondary character is suggested by the fact that they serve no real grammatical function connecting consecutive things

or actions (here in v 3a and in v 19a, *yśm*). In a few cases, I have removed them for stylistic and metrical reasons because they occur at the beginning of poetic lines and add unnecessarily to the length of the line (vv 3b, 5, 17). One might argue that the conjunctions in v 17 be retained because they connect consecutive images, but conjunctions were not considered necessary in the series of images immediately preceding in v 16.

9. The MT (with Barb, Aq, Sym, and Th: *pharan*) carries the original reading. The origin of the unusual translation in the OG, *orous kataskiou daseos*, "the shady, bushy mountain," is impossible to determine with certainty. The OG may have contained the explanatory gloss *ś'yr* which eventually replaced *p'rn* in its text. The close association between *p'rn* and *ś'yr* in Deut 33:2 and the need to explain the difficult designation *p'rn* may have led to this gloss and the subsequent confusion. Later, the geographical term *ś'yr* was understood as the common noun *śē'ār*, "hair." *dasys* is in fact used to translate *śē'ār* elsewhere (Gen 27:11, 23; cf. Gen 25:25 and 2 Kgs 1:8), and it can be used in Greek to describe both hairy and leafy surfaces that have a shaggy, bushy appearance. *kataskiou* may be an alternate interpretation of this same term (it translates *r'nn*, "luxuriant, fresh," and *'bt*, "foliage," when these are used as descriptive terms for *'ṣ*, "tree;" e.g. Jer 2:20; Ezek 20:28).[20] It may represent another attempt to deal with *ś'r* as an adjective describing *hr*.

It has been suggested that *kataskios* and *dasys* are attempts to render *p'rn* by understanding it in relation to *p'rh*, "branches" (see Isa 10:33; Ezek 31:5). But neither *kataskios* nor *dasys* ever translates *p'rn* or *p'rh* elsewhere. And the Greek words which do translate *p'rh* are not synonymous with *kataskios* and *dasys*.

Whatever the *Vorlage*, the translation of OG is peculiar and likely secondary. Everywhere else in the Septuagint both *p'rn* and *ś'yr* are rendered as proper names usually transliterated. This is the only place *p'rn* (or *ś'yr* ?) occurs in the Minor Prophets, and the unusual interpretive character of the translation indicates an attempt on the part of the translator to clarify a geographical term which was not understood.[21]

10. *mālĕ'â* may be read as the predicate of *thltw* or *'rṣ*. Though the versions prefer the latter (Barb, Vg, Tg; the OG contains an adjective), the parallelism of this line with the previous

one suggests the former.[22] *ksh* and *ml'* are paired in the description of God's glory (*kbd*) filling the tabernacle in Exod 40:34.

11. Articles, like conjunctions, are suspect in poetry as prosaic additions.[23] In a number of instances (v 8: *bnhr-m*; v 18: *byhwh*) the Masoretes introduced them into Habakkuk 3, as their vowel points indicate, where the versions lack them. In this case, v 3b, the article appears to be an unnecessary and secondary addition since the term parallel to *'rṣ*, *šmym*, lacks one and since elsewhere (vv 6, 12) *'rṣ* is used without the article.

12. Although the versions, together with the MT, understand *ngh* as a noun, the comparison of "brilliance" to "light" which this interpretation necessitates is awkward. Furthermore, the understanding of this (presumably) masculine noun as the subject of the feminine verb *tihyeh* at the conclusion of the line is suspect. A better interpretation of *ngh* is to read it as a verb, the Qal perfect 3ms, *nāgah*.[24] God's shining advance is expressed in other theophanic contexts by synonyms of *nāgah*: *yāpa'* (Deut 33:2; Ps 50:2) and *zāraḥ* (Deut 33:2).

13. Translate *'ôr* as "flame, fire" rather than "light." For the use of *'ôr* as the "fire" of God, see Isa 31:9. Fire is a frequent aspect of theophanies (cf. Pss 18:9; 50:3; 97:3). The construct chain *'ôr hawwâ* (see textual note 14) translated literally, "fire of destruction," can be more idiomatically rendered, "a destroying fire."

14. Read *hawwâ*, "destruction," as the *nomen rectum* of *'ôr*; thus, "like a destroying fire." *hawwâ* is used similarly in the expression *dbr hwh*, "the destroying Deber/Pestilence" (Ps 91:3). The devastation accompanying God's advance is the central idea in this section of the poem (vv 3–7). The *w/y* confusion which this reading involves is very common, but the intrusion of *taw* in the MT is more difficult to explain. The use of the past tense in the Tg, *'tgly*, might be taken to indicate an original *hyh*, but this may be questioned in light of the tendency in the Tg to read all verbs in the past tense.

15. The bicolon which this term begins is one of the most difficult in Habakkuk 3. The text is certainly corrupt. This is evidenced by the problems in reading the Hebrew text as it stands and by the variety of readings in the versions.

With few exceptions, commentators wish to interpret *qrnym* here as "rays of light." They defend this interpretation by reference to the previous line where *ngh* and *'wr* appear and by accepting the old convention that *qrn* appears as a denominative verb in Exod 34:29, 30, 35 meaning "to send out rays of light."[25]

But this is a forced interpretation. The noun *qrn* is used nowhere else in Hebrew literature to mean "ray of light." It always refers to the literal horn of an ox or ram (or of the altar) or to the figurative horns of a human being, a metaphor suggesting the strength or power of an ox or ram (Deut 33:17 combines both usages).[26] Furthermore, the denominative use of *qrn* as a verb in Exodus 34 probably does not mean "send out rays" but rather "be horny, gnarled."[27] If the previous line in Habakkuk 3 is understood as the conclusion of the preceding tricolon rather than as the opening line of this verse, as it should be, then the contextual motivation for reading *qrnym* as "rays of light" is removed.

qrnym must mean simply "horns." The only commentator to take this line of thinking seriously is W. F. Albright, who reads in v 4: (*yhwh*) *yngḥ k'br/ thyh qrnym mydwt lw*. "Yahweh attacked like a bull/ Provided with tossing horns."[28] Albright's reading must be closer to the original than the understanding of most current commentaries, but some of his emendations are adventuresome. An entirely satisfactory solution to this verse is still lacking.

The key to a solution, it seems to me, must be in the use of *qrnym* at the beginning of this line in parallelism with *'zh* at the conclusion of the following line. These terms appear elsewhere as a parallel pair in Hebrew poetry (1 Sam 2:10; Ps 89:18). If that is the case here, then the point of this bicolon must be the strength of *'ĕlôah*. And the horns must be those of God himself. An image of Yahweh with horns appears in Ps 18:3. A number of the gods of Ugarit possess horns.[29] The dual form *qarnayim* should be read with the MT. Both the OG and Barb mistakenly read this as plural *kerata*. The plural form of *qrn* is *qrnwt*.

Unfortunately, the rest of this line does not make sense as it stands and no satisfactory solution has yet been proposed.

16. The enigmatic character of this line in the MT and the variations among the versions indicate a corrupt text. For the first term, the MT, Vg (*ibi*), and Th read *wĕšām*, while the OG (*etheto*), Aq, and Sym read a form of the verb *śîm*. Barb has a double reading with both alternatives. For the second term, where the MT (followed by the Vg, Tg, Aq, Sym, and Th) reads *ḥbywn* as a form of *ḥbh*, the OG reads *agapēsin krataian*, indicating a

Vorlage with *ḥbywn* (understood as a form of *ḥbb*) or *'hbh* (from *'hb*). The translation of the final two words of the line in Barb, *hē dynamis tēs doxēs autou*, does little to clear up the confusion.

The most satisfactory solution is that adopted by W. F. Albright: *yiśmaḥ bĕyôm 'uzzōh.*[30] The present state of the MT can be accounted for by several simple errors: the misdivision of the first two words, and the common graphic confusions of *w/y* (*wśmḥ* for *yśmḥ*) and *m/n* (*bywn* for *bywm*: 7th c.: *m* = 𐤌 : *n* = 𐤍). The construction, *bĕyôm 'uzzōh*, is, as Albright points out, characteristic of old poetry (e.g. Pss 18:19; 110:3, 5). In addition to these and other examples he cites from biblical and Ugaritic literature, may now be added two lines from a new "theophanic" text from Kuntillet 'Ajrud: *b'l. bym. mlḥ/mt//'l. bym. mlḥ[mt]*, "Ba'l in the day of battle/'El in the day of battle."[31]

The 3ms suffix *-h* on the final term in this line, *'z*, represents an old spelling. The 3ms suffix was represented by *-h* between the 9th and 6th centuries B.C.E.

17. Read with the MT Deber (in pause here, *dāber*: usually translated "pestilence") rather than with the OG "word" (*logos* = *dābār*). All translators except the translator of the OG understood this as part of the retinue accompanying Yahweh in his theophanic march. That the OG interprets *dbr* in this way may arise from the influence of the phrase *lĕpānāyw yēlek* which precedes it: "from his face went out a word." For a fuller discussion of the god Deber, see Chapter 3.

18. The OG is confused and unclear. A variety of readings which are phonetically similar show an inner Greek corruption. The probable original, *eis pedia* (=*bšplh* ?),[32] is an inferior text which appears to have been motivated by the following terms *rglyw* and *'md*.

19. Read the Polel imperfect 3ms of *nûd*, *yĕnōdēd*, on the basis of the OG. A discrepancy exists between the reading in the MT, *ymdd*, "he measured" (supported by Barb, *diemetrēse*, "he measured, surveyed," and by the Vg, *mensus est*, "he measured"), and the reading in the OG, *esaleuthē*, "he shook" (supported by the Tg, *'āzîa'*, "he shook"). Two concerns argue for the primacy of the OG: the parallelism of this term with *ntr*, "to start, jump," in the following line, and the usual way in which nature responds to the theophanic appearance of the deity (note the reaction of the mountains/hills in v 6). Such proposals for the Hebrew *Vorlage* of

the OG as *m'd*,[33] *mṯṯ*,[34] *mgg*,[35] and *ymwt*[36] involve writing or hearing confusions that are not customary. One proposal, *myd*,[37] involves the use of an Arabic cognate, *mwd*, not found elsewhere in the Semitic languages. The best proposal, suggested by both Margolis and Albright but accepted by neither, is to posit *wyndd* as the original reading.[38] This would involve only the common *m/n* confusion (see textual note 16) to produce *wymdd* (possibly triggered by the *md* of *'md* which precedes it). *nûd* is in fact used elsewhere (Isa 24:20) to depict the reaction of earth to God's appearance.

20. Read with the MT *yattēr*, the Hiphil imperfect 3ms of *nātar* I, "to spring, start up." Barb reads *exeikase*, "make like, represent; size up, compare," which probably reflects the MT but interprets it in light of the root *twr*, "seek out, explore," in order to preserve the parallelism with *mdd*, "measure," in the preceding line. The reading of the OG, *dietakē*, "melt," which is supported by the Vg (*dissolvit*), is difficult to understand unless it is a figurative translation of *nātar* II, "to free, loose,"[39] or a confusion with *nātak*, "to pour out" (Hiphil: "melt;" cf. Ezek 22:20).

The verb *nātar* I is used to describe the response to a theophany elsewhere in biblical literature in Job 37:1 (cf. Lev 11:21). Cassuto has also suggested reading this verb with the same meaning in a Ugaritic text in which the monsters which helped Mot are cast into the sea (*CTA* 6.6[62.2].52).[40]

21. Translating *ytpṣṣw* as the Hithpoel imperfect (preterit) 3mp of *pṣṣ*, "break," is supported by the OG and Barb (*diethrybē*) as well as the sense of the passage. Not quite as apt in my judgment is the alternative reading, the Hithpolel imperfect (preterit) 3mp of *pwṣ*, "be scattered, dispersed."

22. Both the OG (*biq*, "by violence") and Barb *thrausthēsetai*, "were broken in pieces") have variant but inferior readings. The OG may have read *'z* in its text instead of *'d*,[41] and Barb represents a doublet for the verb which begins the line.[42] *hrry 'd* //*gb'wt 'wlm* are a common parallel pair in archaic Hebrew poetry (Gen 49:26; Deut 33:15).

23. W. F. Albright's suggestion that *hlkwt* should be understood as the paths or orbits of the celestial bodies has been adopted here.[43] *hlk(t)* is used in both Ugaritic (e.g. *CTA* 19[1 Aqht].2.52) and Akkadian for the orbits of the stars. The disruption of the fixed movements of the heavenly bodies fits in well with

the cosmic turmoil pictured in the preceding lines.

24. Scholars have long been dissatisfied with v 6b and the beginning of v 7 because of problems with sense, grammar, and poetic style. The first phrase of v 7 in the MT, *tḥt 'wn*, is particularly awkward. The use of the preposition *taḥat* with *'āwen* is attested nowhere else in the Hebrew Bible and, judged by its usual meanings, does not seem appropriate here. J. Lachmann has asserted that this phrase "ist sicher ein alter Fehler."[44]

Difficulty in the interpretation of this section of the poem can already be detected in the earliest Greek translations. The translator of the OG version understood v 6b as a part of the line preceding it: *bouvoi aiōnioi poreias aiōnias autou*. "the eternal hills of his eternal march." Barb adds the verb *alloiōthēsontai*, "will be changed, altered," to the final phrase of v 6 and seems to link the last work of v 6, *lw*, with the first two words of v 7: *autou heneka seisthēsetai hē oikoumenē*, "regarding it, the inhabited region will be shaken" (=*lô tēḥat 'iyyin/'iyyim)*.

The best proposal put forward for this problematic text is that of W. F. Albright, who reads the final word of v 6, *l* (), as an emphatic *lamed* and the first two words of v 7 as the Qal passive 3fp form of the Semitic verb, *ḥt'*, the original pronunciation of which was probably **tuḥta'na*.[45] The verb *ḥt'*. "to crush, ruin, vanquish," though not attested elsewhere in biblical Hebrew, is a common Semitic verb. It is present in Ugaritic literature (*CTA* 6[49].2.23; 4[51].8.20; 53[54].7,8,10) and in the Amarna correspondence (EA 102:11–13). Also to be noted are the Akkadian *ḫatû* (for *ḫata'u*), "smash," and the Arabic *ḫata'a*, "to be broken, humbled" (8th form). Barb does not directly support this reading, but it comes very close to the original sense of the text when it reads *tḥt* from the Hebrew *ḥtt*.

The secondary reading *taḥat 'āwen* is readily understandable. The obscure verb *ḥt'* would easily have been forgotten. Then the verb *rgz* and the name Midian in the context would have suggested the motif of distress and trouble. The early close ties between Israel and Midian were soon forgotten and throughout most of Israelite history Midian was considered the archetypal enemy of God. That the appearance of God should place Kushan/Midian "under trouble" would have fit in nicely with prevailing conceptions. The reading *'wn* (with the addition of *w*) may have been influenced in addition by the phrase *tar'ēnî 'āwen* in Hab 1:3 after

Chapter 3 was attached to the text of Habakkuk.

25. Delete *rā'îtî* as an explanatory gloss. The presence of this term in this line has troubled many exegetes.[46] The first person form is anomalous in this section of the poem which rehearses the acts of God with third person verbs. Furthermore, this term is an orphan without a poetic line, once *tḥt'n* in v 7 is recognized as the conclusion of the previous tricolon and the following bicolon is divided as suggested below. *rā'îtî* likely arose on the basis of the theophanic character of the poem as a whole (or the later prophetic vision interpretation of the poem)[47] and the first person forms in the framework of the poem (vv 2, 16–19), and together with the development of the reading *taḥat 'āwen* (cf. Hab 1:3: *tar'ēnî 'āwen*).

26. The redivision of the lines in the MT which is suggested here was proposed long ago by B. Duhm.[48] Though it has been accepted by few modern scholars, it has much to commend it. It follows the MT exactly, solves a variety of grammatical and poetic problems, and suggests, as most scholars have suspected, that the problem with v 7 in the MT lies at the beginning of this verse.

The grammatical problem solved by this arrangement is the lack of agreement between subject (f. *yry'wt*) and verb (m. *yrgzwn*) in the second half of this verse as it stands in the MT. This difficulty is resolved if the subject of *yrgzwn* is identified as the masculine term *'hl* which precedes it rather than the feminine one *yry'wt* which follows it.

The major poetic problem solved by this arrangement is the length of the line in v 7 as it stands in the MT. V 7 has always been considered too full metrically when compared with the rest of vv 3–7. This division reveals a bicolon with a meter consistent with the rest of the poem (8/6). Several other poetic conventions support this arrangement. First, the order of the parallel pair *'hly/yry'wt* remains consistent with its conventional use in Hebrew poetry, where *'hly* is always the initial (A) word and *yry'wt* the second (B) word (e.g. Isa 54:2; Jer 4:20; 10:20; 49:29; and Cant 1:5). The suggestion to reverse the order of these two words in order to solve the grammatical problem raised by the masculine verb *yrgzwn* disregards this convention.[49] Second, the common practice of pairing a geographical term (*kwšn*) with a ballast variant (*'rṣ mdyn*) is preserved (cf. the opening bicolon in this section of Habakkuk 3 [v 3a]; Judg 5:4; Exod 15:14; and Amos 1:5,12; 2:5). The suggestion to delete *'rṣ* to shorten the poetic line disregards this convention. The extra material in v 7 is to be found at the beginning of the verse, not here. Finally, this arrangement reveals the same type of parallelism as that found in the opening bicolon (v 3a) of this section (vv 3–7) and thus provides a perfect inclusion for this part of the poem.

This division of v 7 may still be reflected by a small detail in the OG text, even though its translators have divided the verse in the same way the Masoretes have. The second line in Greek reads *ptoēthēsontai kai hai skēnai gēs Madiam*. The only way to explain the unusual location of *kai* in this phrase is as a literal translation of *yry'wt* preceded by a conjunction in the *Vorlage*. And the best explanation for the presence of a conjunction here is that *yry'wt* was at one time understood as the beginning of a new phrase. The conjunction was not original, but the understanding of the division of these lines which gave rise to it was accurate.

27. Read the *-m* on *nhr* as the old enclitic *m* rather than as the masculine plural.[50] The more frequently used plural of *nhr* is *-wt* as is the case seven lines later in this poem (v 9b). One could also read the dual of *nhr* which is used at Ugarit to refer to the cosmic sources of the deep (e.g. *CTA* 4[51].4.21; 6.1.33[49.1.5]).[51] Either way, in parallel relationship to *yām* in this tricolon, this term designates the waters of chaos, Yahweh's cosmic foe. Given the parallel position of *yām* here and the typical designation of the water monster at Ugarit as *ym/nhr*, I slightly prefer *nhr-m* as an enduring reflection of the ancient name of the dragon of chaos.

28. Read the Qal perfect 3ms of *ḥrh* with the MT against the 2ms form read by the OG (*ōrgisthes*) and Barb (*orgisthes*). The subject of the verb is *'p* in the following line, the only subject employed for *ḥrh* in biblical Hebrew. Normal usage is to state the subject *'p* directly, or indirectly in the cliche *ḥrh l*... An individual is never the subject of this verb, except in the reflexive conjugations (Niphal and Hithpael). The Greek readings represent the influence of the vocative *yhwh* when the sense of a subject which was postponed due to poetic conventions was forgotten.

29. Read *he* interrogative twice for stylistic reasons.

30. The tricolon in the MT, represented by v 8a, is original. It is supported in all the versions. Where a few mss. omit one or the other of the first two lines, the omission can be explained

best as an inner textual corruption, not a witness to a *Vorlage* with a bicolon. The Greek mss. which omit the second line of v 8b, for example, contain perfect examples of inner Greek haplography. The primary impetus behind the frequent attempt among modern commentators to reduce this tricolon to a bicolon seems to come more from an outdated view of poetic conventions than from a careful use of the versions.

31. According to normal biblical usage, *rkb* means "to mount" rather than "to ride" (from one place to another). It is a vertical rather than a horizontal movement.[52] This sense of *rkb* can also be seen from its use in Ugaritic literature (CTA 14[Krt].2.74–75; 14[Krt].4.165–167).

32. P. Humbert, suggesting that it is customary for the warrior in the ancient Near East to mount his chariot rather than the horses that draw it, reverses the order of the parallel pair *swsyk/mrkbtyk*.[53] He has some support for his position in that Barb appears to reflect this same reversal. But all other versions support the MT. The usual sequence of the parallel pair *swsym/mrkbh* in biblical poetry favors the order here (e.g. Isa 2:7; Mic 5:10; but cf. Jer 4:13), as does the meter. The regular line lengths in this bicolon would be destroyed. It is best to understand this bicolon as containing "imagistic parallelism," common in biblical and Ugaritic poetry, in which the poet does not seek to refer to two separate acts but to a single act described with two related images.

33. Read the singular construct, *mirkebet*, with the OG. It makes less sense to describe Yahweh mounting several chariots. The plural reading in the MT and the other versions may have arisen under the influence of the plural *swsyk* in the preceding phrase.

Also suspect in the MT is the suffix on *mrkbt* which interrupts a construct chain. Better than treating this as a construct chain in which the *nomen regens* contains a suffix (GKC, no. 128d) or as an epexegetical substantive added to a substantive with a suffix (GKC, no. 131r) is to recognize it as bad grammar and move the suffix, as does the Peshitta, to the *nomen rectum*, *yĕšû'â*; thus, *yĕšū'ātekā*. The suffix on *mrkbt*, as the plural discussed above, may have arisen under the influence of the parallel term *swsyk* in the preceding phrase.

34. The terms *yĕšû'â* (here in v 8) and *yēša'* (vv 13, 18) may refer specifically to "victory" in biblical usage (e.g. Pss 18:51;

20:7; Isa 59:17). In the context of this poem in which the divine warrior goes out to battle, this is a more precise and appropriate translation than "salvation." The frequent repetition of *yš'h/yš'* identifies "victory" as a key motif in this poem.

35. Read the Piel infinitive absolute followed by the Piel imperfect 2ms of *'rh*, "lay bare." It is clear from the various Greek renderings that their textual bases contained a phrase based upon a weak verb with the consonants *'r*. Barb (*exēgerthē*, "was awakened") and R (*exeg er eis*, "you will awaken"), as well as the Vg (*suscitabis*, "You will arouse"), understand this phrase on the basis of the middle weak root *'wr*, "to rouse, awake." The OG (*enteinōn*, "you will string;" cf. the OL) might be thought to represent *drk* on the basis of the customary practice of the Greek translators who use this expression 13 of 21 instances for *drk*. But since *enteinein* is also used to translate other actions related to the use of a bow (*mšk*, "draw," *nṭh*, "bend, bow," and *nšq*, "handle, be equipped with"?), it is likely that the OG represents here a free translation of a text similar to the MT. The MT contains a reading based on the final weak root *'rh*, "be naked, bare;" it contains the noun *'ryh*, "nakedness," and thereby implies that the Niphal imperfect 3fs verb which follows is to be understood on the basis of a second meaning for *'wr*, "be naked, bare," though this would be the only case of this meaning in biblical Hebrew.

Most modern interpreters prefer the sense of *'rh* in this context and emend suitably, often to *t'rh* for the finite verb here. The confusion represented in the MT and many of the versions may be easily explained on the basis of old orthography. The consonants *t'r* in early orthography could be either a form of *'wr*, "to awaken," or of *'rh*, "to be bare," in the latter case the short preterit form of a final weak verb. This second possibility was likely original. When the preterit use of the imperfect became confined to cases following the *waw* consecutive this form could only have been understood as being derived from a middle weak verb, and the readings in the MT and the versions arose.

The initial word may have been the noun as it appears in the MT, *'ryh*. A number of examples are noted in GKC (see no. 117g) in which an internal or absolute object in the form of a noun derived from the same stem of the verb may accompany the verb to strengthen the verbal idea. This object may precede (cf. Isa 24:6; Jer 46:5; Job 27:12) or follow the verb. A better alternative, however, is to read the initial word in this colon as the infinitive absolute, *'rh*, used to strengthen the verbal idea. Once the sense of its relation to the verbal root of *t'r* was lost, it could have been understood as a noun and spelled accordingly.

Though in the MT and Barb *qšt* is assumed to be the subject of *t'r* which is therefore read as a 3fs form, it is more sensible to understand Yahweh as the subject and read *t'r* as a 2ms form (with R, the OG, OL, and Vg). In the immediately preceding and following lines Yahweh is the subject of the verbs, all of which are active. To read a passive form here would be inconsistent with the context and weaken the force of the other active verbs in the vicinity.

The image of the chariot warrior baring his bow corresponds with the practice of warfare in the Late Bronze and early Iron Ages as it has been reconstructed by historians and archaeologists. The bow by this time had become the principal weapon of the chariot warrior, and chariots were outfitted with bow cases and quivers to carry weapons not in use.[54] The description of the divine warrior in Hab 3:8–9 mounting his chariot, baring his bow (drawing it from the bow case), and firing the arrows drawn from the quiver (see the reconstruction of the following colon of Hab 3:9 below) is what one would expect from an Israelite poet drawing images from the concrete world of human conflict with which the poet was familiar.

36. Franz Delitzsch has wondered whether the second line of v 9 should not be considered the most difficult in Habakkuk 3, if not in the entire prophetic corpus, as least when one considers the labyrinth of more than one hundred interpretations which have been proposed for it.[55] The most extensive, and unusual, examination of this colon is that of H. St. J. Thackeray, who has suggested that it is not a line of poetry but an intrusive prosaic gloss containing three separate rubrics which mark the end of a lectionary text.[56]

There is, however, strong evidence for the poetic character of this colon and for its appropriateness in this literary context. The key to understanding this line is the relationship between *mṭ* in this line and *qšt* in the preceding line. Based on parallels in Akkadian and Ugaritic literature, as well as the context here, *mṭ* must be understood together with *qšt* as part of the arms of the divine warrior. In Akkadian literature *miṭṭu* is a divine weapon, linked together with *qaštu*, "bow," as part of the weaponry Marduk takes into battle against Tiamat (*Enūma eliš* 4.37–38). In Ugaritic literature, *mṭ* is also a divine weapon, identified with 'El (CTA 23[52].37) and with 'Anat (*CTA* 3['nt].2.15–16). In the latter text, *mṭm* appears in poetic parallelism with *qšt* to depict 'Anat's weaponry in a bloody battle. The parallelism of *mṭ/qšt* in *CTA* 3['nt].2.15–16 and in Hab 3:9 has led to the suggestion that these terms should be considered a formulaic parallel pair in the literary conventions of Northwest Semitic poetry.[57] M. Dahood is undoubtedly correct when he observes that "though the line remains obscure . . . any advance in its understanding must take this parallelism into account."[58]

With this in mind, the most satisfactory reading for the opening term of this line is the Piel perfect 2ms of *śb'*, "be sated, satisfied." The consonantal text is firm here. The different interpretations stem only from the fact that these consonants can be read in a variety of ways. The MT reads the plural of *šĕbū'â*, "oath," and the OG the construct of *šib'â*, "seven" (*hepta* should be considered the original Greek rendering and *epi ta* a corruption within the Greek and not an indication of a different *Vorlage*).[59] Barb reads the 2ms perfect of *śb'*, "to be sated." Of these possibilities, the third is the most appealing in this context where the divine warrior moves into battle with his weaponry. The verb *śb'* can be used in Hebrew to describe the satiety of a weapon as it "devours" its victims in battle (cf. Jer 46:10 where it is used of *ḥereb*).[60] The same verb is used of 'Anat when she takes her bow (*qšt*) and arrows (*mṭm*) into the fray. She is described as becoming sated (*šb't, tšb'*) in her battle (*CTA* 3['nt].2.19,29).

37. The Greek translators were unanimous in understanding this term as shafts of some kind: OG, *skēptra*, "scepters;" Barb, *bolidas*, "missiles;" R, *hrabdous*, "rods." The main interpretive question is whether these shafts should be considered the arrows shot by the bow or the lance or club which the warrior carries into battle along with the bow. The latter option is taken by the OG and R whose translations both indicate some kind of scepter or staff. This understanding is in fact supported by the customary usage of the term *mṭ* in Akkadian, Ugaritic, and Hebrew where the term occurs usually in the singular and must be understood as a mace or scepter.

Barb, however, understands these shafts to be arrows, as

the translation, *bolidas tēs pharetras autou*, "missiles of his quiver," indicates. Two features of the Hebrew text support the interpretation in Barb: the plural form of *mṭ*, and its use with *nqb* in v 14a. The divine warrior is never pictured carrying more than one mace into battle. Moreover a mace would not "pierce," *nqb*, the head of the enemy, while arrows would. The use of *mṭ* for arrow can also be supported by Ugaritic usage where twice it appears to have this meaning, once when it is used by 'El to shoot down a bird (*CTA* 23[52].37,40,44,47)[61] and another time when it occurs in the plural, *mṭm*, together with bow as part of 'Anat's weaponry (*CTA* 3['nt].2.15–16). This second possibility, *mṭ* as the "arrows" of the bow, is the more likely one here.[62]

On the basis of the masculine plural form of *mṭ* in v 14a and in Ugaritic literature, it is best to read the masculine plural construct here, *mṭy*. A confusion between *w/y* may account for the *waw* in the MT.

38. The real problem with this line is its conclusion. The OG and R contain the reading of the MT *'mr* (or perhaps *y'mr: legei*) as well as the divine name *yhwh* in their textual bases. If the reading of the first two terms in this line which has just been proposed is correct, *'mr (yhwh)* cannot be original. U. Cassuto has suggested that *'mr* reflects the name of one of the Ba'l's clubs, *'aymr* (*CTA* 2[4 68].19), more properly *'ay-ymr* ("Ho! Let him rout").[63] However, if the parallelism *qšt//mṭm*, "bows//arrows," is accurate, the name of one of Ba'l's clubs would not be appropriate here.

A better solution, though provisional, is to adopt the reading of Barb, *tēs pharetras autou*, "his quiver," and replace *'mr* with *'šptk ('ašpātĕkā)*, "your quiver" (the 3ms suffix in Barb could not have been original in this context).[64] The origin of the reading *'mr (yhwh)* is hard to determine, but it has all the earmarks of a gloss[65] and may have arisen together with the interpretation of *śb't* as related to the verb *šb'*, "swear."

39. I prefer the translations of R and the OG which take *'rṣ* as the subject of this sentence and read *tbq'* as a Niphal 3fs form. The scene has shifted here from the divine warrior to the cosmic response to his appearance, and *'rṣ* provides a nice parallel to *hrym*, the subject of the following parallel line. *nhrwt* must be understood as a circumstantial accusative specifying the manner in which the action described here, the splitting of the earth, took

place.[66]

The translations of the MT, Barb and Aq which read *tbq'* as a Piel 2ms form, taking Yahweh as the subject, are not as felicitous because they obscure the parallelism between this line and the next as well as the shift in scene from Yahweh to the cosmos. The interpretation of *tbq'* as a 2ms verb probably arose under the weight of the series of 2ms verbal forms immediately preceding.

40. There exists some discrepancy among the versions about the tense of *r'wk* and *yḥylw*. The MT has two different tenses, a perfect followed by an "imperfect." The OG has two verbs in the future (*opsontai* and *ōdinēsousi*; cf. the OL, *videbunt* and *dolebunt*). R has two verbs in the aorist (*eidos[an]* and *[ōdinēs]an*; cf. Vg, *viderunt* and *doluerunt*). And Barb has a prepositional infinitive phrase followed by a verb in the future (*en tǭ antophthalmein, tarachthēsontai*).

Of these possibilities, the MT is likely original. The juxtaposition of the suffixal (perfect) and prefixal (old preterit) forms here reflects the use of verb tenses which is characteristic of the entire poem. The shift from suffixal to prefixal forms here, as well as in the rest of the poem, is to be understood not as a shift between perfect and imperfect states but as the archaic use of perfect and preterit forms to convey past narrative, a practice best exemplified in Ugaritic poetry.[67] The same sequence of these two verbs is in fact found in Ps 77:17 (*r'wk mym yḥylw*), part of an archaic theophany very similar to Hab 3:8–15.

Preserving as it does an archaic practice for past narrative which was later replaced by the *waw* consecutive form, the MT represents the *lectio difficilior*, and the renderings in the OG and R can be understood as reflections of the attempt to level the forms through (either in the transmission of the Hebrew text or by the Greek translators) and make the sense consistent. The infinitive phrase followed by a future form in Barb is likely an attempt to render two finite verbs in idiomatic Greek (cf. v 6 in Barb).[68]

41. The versions attest two possibilities here: the MT (with R, Barb, Aq, Sym, Th, the Tg and Vg) reads *hrym*. The OG (with the OL) reads *'mym(laoi)*. The MT is to be preferred. It has, in the first place, the weight of the versions behind it; only the OG and the versions dependent on it represent *'mym*. Furthermore, the theophanic context, in which nature is disrupted by the divine appearance, as well as the parallel term *'rṣ* argue

for the appropriateness of "mountain" here. The disturbance of nature in this context frequently contains reference to the earth, often including the mountains (e.g. Judg 5:4–5; Ps 18:8; Nah 1:3–5; Mic 1:3–4) and the waters (see the following lines of Habakkuk 3). The OG may be described as interpretive.[69] In two other texts, Mic 6:2 and Exod 19:18, the OG has *laoi* where the MT has *hrym*. In both of these cases, as here, the context, and in the case of Mic 6:2 the poetic parallelism, suggests *hrym* as original and *'mym (laoi)* as exegetical.

42. Read the Poel perfect 3mp *zōrĕmû*, from *zrm*, "to storm." One wonders, with J. H. Eaton, whether the difficulty of the MT should be counted for or against it.[70] The combination of an obscure meaning and an extraordinarily short line (only 4 original syllables), however, suggests that some disruption of the MT has occurred. The majority of scholars for some time have preferred to emend this text on the basis of the closely parallel expression in Ps 77:18.[71] Since the recently discovered Hebrew manuscript from the Wadi Murabba'at also contains this reading, there is now further evidence that this proposal represented the original reading here.

43. Read *'ābôt*, "clouds," with the Murabba'at manuscript and Ps 77:18. Compare the expression, *'ābîm nātĕpû māyim*, from a similar theophanic context in Judg 5:4.

44. *šemeš* should be read with this line rather than with the following one with which it is connected in the MT. The Masoretic misdivision of these lines has resulted in both grammatical and stylistic problems. The poetic line in v 11a is saddled with two subjects, *šemeš* and *yārēaḥ*, which 1) lack a conjunction to connect them, 2) are related to a singular verb, *'āmad*, and 3) provide a plural antecedent for the 3ms suffix on *zbl*. Furthermore, v 11a is left as a single line unrelated to the lines which precede and follow it, an unconventional situation in Hebrew poetry.

The origin of these problems lies in the punctuation of the MT, which concludes v 10 with *nś'* rather than with *šmš*. Both the OG and Barb take *šmš* with the final line of v 10 which precedes it rather than with v 11a which follows it. The rendering of the Greek versions is clearly preferable to the MT, as many modern commentators have realized.[72] Understanding *šmš* as the last word and subject of the final line of v 10 relieves the grammatical problems introduced by the punctuation of the MT and provides a bicolon with two nicely balanced cola.

It should be noted that there is no support in the versions for the very popular modern idea that these two lines describe the darkening of the sun and moon. The versions add nothing to the MT in this regard. Rudolph is wrong in my opinion in translating Barb's *epesche* as "stopped."[73] It must mean "held out" rather than "held back" in reference to the sun's light, because the adversative *de* begins the next line. This next line in Barb is difficult to interpret. The moon's light is described as being "fixed, set" (*estathē*).

The image of the sun with its hands outstretched is not uncommon in ancient Near Eastern iconography. It is particularly known from Egyptian art.[74]

45. Read the noun *zbl*, "lordly dais," with the 3ms suffix, *zĕbulōh*. The MT contains the preexilic spelling (9th – 6th centuries B.C.E.) of this suffix. This interpretation of *zbl*, suggested by W. F. Albright, is certainly the best so far, based on its usage in other biblical texts (1 Kgs 8:13[=2 Chr 6:2]; Isa 63:15; Ps 49:15[text problematic]).[75]

46. The translation of this line hinges on the interpretation of the relationship between the terms in it. Barb (*kata to pheggos tōn bolidōn sou)* and the Vg (*in luce saggittarum tuarum*) take *ḥṣyk* as the *nomen rectum* of *l'wr*, "at the light of your arrows." By contrast, the MT (note the accent marks), the OG (*eis phōs bolides*), OL (*in luce jacula tua*), and Tg (*'mk bmymrk 'tgbrw* ?) do not understand *ḥṣyk* to be governed by *l'wr*. They read *ḥṣyk* as the subject of the verb *yhlkw*. It has been quite popular among recent scholars to disregard the MT and OG and accept the alternative interpretation of Barb and the Vg.[76] One is however then forced to identify a subject other than *ḥṣyk* for the verb *yhlkw*. None of the alternatives which have been offered—the sun and moon, the enemies of Yahweh, the cosmic waters, the divine procession—is completely satisfactory.[77]

It is preferable to accept the interpretation of the MT and OG and understand *ḥṣyk* as the subject of *yhlkw*. The verb *hlk* is also used to describe the movement of the divine arrows in the remarkably similar theophanic poem in Psalm 77 (v 18). In Job 37:12, *hlk* describes the movement of God's lightning (*'wrw*), as B. Duhm has pointed out.[78] This idea of speeding arrows is common in theophanic poems where they are also described as being sent (*šlḥ*) by Yahweh from the skies (Pss 18:15; 144:6). Furthermore, this bicolon is an independent unit and it is dubious whether this verb should apply to a subject elsewhere. The sun and moon in the preceding line are particularly unlikely candidates since they are described as standing (*'md*), not moving. The Piel form of *yhlkw* is appropriate here, expressing as it does the idea of continuous activity rather than a single act.[79] The arrows of lightning do not go out once but dart out over and over from the thunderclouds.

The problem which this interpretation raises—if *l'wr* is not taken as the *nomen regens* of *ḥṣyk*—is the meaning of the preposition *lĕ*. The OG (*eis*), OL (*in*), Vg (*in*), and Tg (*b*) all translate "in(to) light." Barb (*kata*) translates, "according to light." BDB has suggested that *l* be understood here by the general idea of having "reference to," in this case "reference to a condition, state, or concomitant circumstance" (cf. Job 29:3); thus, "with reference to a state of light/in the presence of light."[80] Though all of these alternatives are possible, none yields completely satisfactory sense.

J. Lachmann has suggested the translation, "as light," citing a number of texts (Num 22:22; Deut 31:21; 1 Sam 22:13; Ps 48:4; Isa 60:19) in which he believes the preposition *l* carries this meaning.[81] The gist of Lachmann's interpretation is correct but the function of the preposition can be more carefully defined. The preposition *l* here, to use one of the categories in BDB, is "denoting the principle with regard to which an act is done."[82] With this function of *l*, the noun following takes on adverbial force (e.g. *lṣdq ymlk-mlk*, "the king will rule justly (according to justice)," Isa 32:1). This adverbial function of the preposition *l* has also been identified in Ugaritic literature (*CTA* 14 Krt .92–93, 180–181).[83] According to this interpretation, *l'wr* may be translated "brightly," and *lngh* in the following line "brilliantly."

47. The translation of *ḥynt* as plural in the OG (*hoplōn*) should not be accepted as original. Several OG and OL mss. and the MT (which never understands *ḥnyt* as plural) all attest the singular form. The OG itself is not consistent, using *hoplon* in both singular (e.g. Pss 45[46]:9; 56[57]:4) and plural (e.g. Nah 3:3; Hab 3:11) forms to represent *ḥnyt*. Perhaps it has been influenced by the plural of *ḥṣ* in the previous line.

48. The suggestion has been made that the reading of the OG, *oligōseis*, "you will diminish" (cf. the OL, *imminues*, "you will diminish"), represents *tṣ'r*.[84] This is undoubtedly correct. In

Job 8:7; 14:21; and 2 Chr 24:24 *oligoō* renders *ṣ'r*. Furthermore the translators of the OG consistently render *ṣ'd* as "march, walk" (e.g. Judg 5:4, *apairō*, and Ps 67[68]:8, *diabainō*). Finally, the *d/r* confusion which would lead to these variants is common in this poem (e.g. v 10b).

Of these two variants, the MT is the superior reading. It is used elsewhere (e.g. Judg 5:4=Ps 68:8; 2 Sam 5:24) to describe the march of Yahweh into battle for his people. In these cases it is in parallelism with *yṣ'*, the same verb which begins the following bicolon (v 13a). And it provides a good parallel to *tdwš* in the following line, both verbs picturing Yahweh's treading on the earth. Of all recent commentators, only J. Lachmann considers the OG the superior reading, unconvincingly believing *ṣ'r* a better parallel to *dwš*.[85]

Different textual bases for the reading in Barb, *egerthēsę*, "you will rouse yourself," have been suggested, among them *tṣ'r*, *t'wr* and *ṣ'd*.[86] Of these *t'wr* was probably in Barb's textual base. It is an inferior reading to that in the MT, for the same reasons the OG reading is, and it can be explained by the simple haplography of *ṣadeh* from the *tṣ'r* of the OG *Vorlage*.

49. The MT is supported by Barb's *aloēseis*, "you will tread, thresh." The OG *kataxeis*, "you will shatter," probably also supports the MT, though other suggestions have been made.[87] The OG and Barb both contain the idea of "crushing" which is inherent in *dwš*. R. Sinker has explained the variations in the versions which render the OG in the following way: the OL takes *kataxeis* from *katagō*, "lead, bring down" and translates *detrahes*, "draw off, down;" the Syriac, on the other hand, takes *kataxeis* from *katagnumi*, "to shatter, break in pieces," and translates "beat, strike."[88] The Vg, *obstupefacies*, "you will render senseless," is probably an interpretive translation of the MT.

50. The verb *yṣ'* is frequently used to describe Yahweh's advance into battle for his people (Judg 5:4 = Ps 68:8; 2 Sam 5:24; Isa 42:13; Zech 14:3; Judg 4:4; Ps 108:12). In Judg 5:4 and 2 Sam 5:24 this verb follows the verb *ṣ'd* as it does here (v 12). Since it is used also of the king's advance into battle before his people (1 Sam 8:20) and of the advance of the army itself (Judg 2:15; 1 Sam 17:20), *yṣ'* appears to have technical military connotations in contexts such as these.[89]

51. For the use of *'am* as a reference to the militia of Israel,

see Chapter 3.

52. Though the Barthélemy scroll from Naḥal Ḥeber is not extant for the first bicolon of v 13, R can be reconstructed from the seventh column of Origen's Hexapla which is cited by Jerome:[90] *egressus es in salutem populi tui/in salutem cum christo tuo* = *R: exēlthes eis sōtērian laou sou/eis sōtērian syn christǭ sou.* As would be expected on the basis of Barthélemy's study, R here is the exact equivalent of Aquila's translation.

There are two popular alternative readings for the term *lyš'*: 1) the infinitive construct expressing purpose or result ("you went out ... to save"), and 2) a prepositional phrase ("you went out ... for victory"). *yṣ'* can be used in fact with either of these constructions (cf. 1 Sam 23:15; 1 Kgs 20:18).

The former alternative was taken by the OG *(tou sōsai)* and by Barb (*hrysasthai*). These versions apparently felt it was grammatically impossible to translate this expression as they had the same one in the previous line—as a prepositional phrase with a noun in the construct state ("for the victory of ...")—since it was followed by *'t*, which they interpreted as the sign of the direct object. Sym and the Tg also read the infinitive construct here.[91] Since this alternative was embraced by J. Wellhausen in the last century, it has been accepted by most modern textual critics.[92] Most in fact now think both instances of *lyš'* to be infinitives construct, following the reading of Sym and the Tg.

But there are problems with this interpretation. The first is grammatical. Since *yš'* occurs only in the Hiphil (or Niphal, but not Qal) in biblical Hebrew, one would expect *lhwšy'* here if this were the infinitive construct.[93] The second problem is stylistic. In the repetitive poetic parallelism which is in effect in this bicolon one would expect the sense of *lyš'* to be identical in both lines. Since it is understood as a prepositional phrase in the previous line by the major versions (the MT, OG, Barb, R, Aq, Th, OL, Vg), one would expect the same sense in this line. Of course, one might suggest, as do most modern interpreters (following Sym and the Tg), that the poet intended infinitives construct in both cases, but this goes against the major versions, does not solve the grammatical problem just mentioned, and assumes the poet was inconsistent in his use of the sign of the direct object.[94]

The second alternative, to read *lyš'* in the second line of v 13 as a prepositional phrase, was taken by the MT, R, Aq, and the Vg. This alternative provides the better translation of *lyš'*. It follows the consonantal text and is stylistically apt as a parallel for the same expression in the previous line. Moreover, the sign of the direct object *('t)*, which has provided the only problem for this translation, was likely not original in this text, as will be proposed in the following textual note.

53. Read *'am*, "people, militia," with F. Horst and W. F. Albright.[95] The sign of the direct object is a prosaic particle which does not belong in archaic poetry.[96] Furthermore, the poet's penchant for repetitive, or climactic, parallelism (vv 2, 8) favors this emendation.

The corruption in the MT could have arisen by one of two developments. The sign of the direct object could have been inserted for the sake of rhythm or grammatical sense after *'m* was lost by haplography. The two letters of *'m* are identical with the preceding and following ones.[97] Or *'m* could have been misinterpreted as *'im*, the preposition "with," and then replaced with the alternate preposition for "with," *'ēt*, which was later taken to be the sign of the direct object by some translators (e.g. the OG, Barb, Sym, and the Tg).[98] This development may still be reflected in R, Aq, and the Vg which translate *'t*, "with."

54. While the singular form of the MT is attested in R, Aq, Sym, Th, the Vg, and the Tg, both the OG (followed by the OL) and Barb read the plural form. The reading of the MT is superior. Only once is *mšyḥ* found in the plural, where it is applied together with *nby'ym* to the patriarchs (Ps 105:15). Elsewhere this term designates an individual who has been designated for a sacred office, the High Priest (Lev 4:3, 5, 16; 6:15) and the King (e.g. 1 Sam 2:10; Pss 2:2; 18:51; 132:10, 17; cf. Isa 45:1 where it is used of Cyrus). That is how it should be understood here. The particular official referred to here, as is proposed in Chapter 3, I believe to be the military commander of the league militia.

The plural form of the Greek versions is probably interpretive. The OG has a habit in this chapter of reading the plural where the MT contains a singular form (v 2: *erga*, v 4: *chersin*, v 7: *kopōn*, v 11: *hoplōn*, v 13: *desmous*, v 14: *kephalas*).[99] Barb's unusual rendering (*tous eklektous* where the OG has *tous christous*) in the opinion of M. L. Margolis who considers Barb a late translation, reflects an avoidance of *christos* because of its Christian associations.[100] It is strange that Aquila, who elsewhere replaces *christos* with *ēleimmenos* (Ps 2:2; Dan 9:26), ostensibly for the same reason, uses *christos* here.[101] The Christian implications of this term can be seen in Jerome's comment on Aquila's rendering: *Iudaeus Aquila interpretatus est ut Christianus.* It can also be seen in the translation found in the eighth column of the Hexapla *(Sexta:) dia iēsoun ton christon sou*, "through Jesus your Christ."

55. Some have questioned whether the OG, *ebales*, represents *mḥṣt*,[102] but there is no reason to doubt seriously that it does. *ballō* renders other Hebrew roots which are similar in meaning to *mḥṣ* (e.g. *nkh(Hiph)*, *tq'*, *śwm*, *npl(Qal, Hiph)*). Furthermore the OG does not translate *mḥṣ* consistently, using a different word for this root almost every time it occurs. The fact that Barb's translation, *katetoxeusas*, is also used to render *mḥṣ* elsewhere (Num 24:8) makes it quite definite that *mḥṣt* begins v 13b.

56. Read *bāmat*, the 3fs construct form of *bāmâ* (Ugaritic: *bamtu*), with the translation "back" rather than the usual rendering "height". The variations among the major versions at this point in the poem indicate a disturbance of the text from very early times. Following the verb *māḥaṣtā* are three alternate readings: 1) MT (followed by R and the Vg): *rō'š mibbêt rāšā'*, *r'š mbyt rš'* 2) OG (followed by OL): *eis kephalas anomōn thanaton* = *(b)r'š(y) rš'(ym) mwt* or *(b)r'š mwt rš'(ym)*; Barb: *katetoxeusas kephalas anthrōpōn hyperēphanōn* = *r'š(y) mty rš'*.

All three witnesses attest to the terms *ro'š* and *rāšā'*, though the differences between singular and plural present a problem. For the remaining term, however, three variants are reflected: the MT *mibbêt*, the OG *môt*, and the Barb *mĕtê*. What was the original reading? The alternative in the MT, R and Vg, *mibbêt*, accepted as representing the original reading by R. Sinker and J. H. Eaton,[103] appears to describe Yahweh's blow directed against a particular human individual, "(the) leader/chief from (the) house/dynasty of the wicked." This reading is not likely however because it is awkward grammatically. One would expect a construct chain or the preposition *lĕ* to link *rō'š* and *bêt* rather than the preposition *min*. The alternative of Barb, *mĕtê*, accepted as the original reading by P. Humbert and B. Margulis,[104] appears to describe Yahweh's blow directed against a group of evil men, "the heads of arrogant men." This reading too is unlikely because it is plural and the enemy in the rest of the attack (vv 13b–14) is clearly singular.

That leaves the alternative of the OG: *môt*. Understood as did the translator of the OG, "You flung into the heads of the wicked ones death," it is hardly attractive. The expression is peculiar, and the enemy is wrongly understood as a group. But understood, as U. Cassuto and W. F. Albright have, as a reference to Mot, one of the names of the primordial enemy of the storm god, it provides an appealing solution to this textual puzzle. On the basis of the OG, Albright has offered the following reconstruction: *r'š m()wt rš'*, "the head of wicked Death."[105]

Of these alternatives, Mot, understood as Albright has, is the most attractive reading. The identification of the cosmic adversary as the object of Yahweh's blow best fits the context of the poem (vv 8–15). In Habakkuk 3, River/Sea is identified as the enemy of Yahweh in the verses which provide the inclusive framework for this section of the poem (vv 8, 15). At Ugarit these same designations, Prince Sea/Judge River and Mot, Death, are all names of the cosmic foe of the storm god Ba'l.[106] Furthermore, the arming of the divine warrior and his advance into battle which precede v 13 (vv 8–11) recall conflicts between Marduk and Tiamat in *Enūma eliš* and Ba'l and the monster in the Ugaritic myths.

One other possibility deserves consideration. The term in question may be a part of the body of the adversary, described in detail in the following lines, which receives Yahweh's blow (*māḥaṣtā*). As an alternative to Albright's solution, I suggest the reading *bmt*, "back," as the original reading which stands behind the variants, *mbyt*, *mwt*, and *mty*. In classical Hebrew the old feminine singular construct *bmt* would probably have been understood as a plural, since this is the customary usage of this term in the Hebrew Bible, and have been written *bmwt*. The corruption of the MT could then be accounted for by a metathesis of *bet* and *mem* and the common confusion of *waw* and *yod*. A nearly identical corruption in fact occurred in the Hebrew text of Hab 3:19 from which the Tg was translated. The original *bmwt* has been rendered *byt*, showing the *waw* / *yod* confusion and the loss instead of the transposition of *mem*.[107] The corruptions in the Greek versions are also readily explained. The reading of the OG involves the haplography of *bet*, a corruption attested in the Hebrew text of 2 Sam 1:19 from which the OG was translated, where the original *bmwtyk* has been replaced by *mwtyk*. Barb's reading *mty*, reflecting the haplography of *bet* in the OG and the *waw* / *yod* confusion in the MT, also suffered from the metathesis of *yod* and *taw*.

The reading *bmt*, "back," makes no sense of course following the word *rō'š*, "head." If *bmt* is correct, this text must represent an ancient conflate text with a double reading: two different parts of the body of the enemy, head and back, both possible objects of Yahweh's blow, have been combined from different traditions. Of the two, *rō'š* is likely the intrusive member. It could have encroached here because of its use nearby in v 14a as the object of Yahweh's second blow and/or because it is used as the object of *māḥaṣ* elsewhere in Hebrew poetry (e.g. Pss 68:22; 110:6).

Other evidence supports this proposal that *bmt* was the original member of the doublet, *rō'š bāmat*. First, if the back of the wicked monster receives the blow of Yahweh, then the relationship between this line and the following one is clarified. The divine warrior strikes the back or trunk of his adversary, and then he lays it bare, or exposes it, from one end to the other, from buttocks (*yswd*) to neck (*ṣw'r*).[108] Second, the twofold blow to the enemy—first to the body (v 13b) and then to the head (v 14a)- which this reading would suggest is paralleled in the description of the struggle with the primordial monster in Ugaritic and Akkadian literature. In the Ugaritic myth Baʿl strikes *ym* / / *nhr* first on the back (*klp* / / *bn ydm*; cf. Zech 13:6) and then on the head (*qdqd* / / *bn ʿnm*).[109] In *Enūma eliš* Marduk first shatters the body of Tiamat (4.97-104) and then returns and smashes her skull (4.128-132).

Two alternate suggestions for the reading of v 13b deserve to be mentioned in order to be set aside as realistic solutions. One is that of F. Stephens, who proposed *bhmwt*, Behemoth, as original and considered the MT and the OG (Stephens: *hmwt*) corruptions of this.[110] Stephen's inclinations that Yahweh's foe was a cosmic adversary were correct, but contrary to his opinion, Behemoth is not an appropriate designation for this adversary. It is not used for the primordial dragon of chaos in biblical literature.[111]

The other suggestion is even less satisfactory, though it has now been adopted in some recent English translations of the OT (*NEB*, *JB*). According to this suggestion, defended by a number of past and present scholars,[112] *rō'š* should be taken to mean "peak" or "roof," *bêt* to mean "house" in its ordinary sense, *yĕsôd* to mean "foundation," and *ṣawwā'r* should be emended to *ṣûr*, "rock," yielding the following reading for v 13b: "Thou dost shatter the wicked man's house from the roof down, uncovering its foundations to the bare rock" (*NEB*). According to this interpretation the destruction of a building is to be understood as a metaphor for the defeat of Israel's enemy.

This suggestion faces serious difficulties. A major problem, as E. Delitzsch recognized long ago, is the fact that, except for *yĕsôd*, the terms describing the enemy here are not technical architectural terms.[113] The terms in v 13b and 14a are rather transparent "body" language. Yahweh pierces the head (*rō'š*) with arrows, lays the body bare from neck (*ṣawwā'r*) to buttocks (*yĕsôd*), and, if my suggestion is correct, strikes its back (*bāmat*). Even *yĕsôd* which can be used as an architectural term, "foundation," likely has a broader meaning in Hebrew and may be applied to the body.[114] The scene just described is reminiscent of the slaying of the dragon of chaos in ancient conflict myth.

Another telling bit of evidence against the building interpretation is the use of the verb *māḥaṣ*. *māḥaṣ* is an ancient West-Semitic verb found in Akkadian, Ugaritic, Hebrew, and Aramaic. It means, as Moshe Held has observed in his study of the term in the cognate literatures, "to strike/slay (by striking down)."[115] Though it is used in a wide variety of contexts in Akkadian literature, in the Ugaritic epics, and in Hebrew poetry, *māḥaṣ* is used exclusively to describe inflicting a wound in combat. The object of the blow is always an animate adversary. It is used of the divine warfare of Ba'l (e.g. *CTA* 2.4[68].9), 'Anat (e.g. *CTA* 3['nt].2.7), Mot (e.g. *CTA* 6[49].6.24) and of Yahweh (e.g. Ps 68:22: and Job 26:12, with the direct object, *rahab*).[116] The usage of this term does not favor its use with an inanimate direct object like the roof of a house.

bmt should be translated here and in v 19 on the basis of the Ugaritic cognate *bmt*, "back," rather than on the basis of its customary (and derived) use in Hebrew for "heights." In Ugaritic, *bmt* always refers to the back of an animal or god (e.g. *CTA* 4[51].4.14, 15; 6[62].1.5). And the proposal has been made that *bmt* carries the old literal meaning "back" in a number of cases in Hebrew poetry, in particular, cases in which a victorious warrior stands on or tramples the back of his vanquished foe. F. M. Cross and D. N. Freedman have suggested "their backs" for *bmwtymw* in Deut 33:29 where the victorious nation of Israel tramples (*drk*) on the backs of its foes.[117] And M. Pope defends the interpretation "back" for *bmwty* in Job 9:8 where the victorious 'El tramples (*drk*) the back of Sea (*ym*).[118]

57. "The wicked one" (*rāšā'*) is either an original epithet for the dragon of chaos (cf. *Enūma eliš* where Tiamat is described as wicked (4.18, 83–84)) or a later substitution for the actual name of the dragon in order to mute the high mythology.

58. Read with all of the versions against the MT the Piel perfect 2ms form of *'rh*. *'ērîtā* (OG: *exēgeiras* = *'rt* from *'wr*; R: *exe(kenōsa)s* = *'ryt* from *'rh* Vg: *denudasti* = *'ryt* from *'rh*; Th: *ornasti* = *'dyt* from *'dh* with a *d/r* confusion). Although the infinitive construct of the MT, *'rwt*, has been widely defended,[119] one would expect in this case the normal infinitive absolute *'rh* if the poet had wished to use an infinitive. The finite form *'ērîtā* makes a better poetic parallel to *māḥaṣtā* (cf. v 12, v 2a, etc.).

'rh means "to strip, lay bare, expose" in biblical literature. It frequently takes as its direct object human beings (Lam 4:21) or parts of their bodies (e.g. *š'r*, "flesh," Lev 20:19; *mqr*, "fountain (genitals)," Lev 20:18; *npš*, "throat" (? cf. the Akkadian), Ps 141:8, Isa 53:12). In Isa 3:17 Yahweh strikes the head (*qdqd*) of the Jerusalemite women and lays their bodies bare (*pthn y'rh*).[120]

59. Although the OG, *desmous* (= *mwsrwt*, "bonds"), and R, *themelious* (= *yswdwt*, "foundation stones"), have the plural form, the singular of the MT, Th, and the Vg is preferable. Plurals in the OG are suspect (cf. vv 2, 4, etc.). The reading of the OG arises from the common confusion and has been influenced by the reading *kephalas anomōn*, "the heads of wicked men," in the previous line and the word "neck" (*ṣawwā'r*) which follows, a part of the body on which bonds or shackles were often placed (cf. Isa 52:2; Jer 30:8).

yĕsôd is the only term in v 13b which is not immediately recognizable as a part of the body. It is primarily used for the foundation of a city wall (Mic 1:6; Ezek 13:14; Lam 4:11; Ps 137:7) or the base of the altar (Exod 29:12, etc.). *yswd* may however refer here to the base of the body, the buttocks. This interpretation is suggested by the juxtaposition of *yswd* with *ṣw'r* another part of the body. M. Dahood has defended this interpretation of *yswd* in Ps 137:7 where he believes Jerusalem is depicted as a woman being stripped to the buttocks.[121] Prov 10:25 may also contain an example of *yswd* for buttocks. W. F. Albright has suggested that *yswd* has the same derived sense in Hebrew as the synonymous *išdu* has in Akkadian, where *išdu* can refer to the foundation of a building but is also used to describe the tail-end or base of Tiamat's body in her battle with Marduk (*Enūma eliš* 4.90, 129). Albright believes v 13b to be "a vivid sketch of the prostrate body of a dragon," translating, "Destroying (him) tail-end to neck."[122]

60. The versions by and large read as the MT. The OG *diekopsas*, "you cut through," though not as clean a translation as *tetrainō*, "bore through" (4 Kgs 12:9[10]; Job 40:19[24]; Isa 36:6 = 4 Kgs 18:21), and *trypaō*, "pierce through" (Job 40:21 [26]; Hag 1:6), which are otherwise used for *nqb*, "pierce," probably renders this root.[123] R more closely renders *nqbt* with *dietrēsas*, "you pierced." The Vg, *maladixisti*, reads *nqbt* but understands it according to *nqb* II, "curse" (Lev 24:16).[124] The Tg *bz't'*, "you split, perforated," also coincides with the MT. The only dissenting reading is Barb's *exedikēsas*, "you avenged," which apparently translates *nqmt* and represents a confusion between *bet* and *mem* in Barb's *Vorlage*.[125] The action of Yahweh piercing his enemy is appropriate in this context. In a number of other descriptions of the vanquishing of the dragon, it is pierced (*ḥll*) by Yahweh (Ps 89:11; Job 26:13; Isa 51:9). In Job 40 *nqb* itself is used of the piercing of Behemoth's nose (v 24) and Leviathan's jaw (v 26).[126]

61. The reading of the MT, *bmṭy-*, "with shafts," which is supported by R (*en hrabdois*), the Vg (*sceptris*), and the Tg (*bḥwṭry-*) is sound. The shafts, *mṭy-* , of Yahweh have already been mentioned in v 9 and it is not surprising to see them mentioned again in v 14 when the battle with the enemy is joined.[127] The sentence structure here, *nqb* + *b* with a weapon + the part of the body of the monster which is pierced, is closely reflected in Job 40:24b, 26b (*b* with a weapon + *nqb* + the part of the body of the monster which is pierced; cf. also Ps 74:13a).

The OG and Barb are both somewhat difficult to explain. The OG *en ekstasei*, "in astonishment," may represent a text very much like the MT: 1) *bmṭw*, "in trembling," taking *mṭw* as a nominal form from **mṭh* = *mwṭ*, "to totter;"[128] 2) *bmṭh*, "in stretching out," taking *mṭh* as the Hiphil participle of *nṭh*, "to stretch out," and considering *ekstasei* to be an inner Greek corruption of *ektasei*, "extension;"[129] or, 3) *bmṭ* /*bmwṭ*, taking *mṭ* as the Qal participle of *mwṭ*, "totter," or *mwṭ* as the noun "shaking." None of these *Vorlagen* for *ekstasei* is attested elsewhere, however, and some have suggested that the OG represents a text different from the MT, e.g. *mhwmh*,[130] or *zw'h*.[131] None of these possibilities is preferable to the MT. Barb's *meta dynameōs*, "with strength," is generally considered to be a paraphrastic rendering of the MT.[132] Barb may have been influenced in its translation by similar contexts in which God's strength is emphasized (Pss 74:13a; 89:11b; Job 26:12; cf. Isa 51:9a). The concrete description of Yahweh's destruction of the dragon has been muted in both the OG and Barb.

There is wide disagreement about the suffix attached to *mṭy-*. The MT, R, Vg, and Tg read the 3ms suffix, which can only mean that these shafts belong to the enemy. The OG reads no suffix, but two Ethiopic translations of it read the 3mp suffix. Barb reads the 2ms suffix. Since the context suggests these shafts to be Yahweh's and since they are mentioned previously (v 9) as belonging to Yahweh it is best to read with Barb, as do many commentators, the 2ms suffix: "your shafts."[133]

62. The only discrepancy among the versions is whether this term should be read as singular (MT, R, Vg) or plural (OG, Barb, OL, Tg). The plural readings may be accounted for by the fact that *r'š* was understood to be in construct with a plural noun which followed and thus was itself rendered plural.[134] It is likely that the MT represents the original reading and describes the head of the monster being killed (cf. the body terms in v 13cd).[135] Many commentators who accept the singular feel that sense demands a suffix, *r'šw*, referring to the figure smitten in v 13b.[136] There is reason to question the addition of a suffix, however. It is attested in none of the versions. It is not used (where sense might suggest it) when such other parts of the body as *ṣw'r* and *yswd* (v 13b) are mentioned. And, finally, it is not used at this place in a remarkably similar phrase in *Enūma eliš*.

This phrase in *Enūma eliš* deserves some comment because of its striking similarity to v 14a. After Marduk kills Tiamat (4: 94–106) and deals with her companions (107–127), he returns to Tiamat (128) and stands on her buttocks (129: *išdasa*, cf. *yswd* in v 13b). Then: *ina miṭišu la padi ulatti muḫḫa*, "with his merciless weapon he crushed (her) head" (130: translation from *CAD*, vol. 9, p. 148). The warrior's weapon here is identified by the same name, *miṭṭu*, as that in Hab 3:14a, *mṭ*. The verb in *Enūma eliš*, *ulatti* (D of *letû*, "split into pieces"), though not exactly parallel to *nqb*, "pierce," is similar in intent. And the part of Tiamat struck is the head. There need be no direct borrowing here, but the similarities suggest that there could well have been conventional phrases to picture the destruction of the dragon (compare, for example, Isa 27:1 with *CTA* 5[67].1.1,28), one of which is reflected in *Enūma eliš* 4:130 and Hab 3:14a.

63. The remainder of v 14 is the lengthiest textual puzzle of the chapter.[137] The next four words of the MT are understood very differently by the OG, and differently still by Barb. And the final four words of the MT, though confirmed by the OG and Barb, are hard to understand in the context. The disparity among the versions at this point in the poem indicates an ancient disruption in the text which may no longer be possible to correct. All that can be done until more information comes to light is to point out the nature of the difficulties and make some suggestions about avenues along which a solution might lie.

The reading of the OG, *dynastōn*, "rulers, masters," has been considered by some an attractive suggestion for the meaning of the Hebrew term *przw*, and has been supported by noting the Arabic cognate *farz*, "distinguished."[138] The OG is not reliable, however. The fact that the OG translates the root *prz* differently each time it occurs in the MT suggests that the translators were depending upon educated guessing from context rather than upon a consistent understanding of the meaning of this word. Furthermore, *dynastōn* may represent a text different from the MT, e.g. *rznym* (cf. Prov 8:15; 14:28; perhaps *rznym* ʾ*rw* resulting from *w/y* and *m/s* confusions).[139]

The reading of Barb, *tōn hamartōlōn*, "the sinners," is puzzling. It may either represent a different *Vorlage*, e.g. *prṣw*,[140] or it may be a guess at *przw* influenced by the *rš*ʿ of v 13b. The Vg, *bellatorum eius*, "his warriors," must also be a guess, though a popular one (cf. the *RSV*). The Tg is too expansionistic at this point to determine an equivalent reading. The reading of R, *ate[ichis]tōn autou*, "his unwalled (places)," may be the best proposal for the sense of the Hebrew term (cf. Deut 3:5; Judg 5:7; Ezek 38:11; Zech 2:8).[141] But the proposal "his villages" is difficult to understand in this context.

A final problem is the lack of agreement about the suffix for this term among the versions. The OG, Barb, and OL read a plural with no suffix; and the MT, R, and Vg read a plural with the 3ms suffix.

A solution to this situation must lie along the lines of accepting this root in its usual Hebrew sense, "villages/out of the way places," or reading a form of the verb *pzr*, "to scatter," in place of *prz*, a reading which could have been lost from simple metathesis.[142] In any event, this term should not be taken in construct with *r'š* as all of the versions do. V 14a represents a complete poetic line concluding with *r'š*. The addition of another word would overload the line.

The versions concur that a form of *s'r*, as in the MT, existed in their texts at this point. The translation of the OG, *seisthēsontai*, "they will shake," seems at first strange since *seiō* almost always renders *r'š*.[143] But in Amos 1:14 *seisthēsetai* renders *s'r* and in Jer 23:19 *seismos* translates *s'rh*.[144] R, which usually "corrects" the OG to the MT, maintains *seisthēsontai* here (cf. also the OL, *commovebuntur*, "they will be shaken"). Both the Vg, *venientibus ut turbo*, "coming as a whirlwind," and the Tg, *brwḥ 'l'wlyn*, "with the wind of whirlwinds," also point to *s'r*.[145] Barb's *tous pepoithotas*, "those who trust . . .," is the most unusual reading, but it may represent *yissā'ădû* with the confusion of *d/r* which is common in this text.[146]

Most of the versions read this term as a verb, either imperfect plural (MT, OG, OL) or participle (Vg, Sym), and understand it as the activity (shaking, storming) of Yahweh's enemies. The nominal *s'r* or *s'rh*, however, should not be ruled out (cf. the Tg and Vg). *s'r*/*s'rh* is elsewhere used to picture Yahweh's power and his attack upon his foes (e.g. Ezek 1:4; Job 38:1; Amos 1:14; Isa 41:16). This would fit the context nicely. The use of Yahweh's wind to subdue the chaotic waters is alluded to in Job 26:13 and Gen 1:2.[147]

At *lhpyṣny* the three major witnesses, the MT, OG, and Barb, are again at odds. The Hiphil infinitive of *pwṣ*, "to scatter," in the MT has substantial support from the later Greek translators (R: *tou sko[rpis]ai*; Aq: *diaskorpisai*; Sym: *skorpisai*) and the Vg (*ad dispergendum me*), though there is no agreement on the object of the scattering (MT, Vg: *ny*, "me"; R: *hēmas* = *nw*, "us"; Aq and Sym: no object). The OG reads a text similar to the MT but gives it a different sense: *en autę̄. dianoixousi* = *lh ypṣw*, "(they will be shaken) in it; they will open (their bridles)."[148] Barb omits the word altogether.[149]

The reading of the OG, *dianoixousi chalinous autōn*, "they

will open their bridles," may have been influenced by the mention of horses in v 15 and is in any case unusual. A solution here probably lies along the lines of the MT, "to scatter" (possibly the dragon's body, or its helpers, Yahweh's enemies)[150] or of Barb's text which omits the word. The full, prosaic quality of the text of v 14 may indicate explanatory additions or doublets. *lhpyṣny* may duplicate *pzr* if this was the original reading of *przw* above.

The next term in the MT, *'lyṣtm*, "their exultation," again has substantial support from the later Greek translators (R: *to gauriama autōn*; Aq: *gauriama autōn*; Sym: *tous gauriōntas)* and the Vg (*exultatio eorum*). But the OG again differs. *chalinous autōn*, "(they will open) their bridles," most likely represents *mṣlwtm* (cf. Zech 14:20).[151] Barb's *epi tę̄ authadeią autōn*," in their own self–will," is enigmatic. It could represent a text similar to the MT, but divided differently: *'l yṣtm*.[152] The Tg, *wyhbw 'yṣ'*, "and they gave counsel," might reflect *'ăṣātām*, "their counsel."[153]

The diversity here again indicates a disrupted text. One solution is to accept the tradition of the MT but read *'āla()ṣtā()*, "you rejoiced," understanding this as Yahweh's exultation after defeating his enemy.[154] Another is to accept the text of the OG but not its interpretation of it. *mṣwlh* normally means "the deep," not the forced sense the OG applies (possibly influenced by v 15), and this might represent another reference to Yahweh's foe, the sea: *mṣlh*, "the deep," or *mṣlt ym*, "the deep sea."[155]

Considering the diversity in the versions thus far in this verse, there is remarkable unanimity in the reading of the final phrase of v 14: *kmw l'kl 'ny bmstr*. The only differences are the following: 1) some versions omit *kmw* (Barb, Aq, the Peshitta);[156] 2) there is some question whether a participle, *'kl*, was read by some where the MT (Barb, Aq, Sym) has the infinitive *l'kl* (cf. the OG: *esthōn*, R: *esthiōn*, OL: *comedens*, Vg: *eius qui devorat*);[157] and 3) the OG (OL) against all the others understands *'ny* to be the subject of *'kl* rather than its object.[158]

The problem here then is not the diversity of the versions, but the meaning of this phrase in this context. Albright does not venture to translate this line, believing that its "obvious meaning can scarcely be correct."[159] Of the explanations which have been put forward, those of U. Cassuto, who believes this phrase represents the longing of Mot, Death (cf. OG of v 13b), to swallow the living into its recesses, and of W. A. Irwin, who believes the poor are feasting on the body of the slain monster, are most interesting.[160]

The traditional way of understanding the last part of v 14, as reflected in the versions and the opinions of most scholars, is to see here the actions of the cohorts of the enemy against God's people. An alternate interpretation, which deserves more consideration, is to see at this point the annihilation of the dragon which has been slain in vv 13b and 14a. Only W. A. Irwin has attempted a solution along these lines.[161]

Both in the Bible and in the comparative literature there is evidence that after the divine warrior slays his adversary, he disposes of the body. In *Enūma eliš*, after Marduk kills Tiamat, he returns to her to smash her skull and rip her apart so that the north wind bears her blood to secret places.[162] At Ugarit, ʿAnat disposes of Mot by cleaving (*bqʿ*), scattering (*dry*), burning (*šrp*), grinding (*ṯḥn*), and scattering/sowing (*drʿ*) his remains in the field (*bšd*) so the birds can devour (*ʾkl*) his flesh.[163] In another text, ʿAnat scatters the remains on the sea (*bym*).[164] In the two Egyptian tales, "The Book of Overthrowing ʿAPEP" and the "The Myth of Horus at Edfu," the serpent monster is dismembered following its death.[165]

This act is reflected in biblical literature as well. In Ps 74:13–14, after God breaks the heads of Tanin/Leviathan, he gives the monster as food to the animals in the desert (? *lʿm lṣyym*). In Ezek 29:3–5 and 32:2–6, where the king of Egypt is pictured as the primordial monster of the seas, he (the dragon) is killed and then abandoned in the desert to be food for the wild animals and birds.[166] It is possible that the scattering and devouring in Hab 3:14 reflect a similar situation.

64. On the basis of the Greek versions (OG: *epebibasas* [causal of *epibainō*, "to tread"], "you caused ... to tread"; Barb: *anebibasas*, "you made ... go up"), the logic of the Hebrew phrase, and the use of the Hiphil form of *drk* in a similar situation in v 19, many scholars would prefer to read the Hiphil here: *hdrkt*.[167] Though this reading is possible, it is not without problems. When the Hiphil of *drk* is used with a truly causative sense, it occurs only in the idiom, "to lead along a path" (e.g. Pss 119:35; 107:7; Isa 42:16; Prov 4:11; frequently the Hiphil does not appear to carry the causative sense at all, e.g. Judg 20:43; Jer 51:33; Job 28:8). Furthermore, the focus on Yahweh as the victor who treads on his

vanquished foe is in harmony with his being the subject (vv 8–15) in the preparation for battle and the battle itself which precedes v 15. GKC notes the use in Hebrew poetry of "two subjects in a verbal sentence, one of the person and the other of the thing. The latter then serves—whether it precedes or follows—to state the instrument, organ, or member by which the action in question is performed."[168] That is the best way to understand the construction of v 15a. This line would then read "You trampled on Sea with your horses."

65. The preposition *b* occurs commonly with the verb *drk* to identify the thing on which the subject treads (e.g. Isa 59:8; 63:2; Mic 5:4–5; Deut 1:36; Josh 14:9). It should be translated "on" here (with Barb. *epi*, and Tg, *'l*) rather than "in" (with the OG, *eis*, and Vg, *in*). The association of these images with the Exodus from Egypt and the Reed Sea (see the OG renderings in textual note 63) may account for the interpretation of the OG and Vg. *ym* is Sea, the name of the adversary of Yahweh with which this section of the poem opens (v 8a). The image here is that of the victorious warrior trampling on his conquered foe. The most remarkable parallel to this image in biblical literature is the description of God in Job 9:8 as the one "who treads on the back of Sea" (*dwrk 'l bmwty ym*).[169] Other examples of this use of *drk* in the Bible include Deut 33:29 and Judg 5:21 (cf. Judg 20:43; Amos 4:13; and Mic 1:3).[170] This same image is used of Marduk in *Enūma eliš* after he kills Tiamat (4.129). This act, the conquering hero astride the defeated foe, provides the perfect climax for the battle between Yahweh and his cosmic adversary described in vv 8–15.

66. Among the different interpretations given this term by the versions, that of the Greek translators is the best. Both the OG (*tarassontas*, "stirring up") and Barb (*etarachthē*, "was stirred up") understand *ḥmr* as a form of the verb *ḥāmar*, "ferment, boil, foam up." *ḥāmar* is also used to describe the seething of the insurgent waters in Ps 46:4. The seething of the insurgent waters, though described with other verbs, can be seen also in Ps 93:3–4 and Hab 3:10. It may be best to read a noun form from this verb: "the surge/swell (of many waters)." The interpretation of the MT (*ḥōmer*, see BDB, p. 330) and Tg (*dgwr*), "heap," is not as appropriate in this context and is an uncommon meaning for this term in Hebrew. The waters of the Reed Sea and of the Jordan are

elsewhere described as being piled up in a heap (though in different words; e.g. Exod 15:8 [Ps 78:13] of the Reed Sea, and Josh 3:13, 16 of the Jordan) and this may have influenced this interpretation. The reading of the Vg, *in luto*, "in the mire" (*ḥōmer* I, BDB, p. 330) may also arise from associations of this verse with the Reed Sea.

Both the Vg, *in luto*, and the Tg, *bdgwr*, suggest *bḥmr*. The addition of the preposition to this line would make the parallelism between *ym* and *ḥmr mym rbym*, the alternate designation of Sea here, more explicit and would conform to the parallel use of prepositions elsewhere in this poem (vv 2b, 3, 5, 8a, 11b, 12, 13a, 18). It would have the added benefit of making the lines of this bicolon more nearly equal in length. Its omission can be explained by noting the similarity between *b* and *k* in the Aramaic script and positing the haplography of the second of the two.

67. The versions support the MT, the OG *hydōr poly*, "much water," probably being used collectively, and Barb's *ta exaisia hydata tēs abyssou*, "the violent waters of the deep," likely representing a free translation.[171] *mym rbym* is a conventional parallel for *ym* occurring consistently, as here, in the second position (Pss 77:20; 107:23; Isa 23:3; cf. Isa 17:12–13 and Ps 93:4; also Ezek 27:26). It commonly is used of the insurgent waters which Yahweh subdues (e.g. Pss 29:3; 93:4; 18:17; Isa 17:12–13).[172]

Many commentators, both ancient and modern, have considered v 15 to be out of place in the poem.[173] Considered from a literary and thematic perspective, however, it fits perfectly. Literarily, v 15 provides a fine inclusion for this section of the poem which describes Yahweh's battle with the dragon (vv 8–15). The name of Yahweh's adversary, *ym*, and part of Yahweh's entourage, *swsyk*, which were introduced at the beginning (v 8) are referred to again here at the end (v 15).[174] Thematically, v 15 provides a fitting climax for this section. The poem moves from Yahweh's anger against Sea, to his preparation for battle, to the battle itself, and then to his final triumph, pictured here in v 15 as the conquering warrior astride his vanquished foe.

68. There appears to have been some disruption in the texts both Greek translators used. The OG, *ephylaxamēn*, "I kept watch," probably represents *šmrty*.[175] Barb's *etaxamēn*, "I stationed (myself)," on the other hand, must represent *śmty*.[176] The MT (supported by the Vg, *audivi*, and the Tg, *šmʿyt*) is the best

reading of these three alternatives. It provides the most natural sense, it repeats the author's introductory words (*šm'ty šm'k*, v 2a) thus framing the description or report of God's activity in vv 3–15, and it provides an appropriate parallel for *lqwl* for in the following line.

69. Again the Greek translators are at odds with the MT. The reading of the OG, *proseuchēs*, "prayer," may be the result of the translators understanding this infrequent Hebrew verb on the basis of the Aramaic root *ṣl'*, "to pray."[177] This is the way in which the Tg (*ṣl'*) takes the term. Barb omits the word altogether. Again the best alternative is the MT (supported by the Vg, *contremuerunt*). *ṣllw*, "quivered," provides a fitting parallel for *rgz* in the previous line. The reading of the OG which identifies the sound (*lqwl*) as that of the author's own prayer is confusing in this context. And Barb's omission of *ṣllw* makes the poetic line too short.

70. The MT, followed by the Vg (*ingrediator*, "enters," = *ybw'*), preserves the correct reading. The use of the prefix form of the verb for past narrative fits the pattern of verb tenses in the poem as a whole. The OG reading, *kai eisēlthe*, "and entered," likely represents *wb'* which could have arisen from the common graphic confusion of *w/y*. The use of the conjunction, especially at the beginning of a unit, is uncommon in old poetry and in all likelihood not original. Barb, the Vg, and the Tg lack the conjunction.[178]

71. There are two traditions in the interpretation of this term. The MT and the Vg (*putredo*) read "rottenness." The OG (*tromos*), Barb (*tromos*), OL (*tremor*), and the Tg (*zy'*) read "trembling." It has been suggested that the second of these traditions is reading an alternative text, *r'd*, "trembling,"[179] or interpreting *rqb* on the basis of the Arabic root *rqb*, "to fear."[180]

Whatever the case, the former tradition preserves the better reading. The expression "rottenness in the bones" which is used here occurs elsewhere to describe a strong physical and emotional reaction, once to passion (Prov 14:30), another time to a shameful companion (Prov 12:4). This expression also fits the context here. The feeling of rottenness or decay or weakness in the bones in the first line of this bicolon is logically related to the unsteady steps described in the second line.[181] Finally, *rqb*, "rottenness," is in this context the *lectio difficilior*. It is quite possible that the descriptions of trembling in the two previous lines and in the following one led translators to see it in this line as well.

72. The text is not at stake here, but the interpretation is. In Hebrew *tḥt* with a suffix can mean either "under one" (e.g. Ps 18:37, 40; Job 9:13; 36:16; Num 16:31), or "in one's place, where one stands" (e.g. Gen 2:21; Exod 16:24; Deut 2:12; Jer 28:13). The OG (*hypokatōthen mou*), Th (*hypokatō mou*), OL (*subter me*), and Vg (*subter me*) opt for the former interpretation; the MT (note the position of the *'atnaḥ*, Barb (*kat hemauton*, "as for me"), and Tg (*wb'tr dsryn'*, "after resting/where I stand"?) opt for the latter.

The former interpretation is preferable. As a description of the location of the poet's trembling steps (see textual note 74 below), "under me" is the more natural rendering.[182] The shift to the other alternative, "where I stand," was probably made in the MT, Barb, and Tg after the original subject of this line, *'šry*, "my steps," was taken as a relative pronoun (MT: *'ăšer*; Tg: *d*) beginning the next line, and this interpretation was the only reasonable way to relate *tḥty* to the following verb.

73. Read the Qal imperfect (preterit) 3fs of *rgz*, *tirgaz*. The MT (*'rgz*), Barb (*etarachthēn* = *rgzty* or *'rgz*), and Tg (*z'yt*) read a 1cs form of *rgz*, while the OG (*etarachthē* = *rgz/rgzh* or *yrgz/trgz*), OL (*conturbata est* = OG), and Vg (*scateat*, "gushes" = *yrgz/trgz*) read a 3s form. Since *'šry*, "my steps," must be considered the subject of this verb (see textual note 74 below), a third person form of *rgz* must have been original. The first person form is probably a secondary phenomenon. It occurs only in those versions (MT, Tg) which lost the original subject *'šry* by reading it as a relative pronoun related to the next line, and it may represent the attempt to make grammatical sense of the first two words in this line as an isolated unit. It is significant that the Vg, which like the MT and Tg no longer understands *'šry* as the subject, still preserves the third person form of the verb (apparently considering *rqb* in the previous line its subject).

Since *'šwr* is customarily plural (or dual) in Hebrew usage (see textual note 74 below), a plural form of *rgz* might be expected here.[183] This is however contradicted by the versions, all of which read a singular verb. It is also contradicted by the customary use of the plural (or dual) of *'šr* with a singular feminine verb (e.g. Pss 37:31; 44:19; 73:2; cf. Ps 17:5 where the 3ms *tmk* may originally have been *ttmk*). GKC (145k) calls attention to frequent situations in which plurals are construed with the feminine singular of the verbal predicate. Two of his examples (1 Sam 4:15; Mic 4:11) involve another part of the body, the eyes, for which the dual nominal form is used.[184] W. F. Albright has suggested ***trgz*** here, and believes it ought to be understood as a feminine dual form (agreeing with the dual *'šry*, "my steps") rather than the feminine singular form as it was apparently understood later.[185] This may reflect the archaic verbal system of Ugaritic poetry in which the 3cdu could be rendered *tqtl*.[186] The prefix form fits the pattern of verb usage in this poem.

74. Read the dual form of the noun *'aššūr*, "step," with the first singular suffix. The MT, followed by the Vg (*ut*) and Tg (*d*), reads the relative pronoun *'ăšer* and connects it to the following line. The OG, followed by the OL (*habitudo mea*), reads a noun with the 1cs suffix (*hē hexis mou*, "my condition, posture:" variant: *ischys*, "strength"). Barb (*tauta*) either omits the term or construes it as *'lh*.[187] To read a noun here, as the OG and OL, which provides the subject of the sentence in this line, is clearly the best alternative. The relative pronoun *'šr* is a prosaic term not ordinarily found in Hebrew poetry. It could only have been read here after the poetic quality of this text was no longer clearly differentiated from prose. Furthermore, to read this term, as the relative pronoun must be read, with the following line disrupts the poetic meter severely, making this line too short and the following one too long.

The noun in question here is most likely *'šry*, "my steps," as many scholars have pointed out.[188] There has been some question, however, whether the Greek translation, *hē hexis*, "condition, state, posture," actually represents the MT, *'šr*, read as the noun, "step." *hexis* does not translate *'šr* elsewhere but it seems to have no specific referent, translating a different Hebrew term each of the seven other times it is used.[189] It is quite possible that, especially in its sense of "posture," it is a figurative translation of *'šr*, "step."[190] The variant in the OG, *ischys* (largely Lucianic texts), "strength," does not add much clarity. It is however used to render some parts of the body and may represent another way of getting at the basic idea involved here.[191] The variants in the OL seem to represent either *hexis* (*habitudo*, "condition, figure," *qualitas*, "quality, state") or *ischys* (*fortitudo*, "strength," *virtus*, "strength, virtue").

A number of considerations support reading *'šry*, "my steps," as original. The mention of steps, or feet, here fits the context in which the three previous lines have mentioned other parts of the body—belly, lips, bones—which are affected by the poet's deep emotional experience. Furthermore, steps, or feet, would be appropriate for the designation *tḥty*, "under me," which begins the line.[192] The notion of shaking (*rgz*) or unsteady steps is a common one in biblical literature (cf. Pss 17:5; 18:37; 37:31; and Prov 25:19). In one text bones and feet (there *rgly*) are placed in parallel with one another as here (Lam 1:13).

'šry should be read as the dual of *'šr*, "step," since this is its customary use in Hebrew poetry.[193] Also, it provides a close parallel to the plural *'ṣm* in the previous line. The first singular suffix should be read with the OG (*hē hexis mou*), thus maintaining the poetic parallelism operative in the preceding lines: *bṭny*, *śpty*, *'ṣmy*.

75. Of the final bicolon of v 16, S. R. Driver has written, "This and the next line are most obscure and uncertain, the Hebrew being in parts ambiguous, and the text open to suspicion ... the case is one in which it is impossible to speak with confidence."[194] Both the variations in the versions and the variety of scholarly emendations support Driver's conclusion. The suggestions proposed here for these two lines I believe to be the most reasonable readings.

For the initial term in this bicolon read the Niphal imperfect 1cs form of *'nḥ*, *'ē'ānaḥ*, with preterit force ("I sighed, groaned"). The initial *'alep* could have been lost by haplography, there being two *'aleps* in sequence, and the *waw* may be understood as a vestige of late orthography once the *'alep* was lost and the verb was related to *nwḥ*. Though most versions concur with the MT in reading a form of the verb *nwḥ* (OG: *anapausomai*; OL and Vg: *requiescam*), this reading is difficult to connect with the phrase which follows: "I will rest for the day of distress ... "? *nwḥ* does not elsewhere mean "wait quietly" as some (e.g. the *RSV*) would like to translate it here.[195] Furthermore, the act of resting is hardly appropriate in this context of emotional intensity. Barb's alternative, *tauta phylaxeis*, "these you guard" (= *'lh tšmr* ?), does not clarify things.[196] For these reasons, many scholars have suggested reading a form of *'nḥ*, B. Duhm the actual form I have adopted.[197] This interpretation fits with the expression *yôm ṣārâ* which follows and which I take to be the day of battle (see the parallel line), a time charged with anxiety brought on both by the dangers of war and by the theophany described in vv 8–15.

76. Read with the OG and Barb (*en hēmerą*) and the Vg (*in die*) the preposition *bĕ* in place of the preposition *lĕ* of the MT. This is the only preposition used with *yôm ṣārâ* in biblical Hebrew.

77. W. F. Albright's suggestion that *l'lwt* be considered a construction in which the preposition *l* with an infinitive expresses time has been adopted here; thus, "When ... went up" (cf. Gen 24:63; Judg 29:26; 2 Sam 18:29).[198] *'lh* is frequently used to describe the movement of an army into battle (e.g. Judg 1:1; 12:3; 1 Sam 7:7; Isa 36:10), and in these contexts it may carry a technical military meaning. That appears to be the sense of the verb here. The final term in this line should be considered a relative clause in which the attributive relation is expressed by simple coordination (see GKC no. 155).

78. Delete *lĕ*. The preposition results in an awkward construction. *lĕ* may have risen as a dittography of the *'ayin lamed* sequence a few letters before.

79. Read *yĕgûdan*, the energic form without the suffix from the verb *gwd*. The energic form is common in Ugaritic and early Israelite poetry (cf. Hab 3:7);[199] the suffix varies to such an extent among the versions that it may be considered an interpretive addition (MT: *ennû*; OG (OL): *mou*; Vg: *nostrum*; Barb: *polemoun ton laon sou* [either no suffix or the 2ms suffix]). In the other occurrence of this verb in the Hebrew Bible, in the archaic "Blessing of Jacob" in Genesis 49 (v 19), the same corruption is present: *yĕgûdan* has been read *yĕgûdennû*.[200] Barb (*polemoun*, from *gwd*) and the Vg (*accinctum*, from *gdd*) support the MT, while the OG (*paroikias mou* = *mgwry*, "my sojourning") is a late interpretation from the diaspora and may be accounted for on the basis of the common *d/r* confusion.[201]

80. Omit *kî* with Barb. It serves no real consecutive, causal, conditional, or temporal function. I think it may have been added when v 17 came to be interpreted as agricultural drought, and the poet was understood to retain faith in God (vv 18–19) in spite of these adverse circumstances: "when (even though) ... still, let me rejoice...".

81. Read with the MT and Vg. The Greek translations read *tprh*, "bear fruit" (OG: *karpophorein*; with OL, *afferet fruc-*

tum, and Barb, *paradǭ ton karpon autēs*), a variant based on the graphic confusion of *ḥ* and *h*.[202] The Greek variant may have been inspired by the later interpretation of v 17 as a description of the harvest.

82. Though most of the versions appear to read the imperfect form of this verb (OG: *pseusetai*; Barb: *exitēlos estai*; OL and Vg: *mentietur*) the perfect form of the MT is to be preferred. Here, as elsewhere in the poem, are a series of facts which have already taken place and which are narrated by the use of both imperfect (the old preterit) and perfect forms, as was the archaic Canaanite custom. The verb in the following line, *ʿśh*, which parallels this verb is also in the perfect.

It may be that *kiḥēš* here is better understood in light of its meaning in archaic poetry, "cringe, draw back, cower" (Deut 33:29; Ps 18:45) than in light of its usual meaning "deceive." This would be a fitting description of nature recoiling at a theophany (see Chap. 3).

83. The meaning of this term has been widely debated. Many scholars understand the term, along with the early versions (OG: *pedia*; OL: *campi*: Vg: *arva*), to have the basic meaning "fields."[203] Some, such as J. Lachmann, would prefer the idea "vineyard."[204] M. Lehmann has suggested that this term is a compound word, *šd-mwt*, "field of death," an unlikely possibility in light of biblical Hebrew's avoidance of compound words.[205]

Three other suggestions deserve more serious consideration: (1) the branches or limbs of the vine. F. M. Cross has suggested this possibility on the basis of the parallelism with *gpn* in biblical poetry (Deut 32:32; Isa 16:8; and here) and in Ugaritic literature (*CTA* 23[52].10).[206] (2) A variety of grape, differing from or being a specific kind of the *gpn*. A society so dependent on the fruit of the vine might be expected to farm different varieties of grapes and have terms to distinguish them. (3) Terraces. L. E. Stager has recently proposed this translation for 2 Kgs 23:4 and Jer 31:40 (*šadmôt qidrôn*) in the light of the extensive terracing in the Kidron Valley.[207] If the vines were cultivated on terraces and identified with them, this meaning might also fit the poetic contexts of *šdmwt* where this term is parallel to *gpn*. Any translation is still somewhat provisional.

84. There is no reason on the basis of the OG, *exelipon*, leave out, abandon" (cf. Barb, *ekleipsei*), to suggest that its tex-

tual base was different from the MT. Though *ekleipein* translates *gzr* only this once in the LXX, it is used to translate other roots with the same sense *gzr* has here (cf. Isa 55:13 and 56:5 where it translates the Niphal of *krt*). The OL, *desecerunt*, "cut off," and Vg, *abscidetur*, "torn off," lend further support to the MT.

A valid debate does arise, however, about the form of *gzr* which ought to be read. Since the transitive meaning, which the Qal form of *gzr* has elsewhere, is awkward here, most commentators have questioned the originality of the Masoretic pointing. In order to obtain the passive sense, which seems to be demanded by the context, many commentators have followed J. Wellhausen in emending the text to the Niphal *ngzr*.[208] It is more likely, however, that *gzr* here is to be read as an internal Qal passive. **guzar(a)*, an archaic form with which the Masoretes were no longer familiar.[209]

85. The reading of the MT, *mklh* (an orthographic error for *mkl'*), "sheepfold," is supported by Barb (*mandras*, "fold") and the Vg (*ovili*, "sheepfold"). The reading of the OG, *brōseōs*, "eating, meat" (OL: *comederent*, "[that which] they used to eat"), is likely based on an alternative text, *m'kl*,[210] which is less satisfactory in a number of respects. In the first place, it disrupts the parallelism with the following line in which the stalls of cattle are mentioned. Secondly, it can be explained as originating under the influence of *'ōkel* which concludes the previous line. Thirdly, as the following line makes clear, the intent of this bicolon is to say that the distress in the animal world parallels that in the world of vegetation (v 17a), not to suggest specifically that the sheep have nothing to eat.[211] *mklh* in the MT must be incorrect spelling for *mkl'* or *mkl'h*.[212]

86. Though this term occurs only once in the Hebrew Bible, and has no cognates to clarify its meaning, the translators are unanimous in understanding it as a place where cattle are kept: the OG and Barb, *phatnais*, "mangers"; the OL and Vg, *praesepibus*, "stalls." Its place in parallel relationship to *mkl'*, "sheepfold," supports this interpretation. A number of Greek texts appear to have been translated from a *Vorlage* with a double reading at this point. These texts add *ex iaseōs autōn*, "from their healing,"[213] which must have translated *mēripu'tām*.[214] This term does not fit the context here and likely arose as an attempt to explain the difficult *rptym*.

87. A difference of opinion exists within the Septuagint traditions about the force of the pronominal suffix, one group of

manuscripts apparently unconscious of it (*ho theos*) and another group presuming it (see also Barb). Since the treatment of this term as a holy name (in which the pronoun loses its force) rather than the ordinary appellative (in which it retains its force) is probably a late development,[215] it is better to read the pronoun with the latter group of Greek manuscripts and understand the original form to have been *'ădōnî*, "my lord."

88. The Hebrew word *ḥayil*, can be used with the general meaning "strength" or the special military meaning "army." Both meanings must be intended by the poet in this line. The context of the tricolon, in which the victory of a warrior is described, and the context of the poem as a whole, in which God has won the victory for his people, suggest that "army" may have been the primary meaning communicated by this phrase. For this meaning of *ḥayil* in archaic poetry, see Exod 15:4.

89. The parallel in Ps 18:34 (= 2 Sam 22:34) suggests that the simile "feet like the hinds'" was known by Israel's poets and that the MT should be accepted as it stands. The OG, *eis synteleian*, "to completion," is ambiguous and is likely based on a corrupt text which the translators understood as a form of *klh* (perhaps *tklyt*).[216] Barb's reading, *asphaleis*, "safely," may be interpretive.[217] No Hebrew *Vorlage* for Barb which is similar to the MT or the OG can be postulated.[218]

90. At issue is the 1cs suffix in the MT. It is awkward in the MT and omitted in the OG (*ta hypsēla*). This has led to the suggestion that it be omitted as a dittography of the initial *yod* of the term which follows or that it be considered the construct plural in relationship to a noun which has fallen out.[219] These suggestions are both improvements on the MT, but it is striking that *bmwty* appears in exactly this form before the Hiphil of *drk* / *'md* in the three occurrences of this stock expression in archaic poetry (Ps 18:34 = 2 Sam 22:34; Hab 3:19). The similarity between Ps 18:34 and 2 Sam 22:34 is particularly interesting since so many corruptions in these texts show up as variant readings between them. For a mistake to have been responsible for the reading in each of these three texts, it would have to have been made in the same way in each of three different cases. A proposal to make sense out of the texts as they stand is that *bmwty* is an archaic stereotyped phrase in which the old genitive case ending has been preserved and is represented by the final *yod* (**bamāti* > *bāmôtî*, spelled *bmwty*).[220] The Hebrew

text from which the OG was translated no longer contained this anachronistic feature.

Here, as in v 13b (see textual note 56), the old meaning of *bmt*, "back," should be read. In this case, as in the other cases in biblical Hebrew where *bmt* should be rendered "back" (Deut 33:29; Job 9:8), *bmt* represents the part of the body on which the victor treads (*drk*). That the backs in this line are the backs of the poet's foes would be understood: "on (the) backs (of my foes) he made me tread." This in fact was the understanding of Barb: *kai epi tous trachēlous tōn echthrōn mou epibibą me* "and on the necks of my enemies he puts me."

Understood in this way, the final line of the poem establishes a parallel between Yahweh's victory (*drkt bym*, v 15) and the poet's (*ʿl bmwty ydrkny*), and it provides a fitting image for the conclusion of the poem: the victorious warrior empowered by his God (the causative of *drk*) to trample his enemies.

CHAPTER 2

The Literary Structure of Habakkuk 3

Attempts to find a coherent literary structure in Habakkuk 3 have varied widely, from A. Condamin's proposal in the last century that this poem was composed like a Greek chorale with strophes and antistrophes to M. O'Connor's recent suggestion that this poem is composed of three staves which may be subdivided into batches.[1] The great variety among the literary studies of Habakkuk 3 stems in large part from a lack of agreement about the presence in biblical poetry of units larger than the individual verse and about the way in which individual verses combine to form these units.[2] While it is true that biblical poetry does not as a rule contain larger units or stanzas which show the definite regularity of length and structure common in much western poetry, there is much evidence to suggest that clusters of individual verses are frequently combined into larger units which possess their own identity and integrity and exhibit a carefully crafted structure.[3]

In the case of Habakkuk 3, the major poetic technique employed by the poet to provide a coherent literary structure is inclusion. Inclusion, also called cyclic, envelope, or ring composition, is a stylistic device with which the poet effects closure by linking the beginning and end of a unit or subunit of the poem.[4] This connection between beginning and end may involve the repetition of a key word or words or of an entire line or verse, or it may involve the resumption or recalling of a thought or its completion. Although inclusion is a well-known stylistic technique in biblical poetry, no literary study of Habakkuk 3 has yet taken sufficient account of its use in this poem as a structuring device.

An examination of Habakkuk 3 reveals that inclusion is the primary stylistic device with which the poet has given shape to the poem as a whole as well as to the discrete sections within it. Attention to inclusion in this poem indicates that v 2 and vv 16–19 provide a literary framework for the theophany in vv 3–15, and that this theophany is itself composed of two distinct units, vv 3–7 and 8–15. The use of inclusion can be seen operative at almost every possible level. It shapes the poem as a whole, the major units or stanzas within the poem, and subsections within these stanzas. It is apparent in the repetition of themes and motifs, of key words and phrases, of syntactic patterns, of parallelistic verse structures, and of phonetic elements.

The Literary Framework (vv 2, 16–19)

Stanza I (v 2)

The opening unit or stanza of Habakkuk 3 contains a bicolon and a tricolon which are intricately linked by a variety of stylistic devices. For the following analysis of the structure of this stanza, and the following stanzas in this chapter, the cola have been numbered in the left column for easy reference. The text represents the one reconstructed in Chapter 1 without repeated notation of alterations which have been made in the MT. Following the text are the syllable counts (in parentheses) based on reconstructed early pronunciation and the notation of cola type, l (*longum*) for long cola, b (*breve*) for short cola.[5]

1.	*yhwh śmʿty śmʿk*[6]	(7)	l	Verse 2
2.	*yrʾty yhwh pʿlk*	(7)	l	
3.	*bqrb*[7] *śnym ḥyyt*[8]	(6)	l	
4.	*bqrb šnym twdʿ*	(7)	l	
5.	*brgz rḥm tzkwr*	(6)	l	

The metrical character of the introductory stanza may be described l:l::l:l:l. Internal parallelism, that is parallelism within each of the two verse units, is primary. But there are also interlocking structures which unite the bicolon and tricolon to form a coherent stanza.

In the opening bicolon, each unit of the second colon corresponds to one in the first colon, a "non-replacement formula," to use S. A. Geller's terminology, which is particularly frequent in the corpus of early biblical poetry.[9] Especially to be noted is the link between *šmʿk*, the account about Yahweh, and *pʿlk*, the content of that account. This pair of terms is linked by their semantic equivalence, their final position in parallel lines, their grammatical identity (direct objects with 2ms suffixes), and their phonetic correspondence (repetition of *'ayin* and rhymed repetition of the 2ms suffix). The verbs in this bicolon are both third guttural 1cs Qal perfect forms. They establish two motifs central to the poem: the hearing about the acts of God, and the response of great awe which this hearing evokes. The use of the vocative, *yhwh*, identifies at the outset the central focus of the poem, the God of Israel. The verbatim repetition of the vocative initiates the repetitive style employed in the following tricolon and elsewhere in the poem (vv 8a, 13a). Finally to be noted are the phonetic links between the hearing (*šm'ty*) and the account heard (*šm'k*) achieved by use of the cognate accusative in colon 1, and between *yhwh* (**yahwē*) and the awe he inspires (**yari'tī*; MT: *yārē'tî*) in colon 2.

The internal structure of the tricolon in Stanza I is also complex. The overall pattern of this tricolon is one which has been described as repetitive or climactic parallelism.[10] In a tricolon constructed with climactic parallelism, the second line repeats part of the first, with the variation frequently of only one element, usually at the end of the line: the third line is different from the initial two, adding something to them, completing the sense, and thus providing a kind of climax. The repetition in the first two lines of this tricolon, with variation only of the final term, follows the usual climactic pattern, as does the unique character of the third colon. The special character of the third colon is achieved not only by departure from the repetition of the first two but also by its special alliteration produced by the repetition of the phonemes *z*, *r*, and *g/ḥ/k*. Still, this third colon is carefully related to the first two: *brgz* complements *bqrb šnym* in grammatical character (prepositional phrases) and *tzkr* parallels the verbs in the two preceding cola by its position in the line and its 2ms form. Only the infinitive *rḥm* represents a new grammatical element.

Furthermore, an inclusive or cyclic structure overlaps this climactic pattern. The initial verb *ḥyyt* mentions the gracious intent of God's acts as does the final verbal phrase *rḥm tzkr* (note the repetition of *ḥ* and *t* in these terms). Within this envelope are references to the fearful theophany by which God acts, both in the verb *twd'* and in the phrase *brgz* which refers to the turmoil accompanying God's appearance (cf. vv 6–7, 9–10, 16–17). These two characteristics of theophany, its gracious intent and its awful power to disrupt and destroy, become prominent motifs throughout the poem.

It should be clear at this point that the initial bicolon and tricolon in Habakkuk 3 are not isolated verse units but are intimately related to form a coherent stanza. The tricolon explicates the bicolon it follows. The account (*šmʿk*) of God's deeds (*pʿlk*) is identified as the account of a theophany (*twdʿ, brgz*) with salvific intent (*ḥyyt*, *rḥm tzkr*). The awe (*yrʾty*) is identified as that brought about by God's tumultuous (*brgz*) presence. The vocative *yhwh* is developed by three 2ms verbs.

While two line verse units, or bicola, have been universally recognized as part of the repertoire of the Israelite poet, three line verse units, or tricola, particularly when found in a poem composed predominantly of bicola, have not always been given the same recognition. Tricola have been considered inauthentic by some scholars who believe them to be the result of textual corruption (e.g. dittography) or some other error such as the misinterpretation of the text. A number of commentators have tried to remove them entirely from the text of Habakkuk 3.[11]

But the presence of occasional tricola in poems predominantly composed in bicola can no longer be seriously questioned. Since the discovery of the poetic texts from Ugarit, which contain tricola mixed with bicola in single poems, tricola have been recognized as a genuine element in Northwest Semitic poetry.[12] It is common to see in both Ugaritic and Hebrew poetry isolated tricola appearing among the more common bicola. The reduction of tricola in Habakkuk 3 to bicola, which commentators have frequently attempted, is based on a now outmoded understanding of the conventions of Hebrew verse structure. As will be seen in the following study, the tricola in Habakkuk 3 do not occur randomly but are carefully placed to highlight the structure of the poem. Tricola in Habakkuk 3 are used to introduce a stanza (III), to conclude a stanza (I, IV), and in balanced positions within a stanza to contribute to the stanza's inclusive structure (II).

Together with the authenticity of the tricolon in Stanza I, its unique parallelistic pattern deserves comment. Climactic tricola of this kind have been identified as particularly characteristic of archaic Hebrew poetry. The evidence for this lies in the fact that this parallelistic pattern occurs frequently in old Hebrew poetry and in the older poetry of Ugarit but infrequently in later Hebrew poetry.[13] Exodus 15, Judges 5, and such archaic hymns in the Psalter as Psalms 18, 29, 77:17–21, and 93 all furnish fine examples from archaic poetry.[14] In Ugaritic poetry climactic parallelistic style is frequent. A good example, very similar in form to the tricolon in Hab 3:2, is found in *CTA* 2:4(68).8–9:

ht 'ibk b'lm	Behold your enemy, O Ba'l.
ht 'ibk tmḫṣ	Behold your enemy, you shall smite;
ht tṣmt ṣrtk	Behold you shall smash your foe.

Note the verbatim repetition of the first two terms in the first two lines and the beginning of all three lines with the same particle. The vocative in the Canaanite pattern, *b'lm*, has been replaced with a verb in Hab 3:2, the vocative already having been used in the preceding bicolon.

Stanza IV (vv 16–19)

Since v 2 and vv 16–19 provide the literary framework of Habakkuk 3, it will be more efficient to deal with them together before proceeding to the theophany which they frame (vv 3–15). In this way the use of inclusion to link the beginning and ending of the poem as a whole can be more easily seen. Stanza IV itself is composed of several subsections identified by shifts in thought, meter, and parallelistic structure. The first of these subsections is made up of the three bicola of v 16.

1.	*śm'ty wtrgz bṭny*	(8)	l	Verse 16
2.	*lqwl ṣllw śpty*	(8)	l	
3.	*ybw' rqb b'ṣmy*	(8)	l	
4.	*tḥty trgz 'šry*	(7)	l	
5.	*''nḥ bywm ṣrh*	(7)	l	
6.	*l'lwt 'm ygwdn*	(7)	l	

The meter of this opening subsection of Stanza IV may be described as l:l::l:l::l:l. Though all three bicola are interrelated, the links between the first two which describe the poet's response to the account of God's theophany are particularly prominent and complex. Both bicola contain an image of inner turmoil mirrored by an image of outer turmoil related to it. In the first bicolon the trembling of the belly is mirrored by the trembling of the lips. The anatomical connection between these images is drawn literarily by the grammatical (verb + subject with 1cs suffix), semantic (*trgz* // *ṣllw*), and positional (last two units in corresponding lines) parallelism of *trgz bṭny* and *ṣllw śpty*. In the second bicolon the weakness of the bones is mirrored by the unsteadiness of the steps. This connection is enhanced by the grammatical (noun with 1cs suffix), positional (last unit in the line), and phonetic (rhyme and repetition of sibilants and gutturals) parallelism of *ʿṣmy* and *ʾšry*. Note also the internal rhyme in chiastic order of *ʿṣmy* and *tḥty*.

In addition to these parallel mirror images, a number of other devices link these two bicola. Most prominent are the inclusive use of *rgz* in cola 1 and 4 in identical prefix forms and position in the line, and the parallelism of the final terms of the four cola which is operative at the semantic (parts of the body), grammatical (nouns with 1cs suffixes), and phonetic (rhyme and the repetition of sibilants, *ś*/*ṣ*/*š*) levels. Each of these four cola is marked by a unique alliterative pattern: *t* is repeated in colon 1, *l* and the sibilants *ś*/*ṣ* in colon 2, *b* in colon 3, and *t* and *r* in colon 4.

The final bicolon in this subsection of Stanza IV picks up the motif of personal distress highlighted in the first two bicola with its opening verb *ʾnḥ*. Then this bicolon proceeds, in inclusive fashion, to expand upon the account (*lqwl*) the poet has heard (*šmʿty*) which inspired this distress and was mentioned at the opening of the first two lines of Stanza IV. The account which the poet has heard is further identified here as an account of the day of battle in which the poet's people participated.

When this initial subsection of Stanza IV is compared with Stanza I, the prominent occurrence of inclusion to provide a literary framework for the theophany in vv 3–15 becomes apparent. The literary relationship between the first subsection of Stanza IV and Stanza I is nowhere clearer than in the opening colon of Stanza IV. Here every term recalls the opening stanza. *šmʿty* is a verbatim repetition of the verb in the opening line of Stanza I. *wtrgz* echoes two terms in the concluding line of Stanza I, *brgz* and, by its phonetic similarity, the verb *tzkr*. *bṭny* recalls in subtle fashion the third term in the concluding line of Stanza I, *rḥm*, a denominative verb from *reḥem*, "womb."

In the remainder of this subsection of Stanza IV the motifs and vocabulary of Stanza I are continued and amplified. The term in parallel position with *šmʿty* in Stanza IV, *qwl*, echoes the cognate accusative of *šm'ty* in Stanza I. *šm'*. In Stanza IV as in Stanza I hearing this account leads to intense awe. *šm'ty wtrgz bṭny* repeats the logic of the *šm'ty / yr'ty* parallelism of Stanza I. In fact, cola 1–4 of Stanza IV provide an amplification of the verb *yr'ty* in Stanza I. The double use of *rgz* in these four cola of Stanza IV recalls *brgz* of Stanza I. Used in the opening stanza of the poem for the general turmoil accompanying a theophany, *rgz* here refers more specifically to the poet's own reactions. Finally, the description of the event of holy war in cola 5–6 of Stanza IV provides an amplification of the allusion to this event in Stanza I (*twd'*, *brgz*).

One additional, and significant, link between Stanzas IV and I is the first person perspective in which both are composed. First person verbal forms, pronouns, and pronominal suffixes predominate. The focus is on the poet and his situation. This contrasts with the theophany in vv 3–15 where first person forms are absent and where second and third person verbal forms and pronominal suffixes predominate. In this section of the poem the focus is on God and his acts.

The only element of Stanza I not directly recalled by the first subsection of Stanza IV is the gracious intent of the theophany expressed in cola 3 and 5 of Stanza I. But this is deliberate. This motif becomes the focus of the final subsection of Stanza IV, providing a triumphant conclusion to the poem as a whole. The middle subsection of Stanza IV, however, precedes this conclusion and carries forward the motif of the initial subsection.

7.	*t'nh l' tprḥ*	(6)	l	Verse 17
8.	*'yn ybwl bgpnym*[15]	(7)	l	
9.	*kḥš m'śh*[16] *zyt*	(5)	l	
10.	*šdmwt l' 'śh 'kl*	(7)	l	
11.	*gzr mmkl' ṣ'n*	(6)	l	
12.	*'yn bqr brptym*	(7)	l	

The meter of this second subsection of Stanza IV corresponds to the meter of the opening subsection (v 16): l:l::l:l::l:l. It should be noted, however, that the lines in this unit of Stanza IV are slightly shorter than the lines of the unit which precedes and of the unit which follows, setting this unit off from its context and producing a slight staccato effect. A five syllable line, like that in colon 9, is ordinarily too short to be identified as long, but its anomalous position among long cola and its presence in a unit composed of slightly shorter lines suggest that it possesses the same metrical character of the lines among which it is found. Furthermore, the preservation of case endings is attested occasionally in archaic poetry, as appears to be the case in v 19, and the presence of unmarked case endings might have extended the length of particularly short lines like this one (and that in v 12a).

Each bicolon in this section is a distinct unit. In the first, *t'nh* and *gpnym* are semantic equivalents in chiastic order and two particles of negation (*l'*, *'yn*) complement one another. In the second bicolon, *zyt* and *šdmwt* are a semantic pair in chiastic order, and phonetic correspondences link the first terms (repetition of *š*) and second terms (repetition of the root *'śh*) of both lines. In the third bicolon, which turns to a description of the animal world, *mkl'* and *rptym* are a semantic pair as are *ṣ'n* and *bqr*.

But even more remarkable is a pattern which transcends the individual bicola of this section. In this pattern individual cola of different bicola are linked with one another. These correspondences provide a literary substratum of three alternate "bicola" which interlock with one another. Cola 7 and 10 are a pair in this substratum. They are nearly identical grammatically (subject + *l'* + verb [with direct object in colon 10]) and both characterized by a repetition of gutturals (*h*, *ḥ*, ', '). Cola 8 and 12 are identical grammatically (*'yn* + subject + prepositional phrase with *b*) and both characterized by a repetition of labials (*b*, *p*, *m*). Cola 9 and 11 are similar grammatically (verb [+ prepositional phrase in colon 11] + subject) and reflect the repetition of sibilants (*š*, *ś*, *z*, *ṣ*) and *m*.

This subsection of Stanza IV continues the motif of turmoil accompanying a theophany from Stanza I in its description of the devastation of nature.[17] It further amplifies *brgz* from Stanza I, including among the responses to God's appearance the response of the world of nature as well. All living things, human and non-human, recoil before God's presence.

In the final subsection of Stanza IV the focus shifts from the awful character of the theophanic event to its salvific effect. The meter of this unit may be described as l:l::l:l:l, the same metrical pattern as Stanza I.

13. *w'ny byhwh "lwzh*	(9)	I	Verse 18
14. *'gylh b'lhy yš'y*	(9)	I	
15. *yhwh 'dny ḥyly*	(7)	I	Verse 19
16. *yśm rgly k'ylt*	(8)	I	
17. *'l bmwty ydrkny*	(8)	I	

The bicolon of lines 13–14 features chiastic structure, the cohortatives *"lwzh* and *'gylh* being in chiastic order as well as the 1cs pronoun/pronominal suffix (*'ny/-y*) with the parallel pair *yhwh// 'lhy* providing the center of the chiasm. The additional element of colon 14, *yš'-*, combines with *'lhy* to provide a ballast variant of *yhwh*.

A tricolon concludes Stanza IV just as a tricolon concluded Stanza I. The tricolon in Stanza IV is not of the same type, however, as the tricolon in Stanza I in which the "non-parallel" line completes the verse unit. In this tricolon, the "non-parallel" line introduces the verse unit, providing an example of an alternate type of tricolon also present in early biblical poetry.[18] The most prominent parallelism here is between cola 16 and 17 where *yśm rgly* corresponds to *ydrkny* in chiastic order. Even then the initial colon is linked to the final two. It rhymes with the third and provides the subject, with three coordinate titles of God, for the verbs in the second and third cola.

The bicolon and tricolon which comprise this third subsection of Stanza IV are themselves linked in a variety of ways. The divine name Yahweh appears in the initial colon of each, and the 1cs pronominal suffix is used throughout both verse units. In fact, the pronoun *'ny* and the pronominal suffix *-ny* provide an inclusion for this subsection as a whole.

Like the preceding subsections of Stanza IV, this concluding subsection picks up and extends motifs and vocabulary from Stanza I, thus completing the inclusive framework which these stanzas provide for the poem as a whole. The divine name is used twice, paralleling its double use in Stanza I. *yhwh* is the initial word in the closing verse of the poem just as it is in the opening verse unit. In this subsection the first person perspective of Stanza I is again predominant as the verb forms, pronouns, and pronominal suffixes indicate. Finally, the theme of salvation in this concluding section of the poem amplifies the references to the salvific character of God's acts in Stanza I (*ḥyyt*, *rḥm tzkr*). The one who sustained life and remembered to show compassion is here described as the poet's lord and fighting force,[19] as the one who sustained life and was compassionate by giving sure footing in battle and causing the poet to tread the backs of his enemies in triumph.

This final subsection of Stanza IV, though connected directly with Stanza I to provide a literary framework for the poem, also echoes motifs from the theophany enclosed by Stanzas I and IV. One of these motifs is victory (*yšʿ*). The poet's reference to Yahweh as "God of my victory" echoes the use of this term in the theophany where God rides a chariot of victory (v 8b) to achieve the victory for Israel's militia (v 13a). Another motif is the act of treading (*drk*) on the conquered foe. The image of the poet treading the backs of his foes parallels the image in the final line of the theophany where Yahweh treads on Sea in triumph.

A final observation about Stanza IV as a whole is in order before proceeding to the theophany framed by this and the opening stanza. Although Stanza IV is constructed largely as a development of Stanza I and achieves its coherence in this process, it does contain its own internal structure which must not be overlooked. The initial and final subsections of Stanza IV contain contrasting images arranged in a cyclic pattern. The initial subsection opens with an image of unsteady steps (cola 3–4) which is followed by an expression of personal anguish (*ʾnḥ*, a 1cs prefix form). The final subsection opens with an expression of personal joy (*ʾʿlwzh*// *ʾgylh*, 1cs prefix forms) which is followed by an image of steady steps (cola 16–17). The pattern "trembling steps—anguish/joy—firm steps" is thus produced uniting Stanza IV and providing here a literary link between the two aspects of theophany, its awfulness and graciousness, also linked in Stanza I.

The Theophany (vv 3–15)

Although the theophany in vv 3–15 is a continuous narrative of the appearance of the divine warrior to achieve victory for the militia of his people, it has been composed in two stanzas, each with its own literary integrity. The special character of each of these stanzas as well as the relationship between them and their literary framework can be more easily observed by discussing each stanza in turn.

Stanza II (vv 3–7)

1.	*'lwh*[20] *mtymn ybw'*	(7)	l	A	Verse 3
2.	*qdwš mhr p'rn*	(6)	l		
3.	*ksh šmym*[21] *hwdw*	(6)	l	B	
4.	*thltw ml'h 'rṣ*	(8)	l		
5.	*ngh k'wr hwh*	(6)	l		Verse 4
6.	*qrnym . . .*			C	
7.	*yśmḥ bywm 'zh*	(6)	l		
8.	*lpnyw ylk dbr*	(6)	l	D	Verse 5
9.	*yṣ' ršp lrglyw*	(6)	l		
10.	*'md wyndd 'rṣ*	(7)	l	C'	Verse 6
11.	*r'h wytr gwym*	(7)	l		
12.	*ytpṣṣw hrry 'd*	(8)	l	B'	
13.	*šḥw gb'wt 'wlm*	(7)	l		
14.	*hlykwt 'wlm ltḥt'n*	(9)	l		Verse 7
15.	*'hly kwšn yrgzwn*	(8)	l	A'	
16.	*yry'wt 'rṣ mdyn*	(6)	l		

The central literary feature of this stanza is its perfect cyclic, inclusive structure. This structure has been illustrated above by the use of capital letters to identify corresponding verse units. The three opening verse units (ABC) describe the appearance of God, while the three closing verse units (C'B'A') describe the response to God's appearance. The description of the response is perfectly matched through cyclic structure to the description of the appearance. In order to illustrate the care with which this overall structure has been achieved, corresponding verse units will be discussed together rather than proceeding through the stanza from beginning to end.

The opening and closing bicola of Stanza II (A, A') correspond to one another at almost every possible level. They are metrically alike (l:l), and their verse structure is nearly identical. The first colon of each bicolon opens with the subject which is followed by a geopolitical term and the verb (prefix form: preterit) which serves both lines of the bicolon. The second colon opens with a repetition of the subject expressed by a parallel term which is followed by a ballast variant of the geopolitical term in the first colon. The only significant difference is the appearance of the geopolitical terms of bicolon A in prepositional phrases and those of bicolon A' in construct chains. In addition to these similarities should be noted the phonetic parallels between these bicola, particularly prominent between the geopolitical terms *têmān*//*har pā'rān* and *kûšān*//*'ereṣ midyān*. The repetition of *-ān* is particularly apparent. And when the probable historical pronunciation of these terms—*tayman*//*harr pa'ran*, *kūšan*//*'arṣ madyan*—is taken into account, two other types of phonetic correspondence become clear: the identical stress pattern and syllable length of the pairs of terms and the assonance produced by the repetition of "a" in all but two syllables. Also to be noted is the phonetic similarity between the opening terms in each bicolon, *'ĕlôah* and *'ohŏlê*. The content of these two bicola reflects the appearance/response contrast upon which Stanza II is constructed. In bicolon A God leaves his sanctuary, Teman/Mount Paran. In bicolon A' the inhabitants of this area, Kushan/Midian, tremble in awe.[22]

Verse units B and B' which form a concentric circle within the opening and closing bicola (A, A') show many similarities as well. They are metrically alike tricola (l:l:l, l:l:l). In each chiasm is employed as a structuring device. In tricolon B *hwdw* and *thltw* are arranged chiastically as are *ksh šmym* and *ml'h 'rṣ*. A chiastic patterning is apparent also in the final long *a* (represented by *h*) of *ksh*/*ml'h*/*hwh*. In tricolon B' the final colon is related chiastically to the straight order parallelism of the first two cola: *ytpṣṣw*/*šḥw* and *tḥt'n* are arranged chiastically as are *hrry 'd*/*gb'wt 'wlm* and *hlykwt 'wlm*. In both tricola the final line represents the "unique" colon. And in both tricola the subject of the verbs (with one exception, *ngh*, a reconstruction) is not God but a common noun. These tricola also reflect the appearance/response contrast of Stanza II. Whereas tricolon B describes God's majestic and splendorous appearance in heaven and on earth, tricolon B' describes the tumultuous response on earth and in heaven (in cyclic structure).

Bicola C and C' may not be compared as extensively due to the disrupted text of v 4, but some observations may be made on the basis of the partial reconstruction which has been proposed. Three of the four cola begin with verbs of which God is the subject. These bicola also reflect the appearance/response contrast.

Bicolon C describes the strength of God (*qrnym*, *'zh*) and bicolon C' describes the result of his strength: "he stood and shook earth, he looked and startled nations."

At the heart of the cyclic construction of Stanza II lies bicolon D, a description of God's entourage marching out before and behind. It is fashioned with chiasm, *lpnyw* and *lrglyw* being positioned chiastically together with *ylk dbr* and *yṣ' ršp*. Though it represents a unique image within the stanza, this bicolon has links to preceding and succeeding sections of Stanza II. The verbs and the position of *dbr* and *ršp* in relation to *'lwh* recall the opening bicolon of Stanza II describing God's march from his sanctuary. And the prepositional phrases *lpnyw* and *lrglyw* appear to be related in chiastic order to the initial verbs in the two cola which immediately follow (*'md*, *r'h*).

In addition to the unifying cyclic construction which marks Stanza II off as a distinct unit within the poem, several other literary features indicate the distinctive character of this stanza. First, the perspective is no longer the first person perspective of the poet in Stanza I, which reappears again in Stanza IV. First person verbs and suffixes are absent,[23] and the focus is entirely on God's activity and the general response to it. Second, God is not addressed in the second person as he is in Stanzas I and III but is referred to entirely in the third person. Third, the title of God is *'lwh*/*qdš* whereas *yhwh* is used in the other stanzas.

Stanza III (vv 8–15)

Stanza III continues the narrative of God's appearance and of the response to it which was begun in Stanza II. But a variety of literary features mark Stanza III off as a distinct unit within the theophany as a whole. Here as in Stanza II the major literary technique which distinguishes this stanza from its context is inclusion. In order to bring out the use of this technique to structure this stanza, the opening and closing subsections of Stanza III will be dealt with first; then the two inner subsections will be described.

1.	*hbnhr-m ḥrh yhwh*	(9)	l	Verse 8
2.	*hbnhr-m ’pk*	(7)	l	
3.	*’m bym ‘brtk*	(6)	l	
4.	*ky trkb ‘l swsyk*	(6)	l	
5.	*mrkbt yš‘tk*	(6)	l	
6.	*‘rh t‘r*[24] *qštk*	(6)	l	Verse 9
7.	*śb‘t mṭy ’šptk*	(7)	l	
20.	*mḥṣt bmt rš‘*	(6)	l	Verse 13
21.	*‘ryt yswd ‘d ṣw’r*	(7)	l	
22.	*nqbt bmṭyk r’š*	(6)	l	Verse 14
	. . .			
23.	*drkt bym swsyk*	(6)	l	Verse 15
24.	*bḥmr mym rbym*	(6)	l	

The opening subsection of Stanza III describes the preparation of the divine warrior for battle. He turns his anger against his foe (cola 1–3), mounts his chariot (cola 4–5), and makes ready his weapons (cola 6–7). The rhetorical question with which this section begins is a device used by Hebrew poets to introduce new stanzas.[25] The opening tricolon is composed in a climactic style somewhat similar to that of the tricolon in Stanza I. Verbatim repetition at the beginning of the first two lines is paralleled by a variation in the third line. In the final two cola of this tricolon and in both bicola which follow parallelistic structure at all levels—grammatical, semantic, and phonetic—as well as equality of line length is achieved by pairing the final term in one line with a ballast variant in the next. In cola 2 and 3 *’pk* and *‘brtk*, both subjects of the verb *ḥrh*, are paired; in cola 4 and 5 *swsyk* and *mrkbt yš‘tk*, both objects of the preposition *‘l*, are paired; and in cola 6 and 7 *qštk* and *mṭy ’šptk*, both direct objects, are paired. Of particular note is the phonetic similarity among all of these terms achieved by the repetition of the 2ms suffix. In fact, the vocative *yhwh* at the end of colon 1 and the related, rhyming 2ms suffixes at the end of the following cola (2–7) provide the major stylistic feature unifying this subsection of Stanza III. This phonetic pattern is enhanced by additional alliteration in the final terms of these cola: the repetition of gutturals and labials in *’pk* // *‘brtk* and of *š*, *t*, and gutturals in *yš'tk*/*qštk*//*'šptk*.

Whereas the opening subsection of Stanza III describes the preparation of the divine warrior for battle, the concluding subsection describes the battle itself. The divine warrior attacks his foe (cola 20–22) and treads on it in triumph (cola 23–24). The combat of the divine warrior in this subsection is highlighted by the series of 2ms perfect verbs which begin each colon but the last, a colon intended as the climax for the description of the battle. The parts of the body of the enemy struck by Yahweh provide a patterning structure for the attack itself: *bmt*/*yswd 'd ṣw'r*/*r'š*. Finally, the alliteration in the terms concluding cola 20 and 22 (*rš'*, *r'š*) should be noted.

These opening and concluding subsections of Stanza III contain many prominent correspondences which serve to produce an inclusion unifying the stanza as a whole. The relationship of the content of these subsections—the preparation for battle and the battle itself—has already been noted. This thematic association is supported by numerous literary connections. Foremost among these is the identification of the enemy in the opening cola (1–3) of the initial subsection of Stanza III and in the concluding cola (23–24) of the final subsection. The alternate titles of the enemy are arranged in cyclic order: *nhr-m*//*ym*, *ym*//*mym rbym*. The terms *nhr-m* and *mym rbym* are in chiastic position in their respective verse units, making up the first and last words of the stanza as a whole.

Other correspondences occur between the initial two verse units of the opening subsection and the final verse unit of the concluding subsection. Yahweh begins the battle by mounting his horse-drawn chariot (*swsyk*//*mrkbt yš'tk*) and ends the battle by trampling Sea with his horses (*swsyk*). The phonetic and semantic similarities between the verbs mount (*trkb*) and trample (*drkt*) and the semantic similarity between the prepositions related to them (*'l* and *b*) further link these two acts with one another. Finally, the mention of Yahweh's victory (*yš'tk*) in colon 5 clearly anticipates the description of triumph in cola 23–24.

Further connections can be seen between the final verse unit of the opening subsection and the initial verse units of the concluding subsection. The reference to Yahweh's baring (*'rh t'r*) his bow (colon 6) is recalled when Yahweh lays bare his enemy (*'ryt*, colon 21). And the reference to Yahweh's shafts (*mṭy*, colon 7) is recalled when Yahweh pierces his enemy's head with these shafts (*mṭy*, colon 22). Thus, a cyclic construction, including various levels of inclusion, unites the opening and closing subsections of Stanza III.

The two medial subsections of Stanza III are composed of three verse units each, just as the opening and closing subsections. These sections do not mirror one another as do the opening and closing subsections. Rather, they are related to the opening and closing subsections which precede and follow.

8.	*nhrwt tbq' 'rṣ*	(7)	l	Verse 9
9.	*r'wk yḥylw hrym*	(7)	l	Verse 10
10.	*zrmw mym 'bwt*	(6)	l	
11.	*ntn thwm qwlw*	(6)	l	
12.	*rwm ydyhw nś' šmš*	(7)	l	Verse 11
13.	*yrḥ 'md zblh*	(7)	l	
14.	*l'wr ḥṣyk yhlkw*	(8)	l	
15.	*lngh brq ḥnytk*	(7)	l	
16.	*bz'm tṣ'd 'rṣ*	(5)	l	Verse 12
17.	*b'p tdwš gwym*	(6)	l	
18.	*yṣ't lyš' 'mk*	(6)	l	Verse 13
19.	*lyš' 'm mšyḥk*	(6)	l	

The first of these medial subsections pictures the response to the divine warrior's preparation for battle which is described in the preceding subsection. In subsequent bicola, earth and mountains crack and heave (cola 8–9), the waters above and below burst out (cola 10–11), and Sun and Moon stand in the heavens (cola 12–13). The chiastic structure of the final bicolon may be noted: *šmš* and *yrḥ* are in chiastic arrangement as are *rwm* and *zblh*; at the midpoint are the related phrases *ydyhw nś'* and *'md*. Particularly prominent in this subsection is the "water" motif, which is found in three of the six cola (8, 10, 11) of this subsection, and which recalls the titles of God's enemy in the opening and closing subsections of Stanza III. *nhrwt* recalls *nhr-m* in cola 1–2; *mym* anticipates *mym rbym* in colon 24; and *thwm* may echo *ym* in cola 3 and 23. This focus on the agitation of the cosmic waters in the description of the response to the divine warrior here appears to foreshadow the actual battle with the water monster at the conclusion of Stanza III.

The second of the medial subsections of Stanza III anticipates the following subsection. It describes the march of the divine warrior into battle. His lightning flashes (cola 14–15) as he marches on earth trampling nations (cola 16–17) on the way to achieve victory for his people (cola 18–19). Straight order parallelism predominates at the grammatical and semantic levels in these bicola, the first and third employing "double-duty" verbs in the initial colon and ballast variants in the second colon. The repetition of prepositions in parallel cola occurs in all three bicola: *l* in the first and third, *b* in the second. The third bicolon reflects climactic structure, based on the repetition of *lyš' 'm* and enhanced by rhyme (2ms suffixes) and alliteration (repetition of *š*, ', *m*, *y*, and *k*/*ḥ*).

This subsection of Stanza III recalls a number of motifs of the opening subsection and of the concluding subsection which it anticipates. The mention of Yahweh's anger (*z'm*//*'p*, cola 16–17) recalls the reference to it in the opening subsection (*'pk*//*'brtk*, cola 2–3). And the mention of victory (*yš'*. cola 18–19) recalls its use earlier (colon 5). The occurrence of Yahweh's weapons here (cola 14–15) reflects the mention of them in the opening subsection (cola 6–7) and in the closing subsection (colon 22). Finally, the description of Yahweh's march with the use of the verbs *tṣ'd*//*tdwš* in the second bicolon of this subsection anticipates Yahweh's trampling on his enemy (*drkt*) at the conclusion of the stanza.

Stanza III is thus made up four subsections of equal length. Its literary integrity is achieved primarily by the use of inclusion which links the first and last subsections and shapes the character of the medial subsections. In addition to this structural pattern, several other literary features mark off Stanza III as a distinct unit. The title for God is *yhwh*, rather than *'lwh*/*qdš* as in Stanza II. Yahweh is addressed directly in the second person, rather than indirectly in the third person as in Stanzas II and IV. A number of motifs which are dominant in Stanza III—e.g. divine anger and weaponry, the cosmic waters—are absent elsewhere in the poem.

But Stanza III should not be viewed in isolation. It has significant links to its context, particularly to Stanza II with which it is combined to form the heart of the poem, the theophany of vv 3–15. The description of God's march into battle and his victory in Stanza III is the logical sequel to the description of his departure from his sanctuary flanked by military attendants in Stanza II. The narrative sequence of verbal forms, the alternation of suffix and prefix conjugations, continues throughout these stanzas without interruption. In more specific terms, numerous images and words in Stanza III reflect the language of Stanza II. Stanza III opens with the name of God (*yhwh*) as does Stanza II (*'lwh/qdš*). The cracking of earth and heaving of mountains in response to God's appearance in Stanza III recalls the shattering collapse of mountains/hills in Stanza II. The positioning of Sun and Moon in Stanza III echoes both the divine entourage (*dbr/ršp*) and the altered orbits of the stars in Stanza II.[26] The brilliance of the divine warrior's weapons in Stanza III reflects his splendor in Stanza II (note the repetition of *ngh* and *'wr*; vv 4, 11). The image of God trampling earth and nations in his march in Stanza III is directly related to his standing and shaking earth and nations in Stanza II (note the use of the same formulaic pair *'rṣ//gwym* and the similarity of the verbs *'md/tṣ'd//tdwš*; vv 6, 12). Finally, the mention of God's people in Stanza III is, if my interpretation is correct, parallel to the mention of Kushan and Midian in Stanza II.[27]

The Literary Unity of Habakkuk 3

The coherent literary structure of Habakkuk 3, as has been shown in the preceding analysis, derives fundamentally from the use of inclusion. Very often inclusion operates not only as a single circle uniting the beginning and end of a literary unit but as a series of concentric circles carefully fashioned to produce a cyclic structure in which many layers of inclusion may be found. This inclusive structure operates at every level of the poem. It links Stanzas I and IV to provide a literary framework for the poem as a whole. It links beginnings and endings of stanzas, in particular Stanzas II and III, to mark them off as distinct units within the poem. It links the beginnings and endings of some subsections within stanzas. Inclusion is used as a structuring device even within some individual verse units of Habakkuk 3.

Inclusion is a well attested technique in the literature of the Hebrew Bible. Its presence has been noted, for example, in the Psalms, Isaiah, Jeremiah, the Song of Songs, and even in the prose of Deuteronomy.[28] It has also been shown to have been an important structuring device in Israel's oldest poetry. In his literary analysis of Judges 5, M. Coogan has identified the use of inclusion to delineate stanzas within the poem as well as to link the opening and closing stanzas of the poem.[29] In a recent study, F. M. Cross has described the cyclic structure within the archaic material in the Psalm of Jonah.[30] Inclusion was evidently a technique common among Israel's earliest poets which was passed down to succeeding generations of literary artists.

Though inclusion is central to the coherent structure of Habakkuk 3, several other important literary features contribute to the unity of the poem. One of these features is the consistent use of prefix and suffix conjugations of the verb in alternating fashion throughout Habakkuk 3. Usually this alternation occurs between verse units. The poet begins the description of an event in one verse unit with a prefix verb, for example, and then continues this description in the following verse with suffix verbs (e.g. v 3a and b). Occasionally this alternation can be found within a single verse unit (e.g. v 9a–10a), or even within a single colon of a verse unit (e.g. v 10a).

This literary feature of Habakkuk 3 has puzzled exegetes. And a variety of explanations for this alternating style have been given by scholars who have understood these conjugations on the basis of their normal grammatical functions in Hebrew, the suffix conjugation reflecting completed action and the prefix incomplete action. W. Rudolph has recently suggested that the alternation of verb tenses from verse to verse in Hab 3:3–15 can be explained if this text is considered a vision, the perfect tense indicating that the vision had already taken place, the imperfect that the actualization of the vision would take place in the future.[31] J. H. Eaton argues that the alternation of tenses in these verses reflects the liturgical experience of the community in which the past and future met together as the people were reminded of God's past salvation and gained hope for his future work.[32] E. M. Good rejects *ad hoc* explanations like these and simply concludes that no satisfactory explanation has yet been found to account for the verbal syntax in Habakkuk 3.[33]

A plausible explanation does exist, however, if the historical development of the Hebrew language is taken into account. In such ancient Semitic languages as Akkadian and Ugaritic, the prefix conjugation functioned as a preterit form. In Ugaritic it was used together with the suffix form in past narrative. This use of the prefix conjugation to describe the past was lost in biblical Hebrew, with two exceptions. It is still very likely reflected in the use of the converted imperfect for past narrative. And it survives intact in some of the oldest Israelite literature. The most systematic study of the preservation of the prefix conjugation with its old preterit function in ancient Hebrew poetry is that of D. A. Robertson.[34] Robertson has shown that the verbal syntax in Hab 3:3–15 conforms closely to the pattern of verbal conjugations used in past narrative in the Ugaritic epics and myths. Prefix verbal forms alternate with suffix forms to describe events in the past.

In that part of Habakkuk 3 which Robertson analyzed, vv 3–15, only three forms appear to depart from the archaic pattern of prefix/suffix alternation. These are the three *waw* + prefix forms in v 6. The *waw* + prefix form, as Robertson has shown, is characteristic of verbal conjugations in the later Hebrew poetry of the eighth and following centuries, particularly when it initiates a verse unit (*wytpṣṣw*) or is parallel to a suffix form (*'md wyndd*, *r'h wytr*). The fourth instance of a *waw* + prefix form, *wyṣ'* in v 5 (in which I believe the *waw* to be secondary), fits the pattern of archaic narrative since it occurs parallel to another prefix form and within a verse rather than at the beginning of a verse.[35]

Each of the three apparently atypical verbal forms can be shown, however, not to contradict the pattern of prefix and suffix conjugations which make up the remainder of this section of Habakkuk 3. There is the possibility, in the first place, that the conjunctions in none of these forms is original since, as has been pointed out in the textual study in Chapter 1, conjunctions are suspect in archaic Hebrew poetry. In one case, *wytpṣṣw*, there is textual support for this. The OG, Barb, and the OL all lack the conjunction before this verb.[36]

The two other forms in question, *wyndd* and *wytr* are both medial in the bicolon in which they appear. This is typical of archaic narrative. But they both occur, as does *ytpṣṣw* in the following verse, parallel to a suffix form. This is common in later poetry but uncommon in early narrative use where the *waw* + prefix form invariably parallels a prefix form. Robertson has explained this situation by suggesting that it is the result of chance variation. Where the prefix and suffix forms alternate, it is conceivable that some of these forms, regardless of their relationship with one another in parallelistic lines, will occasionally have the conjunction prefixed to them.[37] It should also be pointed out that in Habakkuk 3 the pattern of a suffix verb being followed immediately by a prefix verb in a single line occurs in the second colon of v 9b–10a. In this colon the prefix form lacks the conjunction. The same pattern appears to recur in v 6, but with the conjunction included. *wyndd* and *wytr* are not, therefore, the converted imperfects of later poetry, which the Masoretes took them to be, but old preterits which attracted a conjunction (coordinate, not conversive) because of their medial position in the poetic line.

Though Robertson dealt only with vv 3–15 in his analysis, the verbal syntax of the preceding and following verses deserves consideration in light of his work. With the exception of the cohortative forms of v 18, the verbal syntax of the remainder of the verses in Habakkuk 3 (vv 2, 16, 17, 19) reflects the same pattern as the syntax of vv 3–15. Prefix and suffix forms are alternated with one another. This indicates that like the verbs in vv 3–15 those in vv 2, 16, 17 narrate past events.

The verbal syntax throughout Habakkuk 3 therefore reflects the archaic practice of past narrative. Prefix forms, with preterit force, and suffix forms are alternated to recount a past occurrence. This understanding of the alternation of verbal forms in Habakkuk 3 has significance for interpreting the poem and for dating it. The interpretation of these verses must take into account the fact that they refer to a past event or events. The dating of these verses must take into account the fact that they preserve a syntactic style which predates the syntax of standard Hebrew poetry. Because the verbal syntax of Habakkuk 3 fits archaic narrative usage so closely, Robertson has suggested a date for its composition between the thirteenth and tenth centuries B. C. E., the era before the syntax of later Hebrew narrative took hold.

A final literary feature which provides unity to Habakkuk 3 as a whole is the use of a number of key words to link two or more stanzas together. All of these key words have already been mentioned in the preceding literary analysis, but their pattern of use throughout the poem merits a brief review. One of these key words is the divine name *yhwh* (with the alternates *'lwh/qdš* in Stanza II). Its placement in the poem has been carefully controlled. It occurs only in the opening verse units of the first three stanzas and in the two concluding verse units of the final stanza. It is used twice in Stanzas I and IV: and its vocative use (Stanzas I, III) alternates with its indirect use (Stanzas II, IV).

A second of these key words in the root *rgz*. It is used four times to describe the turmoil created by the divine power in a theophany. Its four occurrences show a careful progression of increased specificity. In the fourth colon of Stanza I it refers to the universal response to theophany; in the penultimate colon of Stanza II it refers to the response of the people (of God) in particular; and in the first and fourth cola of Stanza IV it refers to the response of the poet as an individual. The awful character of God's appearance is thus progressively focused till it affects the individual worshipper of Yahweh.

A third key word is the root *yš*ʻ, describing the victory of the divine warrior. In a hymn of triumph such as that found in Habakkuk 3,[38] this root carries, in a sense, the central motif of the poem. The root *yš*ʻ, like *rgz*, is used four times. And like *rgz* its usage shows a progression of increased specificity. It occurs first in the opening subsection of Stanza III (colon 5) where it refers to the victory of Yahweh. It then recurs twice just before the battle scene at the conclusion of Stanza III where it identifies Yahweh's victory as a victory for Israel's militia (cola 18–19). Finally, it is used at the conclusion of Stanza IV to link Yahweh's victory to the poet's own triumph. As with *rgz*, there is a narrowing here of the experience of victory from Yahweh, to the militia, to the individual worshipper. In the phase *ʼlhy yš*ʻ*y* divine and human triumph are inseparably united.

A fourth key word is the root *drk*. It occurs only twice, though at strategic points in the concluding verse units of Stanzas III and IV. Moreover, there are echoes of it earlier in the poem when Yahweh marches into battle (e.g. *ʻmd*, v 6; *tṣʻd*//*tdwš*, v 12). In its initial occurrence at the conclusion of Stanza III it describes Yahweh treading in victory on his vanquished foe. It thus provides a fitting climax to the theophany of the divine warrior in vv 3–15. In its second occurrence at the conclusion of Stanza IV it describes the poet, empowered by God (the Hiphil form of the verb is used), treading on the backs of his enemies in triumph. As with the word *yš*ʻ divine and human victory are inseparably linked. The two images linked by the verb *drk* identify Habakkuk 3 as a hymn of triumph sung in celebration of a victory which is at once Yahweh's and the poet's.

CHAPTER 3

The Hymn of Triumph in Habakkuk 3

The difficult character of the poem in Habakkuk 3 has been widely recognized. Most commentators introduce their studies of Habakkuk 3 with an admission of the problems involved in understanding and interpreting it. "The psalm in chapter iii of the Book of Habakkuk," writes U. Cassuto, "constitutes, in its general connotation and also in its details, a remarkably strange enigma."[1] W. A. Irwin agrees. "On one point, at least, biblical scholarship seems to be agreed in regard to the third chapter of Habakkuk:" he states, "that it may take its place among the very difficult and obscure passages of the Old Testament."[2] These judgements are representative of contemporary opinion.

One might expect from a difficult text such as this a profusion of interpretations and proposals. But such, ironically, is not the case. What might almost be called a consensus has emerged regarding the form and content of Habakkuk 3. It is broadly believed that Habakkuk 3 is a vision within a prayer of supplication or lamentation and that it stems from the same figure responsible for Habakkuk 1–2. A small minority holds otherwise.[3]

The elements of this consensus, however, as will be pointed out in more detail below, can simply not be sustained on the basis of a close analysis of Habakkuk 3. The conclusion that Habakkuk 3 is a prayer hinges largely on a single word in the Masoretic text, the imperative *ḥayyêhû* (v 2a), which is problematic in its context because of the ambiguity of the antecedent of its pronominal suffix, and which is only a single, and probably secondary, variant of a corrupt text. Furthermore, the view that this "prayer" is a lament runs counter to basic form critical considerations. The poem is so unlike the typical lament—in the arrangement of its parts, in its content, in its overall mood—that one would be forced to draw up new definitions to include it within this genre. Finally, the judgment that vv 3–15 comprise a vision within this "prayer of lamentation" is a secondary interpretation of Habakkuk 3 which can be seen most clearly in the LXX.[4] A careful textual study reveals that all "visionary" elements are not original and that the poem clearly indicates that this text stems rather from a context of recitation.

The consensus that Habakkuk 3 is from the same individual who created Chapters 1–2 also faces difficulties. The differences between Chapter 3 and the first two chapters of Habakkuk—in content, style, vocabulary, political orientation, etc.—are so numerous that studies of Habakkuk have traditionally spent a great deal of time explaining how such diverse material could come from the same hand. The way in which these differences place commentators, who take Habakkuk as the author of Chapter 3, on the defensive causes one at the outset to question the viability of their task. A major difficulty faced by those who assert unified authorship for Habakkuk is the patently archaic quality of Chapter 3, a difficulty which has been dealt with by proposals that the author was archaizing or simply appropriating archaic material.[5] The consistent presence of archaic characteristics, however, makes these proposals of archaizing or appropriation suspect and suggests rather a composition which is genuinely archaic.

The title of Chapter 3 (v 1), of course, supports the present consensus on this poem. But as is recognized today, these titles represent a special problem for the exegete. Where they occur before poetic compositions in narrative contexts, in the Psalms, and in the prophets, they are frequently secondary and reflect a later use of the poem in a context different from the one for which it was originally composed.[6] Members of the current consensus have accepted the title of Habakkuk 3 much too uncritically.

The fact that the major elements of the scholarly consensus on Habakkuk 3 become seriously suspect under a rigid scrutiny of this text indicates that another approach must be sought. This study is an attempt to do that. Its conclusions are 1) that Habakkuk 3, rather than representing a lament or a vision or both, is a fine example of another genre, the song of victory, a genre found elsewhere in biblical texts with close parallels to Habakkuk 3; and 2) that the differences between Chapter 3 and Chapters 1–2 are genuine indicators of separate authorship, and that the archaic qualities of Chapter 3 are authentic attestations of a composition much older than the seventh century prophet Habakkuk.

The Theophany (vv 3–15)

The heart of Habakkuk 3 is the description of the appearance of God in vv 3–15. This description of the arrival of the divine warrior to fight for his people and win for them the victory is the purpose of the poem. Because the theophany is central to the poem it will be treated first, and a discussion of the literary framework which encloses it(vv 2, 16–19) will be reserved until the theophany itself has been dealt with.

The theophany, though based on a single ancient conflict pattern, has two sections which may be distinguished from one another on the basis of form and content: vv 3–7 and vv 8–15. They provide two stanzas or strophes within a unified composition. Each of these sections of the theophany will be dealt with separately to illustrate their distinctive qualities, but the relationship between them will also be carefully defined.

'Eloah came from Teman: The March from the Southeast (vv 3–7)

The Location of God's Appearance

The location of God's appearance is described in the two bicola which provide the poetic framework for vv 3–7. The care with which the poet has constructed these bicola to form an inclusion for the theophany described within them can be seen in their formal identity:

	Masoretic Text	Reconstruction of Historical Pronunciation
v 3a	*'ĕlôah mittêmān yābô'*	*'ilōh mittayman yabō'*
	qādôš mēhar pā'rān	*qaduš mihharr pa'ran*
v 7	*'ohŏlê kûšān yirgĕzûn*	*'uhalay kūšan yirgazūn*
	yĕrî'ôt 'ereṣ midyān	*yarī'ōt 'arṣ madyan*

	Translation	Parallelistic Structure
v 3a	'Eloah from Teman came	Subject/Geographical Term/Verb
	The Holy One from Mount Paran	Subject/Ballast Variant of Geog. Term
v 7	Tents of Kushan shook	Subject/Geographical Term/Verb
	Tent curtains of the land of Midian	Subject/Ballast Variant of Geog. Term

The inclusive character of these bicola can also be seen in the similarity of sound between the two sets of geopolitical terms, especially when the probable historical pronunciation is taken into account: *tayman//harr pa'ran*, *kūšan//'arṣ madyan*. The similarity in syllabic length and accentuation between these pairs of terms and the rhyme, assonance(the repetition of the "a" sound), and alliteration(the concluding "n"s) are striking.[7]

These four designations, linked together poetically within the framework of this section of the poem, locate the appearance of God described in vv 3–7 in an area to the southeast of Canaan. All point to the same area, a region east of the Arabah in the southern section of Transjordan. This is not the judgment of most contemporary commentators and geographers. But a critical evaluation of the biblical evidence and a consideration of archaeological evidence which has become available favors this conclusion.

The location of Teman, according to biblical usage, is in the area of Edom, southeast of the Dead Sea. Yet the biblical references to Teman (Amos 1:12; Jer 49:7,20; Ezek 25:13; Obad 9) are vague enough to make it uncertain whether Teman was considered a city in Edom, a region of Edom, or a synonym for Edom itself.

Most archaeologists and geographers have understood Teman to have been a major Edomite city, apparently because of its association with Bozrah in Amos 1:12. They have identified it with such sites as Shôbak in the vicinity of Petra and Kh. eth-Thuwâneh north of Ma'an.[8] But the most popular suggestion, originally proposed by Nelson Glueck and now accepted by most Bible atlases, dictionaries, and geographies, is that biblical Teman is to be identified with Ṭawilân, a site on the eastern outskirts of Petra.[9]

In spite of the widespread acceptance of Glueck's suggestion, there is now reason to doubt it. Crystal-M. Bennett, who has been directing archaeological work at Ṭawilân, has concluded that there is no evidence to identify Ṭawilân with biblical Teman. She has found that Ṭawilân was not occupied before the end of the ninth century at the earliest, was never fortified, and therefore could not have been the southern capital of Edom, equivalent to Bozrah in the north, which Glueck thought Teman/Ṭawilân was. Bennett considers Ṭawilân "une grande ville édomite anonyme."[10]

Roland de Vaux, reconsidering the biblical evidence, has concluded that Teman never clearly refers to a city.[11] The name, according to de Vaux, was used originally for a region of Edom (Gen 36:34; Ezek 25:13), likely the southern area according to the etymology of the term. Later it was often a synonym for Edom itself (Amos 1:12; Jer 49:7,20; Obad 9). Of these latter instances, Amos 1:12 is decisive for de Vaux's interpretation. There Teman is not to be understood as a city alongside Bozrah in the following line, but as a territory (Edom) in which the city of Bozrah is located. This interpretation is demanded by the literary pattern of the oracle against Edom which parallels the oracles against Moab (Amos 2:1–3) and Judah (2:4–5), where a country or territory is balanced by a city within it. It is also to be noted that Gen 36:34 ("the land of the Temanites") suggests an area rather than a city as the referent for Teman.

The view that Teman originally referred to the southern region of Edom coincides with the evidence about Teman now available from Kuntillet 'Ajrud.[12] Kuntillet 'Ajrud is located in the Negeb, about 40 miles south of the traditional site of Kadesh Barnea on a hill above the Wadi Quraiya. The religious inscriptions and the imported pottery inscribed with blessings and drawings of divine figures have led to the conclusion that the site was an ancient pilgrimage shrine. The fact that Kuntillet 'Ajrud is located at a crossroads of desert tracks supports this judgment. One of these tracks traverses Sinai along the Wadi Quraiya; another branches off to the south in the direction of southern Sinai. But the major road which intersects Kuntillet ʿAjrud is the Darb el-Ghazza which leads from Gaza in the north to Elat in the southeast. The pilgrims who inscribed *yhwh htmn*, "Yahweh (of) Teman," at Kuntillet ʿAjrud were most likely referring to a site in the southern Transjordan to which this major artery leads.[13]

The most common identification of Paran in atlases and dictionaries today is an area south of Canaan and west of the Arabah.[14] This judgment is generally based on the prose accounts of the wilderness journey of Israel to Canaan (Num 12:16; 10:12; 13:2,6) which connect Paran with Kadesh, popularly identified at present with the modern Ein el-Qudeirat. The identification is further supported by reference to the modern Jebel Fārān, located approximately 80 kilometers west of Petra.

This popular position must be challenged first on the basis of the oldest biblical sources which refer to Paran, the old poems. Deuteronomy 33 associates Paran with the area east of the Arabah. In v 2, *har pā'rān* occurs in parallelism with Seir, a designation for Edom. This usage coincides with Hab 3:3 where *har pā'rān* occurs in parallelism with Teman, a designation for southern Edom. The theophany of Yahweh in the south described in Judg 5:4, a text clearly related to Deut 33:2 and Hab 3:3, is also located east of the Arabah. Paran is not used in Judges 5, but Seir and the fields of Edom are identified with Yahweh's appearance.

An old prose source, found in Genesis 14, corroborates the evidence of the old poems. It is generally agreed that this material is not one of the pentateuchal sources, and it has been suggested that it is ancient in origin.[15] In the description of Chedorlaomer's campaign through Transjordan, Chedorlaomer's forces march south through the lands of the Zuzim (later Ammon? Deut 2:20), the Emim (later Moab? Deut 2:10), and the Horites of Seir(the predecessors of Seir/Edom; Gen 34:20; Deut 2:12,22) as far as El-Paran. Here El-Paran, "the terebinth of Paran," appears to be the designation of an area or settlement in southern Edom.[16]

In the younger prose sources of the Priestly Work, Paran is always designated *midbār pā'rān* and is identified as the staging area from which spies were sent by the Israelites to Canaan (Num 10:12; 12:16; 13:2,26). Because the Priestly tradent identifies Paran as the first stop after leaving Mt. Sinai and connects this area with Kadesh (Num 13:26), and because Kadesh has been identified by many with Ein el-Qudeirat in the Negeb, *midbār pā'rān* is usually identified with the area south of Canaan and west of the Arabah.

But there are serious problems with the reliability of this evidence from the Priestly Work and with the usual identifications based upon it. In the first place, the literary interests of the biblical editors have led them to simplify and rearrange historical and geographical details. The Priestly tradent, for example, has artificially systemized the journey from Sinai to Canaan by the technique of stages, like *midbār pā'rān*, which incorporate many obscure stops. The result is not a cohesive itinerary. And this simplification has led to contradictions, one of which identifies Kadesh first with *midbār pā'rān* (Num 12:26), then with the next stage of the journey, *midbār zin* (Num 20:1).[17]

Secondly, the location of *midbār pā'rān* and Kadesh of the exodus with the Negeb has found no corroboration from archaeologists. Evidence of settlement in the Late Bronze Age, when Israelite or proto-Israelite tribes would have been in this area, is so far lacking at the traditional site of Kadesh and elsewhere in this part of the Negeb.[18] Current evidence thus suggests that neither the itinerary in the Priestly Work nor the common identification of sites in this itinerary are reliable sources for locating Paran.

The occurrences of Paran in the Deuteronomistic History are hardly more helpful. The list of sites identifying the location of Moses' final address to the Israelites, within which Paran occurs (Deut 1:1), includes some sites which are obscure and others with no geographical proximity.[19] And the connection of Paran with David's adventures in Carmel (1 Sam 25:1) is in all likelihood not original (cf. the LXX).[20] Only the description of Hadad's flight through Paran (1 Kgs 11:18) is of any significance for locating Paran. Because Hadad travels through Midian and then Paran on his way to Egypt, it has been presumed that Paran is between Midian and Egypt, west of the Arabah. But Hadad may have been travelling south through Transjordan, where Paran was located, before heading west on the ancient road traversing the Sinai desert from the tip of the Gulf of Aqabah to Egypt.[21]

Thus, in the oldest poetic and prose sources, Paran is connected with the area east of the Arabah. The later traditions, and the identification of Paran west of the Arabah to which they have given rise, are not to be trusted as reliable geographical information on the basis of literary and archaeological evidence.

Midian is used in the Bible to refer to a group of people who had contacts with Israel in the Late Bronze and Early Iron Ages, the era of exodus and conquest. The Midianites are pictured as a nomadic people, ranging from Egypt (Gen 37:28) through Transjordan (Numbers 22, 25, 31) into Canaan (Judges 6–9) and perhaps as far to the northeast as the Euphrates (Num 22:5). But they are identified predominantly with the southern part of Transjordan, perhaps as far south as the eastern shore of the Gulf of Aqabah (Gen 25:6; 36:35; Num 10:29; 22; 25; 31; Josh 13:21; Judg 6:3,33; 7:12; 1 Kgs 11:18).

The association of the Midianites with this area may be reflected in the name of a later city in the vicinity of El Bedʿ, east of the Gulf of Aqabah, referred to by Josephus as Madianen. This is not certain however since the origin of the name of this city may as easily be linked to the common terms *dîn*, "judge," and *mĕdînâ*, "province, district," as to the preservation of a historical memory of the ancient Midianites. Eusebius refers to this later city as Madiam, and it is almost certainly this city with which the translator of the LXX (*Madiam*) connected the *midyān* of Hab 3:7.[22]

The distinctive type of pottery called "Midianite Ware," because it coincides with the location and period occupied by the biblical Midianites, may provide further evidence linking the Midianites to the southern part of Transjordan. This ware has been discovered predominantly at sites in the Arabah just north of the Gulf of Aqabah, in Transjordan, and farther south to the east of the Gulf of Aqabah.[23] Debate about the date and cultural source of this ware continues, however, and its relevance for locating the Midianites must still remain provisional.[24]

There is some question whether biblical writers employed the term Midian to refer to a group of people—a tribe or league—or to a definite geographical area. William Dumbrell has made a very complete case for identifying Midian as a league, composed of various tribal groups, which was prominent in Transjordan in the Late Bronze Age.[25] This judgment is not necessarily contradicted by the reference to the land of Midian (*ʾrṣ mdyn*) in Hab 3:7. In the first place, the reference to the tent curtains (*yryʿwt*) of

Midian indicates that the poet has in mind a nomadic people rather than a group permanently settled in a specific location.[26] Secondly, the use of *'rṣ* in the second half of the bicolon in v 7 has poetic rather than political significance. The poet has structured the two bicola framing this section of Habakkuk 3 (vv 3a, 7) in exactly parallel fashion, providing the geographical term in the initial colon of each bicolon with a ballast variant in the concluding colon of each bicolon (*tymn//hr p'rn*; *kwšn//'rṣ mdyn*). The poet may simply be referring to the area in which the Midianites live, not to a country named Midian.

Kushan is the geopolitical designation of the four in Habakkuk 3 about which least is known. It appears only here in this form. The versions have all connected it with Ethiopia, the common referent of biblical Kush (eg. OG/Barb: *aithiopon*; OL: *Aethiopum*; Vg: *Aethiopiae*). This identification cannot be correct and is another example of an old designation having been forgotten and reinterpreted by later translators in light of their own political situation.[27]

Kushan's position in parallel relationship to Midian in the bicolon in Hab 3:7 suggests its association with Midian. This is corroborated by the Moses material in the epic traditions (JE) which identify Moses' wife as Midianite and Kushite (Exod 2:15–22; Num 12:1). As W. F. Albright has shown, there is extrabiblical evidence for a Kush(an) in the southern part of Transjordan which is different from the better known Ethiopian Kush.[28] The Execration Texts from the reign of Ammenemes III (1842–1797 B.C.E.) include among the list of Egyptian enemies references to two "great men of the tribes of *kwšw*."[29] This designation is immediately followed by upper and lower *šwtw*, which Albright has identified as the archaic tribal name of the Moabites on the basis of the *mô'āb//šēt* parallelism in the Oracles of Balaam (Num 24:17). This would place the Kush known to the Egyptians—certainly to be identified with the Kushan in Hab 3:7—roughly in the area of Midian.

While G. Posener considers the Kush of the Execration Texts to designate a country, the reference to tribes and the designation of their leaders as *wr*, "chief, noble one, elder," suggests a league or confederation made up of nomadic groups (cf. Hab 3:7: "the tents of Kushan").[30] The identification of Kushan with Midian in Hab 3:7 and in the Moses traditions may indicate that elements of the ancient Kushites were later incorporated into the

Midianite confederation which dominated the same area in the Late Bronze Age or that Kushan was an ancient term which could still be applied to its successors, the Midianites.[31]

The four geopolitical terms which frame vv 3–7 thus locate the theophany described within these verses at a holy mountain in the southern sector of Transjordan. That all of these designations refer to the southern part of Transjordan is not a new judgment. Alois Musil, one of the earliest geographers of the ancient Near East, held this opinion.[32] But few modern commentators have realized that research since his time has been gradually confirming the basic accuracy of his views. Together with the evidence presented above, other biblical evidence, and extrabiblical evidence as well, support Musil's opinion that the ancient southern sanctuary of Yahweh was located to the east of Sinai in the southern part of Transjordan.

Foremost among the biblical material is the old poetry. The appearance of God in the southeast to set out for battle is pictured in the old war songs in Judges 5 (v 4; Seir//Edom, Sinai: cf. Ps 68:8–9) and Deuteronomy 33 (v 2: Sinai//Seir//Mt. Paran). In these hymns God marches out from a sanctuary in the southeast to fight for his people. Also to be noted are the epic traditions (JE) which link Moses and the mountain of Yahweh with the Midianites. According to these traditions, Moses escapes to Midian and marries the daughter of a Midianite priest (Exodus 2), is first encountered by Yahweh at a holy mountain there (Exodus 3), and returns after the exodus to his father-in-law, the priest of Midian, who offers sacrifices to Yahweh and supplies Moses and Israel with a judicial system (Exodus 18).

Extrabiblical evidence which has come to light reinforces these traditions of a sanctuary of Yahweh in southern Transjordan. Most striking is the mention of Yahweh in a list of place names recorded in the temple of Amon at Soleb, from the time of Amenophis III (1405–1367 B.C.E.) and copied later during the time of Rameses II (1290–1224 B.C.E.) in the temple at Amarah-West.[33] In this list the name *t3 šsw yhw3*, "Yahwe (of the) land of the Shasu," appears alongside the names *s'rr*, "Seir," and *rbn*, possibly "Laban" (cf. Deut 1:1). The association of the toponym Yahweh with Seir indicates its location in southern Transjordan. The name itself, as Raphael Giveon has argued, likely developed from a form such as "Beth Yahweh," which would point to a sanctuary of Yahweh in southern Transjordan in existence in the late 15th and early 14th centuries B.C.E.[34]

This evidence suggests that the old southern sanctuary of Yahweh designated Sinai/Horeb in the epic narratives should not be sought at its traditional site, Jebel Musa, in the southern Sinai, nor at Jebel Helal in the northern Sinai,[35] but in the mountainous terrain east of the Arabah. Archaeologists, to this point, have found no evidence of the occupation of the Sinai, in the north or in the south, during the Late Bronze Age, while uncovering evidence for extensive occupation in Transjordan during this period.[36] This archaeological picture is corroborated by Egyptian records which place the Shasu, among whom the Late Bronze Age sanctuary of Yahweh existed, and with whom proto-Israel must have in some way been related, primarily in southern Edom.[37]

It should be noted, in order to locate Habakkuk 3 correctly within Israelite history and tradition, that the theophany of Yahweh is identified with this southern sanctuary, apart from the historical memories preserved in the epic sources, only in Israel's archaic poetry (Judg 5:4; Ps 68:9; Deut 33:2). From the time of the monarchy, when Jerusalem became Israel's religious center, and the temple of Yahweh was established there, Mt. Zion replaced the southern mountain as Yahweh's abode.[38] When the theophany of the divine warrior marching out for his people—or against them—is described, the divine warrior marches out from Zion. This can be seen in psalms from the Jerusalem cult (e.g. 50:1–4; 2:1–7; 48:2–8; 76:2–4), as well as in prophetic speech (e.g. Amos 1:2; Isa 6:1–5; 29:1–8; Joel 2:1–11; 3:14–16). God was also described during the monarchic era as coming down from his heavenly temple (*yrd*: Ps 18:7,10; Mic 1:2–3), the cosmic equivalent of the temple on Zion.[39]

Moreover, the southeast, from monarchic times on (and perhaps even earlier) is viewed generally with contempt. Teman, for example, when it designates an area of Edom elsewhere in the Bible, occurs only in prophetic oracles of judgment against Edom (Amos 1:12; Jer 49:7,20; Ezek 25:13; Obad 9). When Yahweh does appear to approach from the southeast as a divine warrior in the proto-apocalyptic poetry of the postexilic disciples of Second Isaiah (63:1–6), he does so not on a march from his holy mountain, but on the way back from a battle with Edom which has stained his garments with blood.

The location of God's theophany at his ancient sanctuary in the southeast in Habakkuk 3 links this poem to Israel's most archaic poetry which originated in the era of the league. At the same time it places Habakkuk 3 in tension with the poetic traditions of the temple cultus of the monarchy, with prophetic conventions, and with the motifs of apocalyptic literature.

The Entourage of the Divine Warrior

When 'Eloah goes out from *har pā'rān*, the ancient sanctuary of Yahweh in the southeast, he does not march out alone. He is accompanied by two attendants, Deber and Resheph. Modern English translations and commentaries still continue by and large the tradition of translating Deber and Resheph as common nouns: disease, plague, pestilence, fever. But there is a great deal of evidence that Deber and Resheph ought to be understood as divine beings who are members of God's cosmic army and who march with him into his holy war.

One of these attendants, Resheph, originally pronounced *rašp(u)*, was a deity known throughtout the ancient Near East.[40] Canaanite in origin, he was also worshipped in Syria, Phoenicia, Cyprus, Egypt, North Africa, and also at Ebla.[41] Above all, Resheph was a warrior, an appropriate kind of deity to be included in Yahweh's military retinue in Hab 3:5. Resheph was pictured in his iconography with mace-axe, spear, quiver, and shield; described as fierce in battle; and adopted as a military patron by Syrian and Egyptian kings. He appears to have been a god of the underworld, identified explicitly with Babylonian Nergal at Ugarit, and associated with such deadly forces as plagues and disease.[42] In some biblical references to Resheph he still seems to retain his personalized character of a divinity or demon (Deut 32:24; Ps 78:48; Job 5:7). Even when the term appears to be used more as a common noun depicting the forces associated with the deity Resheph, the mythological roots of the expression are not far from the surface (Ps 76:4; Cant 8:6).

The identity of Deber, parallel to Resheph in Hab 3:5, is less clear. A number of biblical texts present Deber as a destructive deity who, like Resheph, brings plagues and diseases. In texts such as Ps 78:48, where he is also paired with Resheph (reading with Sym), in the catalogue of terrors in Ps 91:5–6, and in the covenant curse of Deut 28:21 (cf. 1 Kgs 8:37; 2 Sam 24:13, 15), Deber retains characteristics of a personalized deity.[43] Recently G. Pettinato and M. Dahood have claimed that Deber (written *dabir*) has been identified in the archives from Tell Mardikh as the patron god of ancient Ebla: ^{d}*da-bi-ir* dinger-*eb-la*^{ki}. This would provide evidence, if Pettinato and Dahood are correct, that Deber was a deity and that the biblical texts under discussion here may well preserve the recognition of this fact, but a final evaluation of the Eblaite material must await further information.[44] In light of the divine status of Resheph, with whom Deber is paired in Hab 3:5, and in light of the suggestions in biblical literature and elsewhere that Deber was a personalized deity, Deber is best understood here as a member of the entourage of the divine warrior.

Viewing Resheph and Deber as members of Yahweh's army in Hab 3:5 is supported by the fact that the military retinue is an extremely common feature of the descriptions of great gods throughout the ancient Near East. Patrick Miller has assembled evidence which indicates that all of the important gods at Ugarit—'El, Ba'l, 'Anat, 'Aṯtart, Yamm, and Mot—and others less frequently mentioned in the texts, were flanked by military assistants.[45] These assistants are often mentioned in pairs, as they are in Hab 3:5. In Mesopotamia great divine figures like Adad, Marduk, and Tiamat are accompanied by divine armies into battle. The description of Adad's theophany in the Epic of Gilgamesh is remarkably similar to Hab 3:5: "With the first glow of dawn,/ A black cloud rose up from the horizon./ Inside it Adad thunders,/ While Shullat and Hanish go in front,/ Moving as heralds over hill and plain."[46]

The military retinue was also an important feature in Israel's understanding of its God. It can be seen in the archaic title for Israel's God, Yahweh Sabaoth, likely to be translated "he who creates the (heavenly) armies." This military title may have been the original cultic epithet out of which the name and character of Yahweh developed.[47] The military retinue can also be seen in the ancient war songs of Israel in which the divine warrior enters battle accompanied by his cosmic army, the holy ones (Deut 33:2), the stars (Judg 5:20), the sun and moon (Josh 10:12–13), the divine chariots (Ps 68:18), and the cherubim (Ps 18:11).[48] These cosmic armies of God become prominent again in apocalyptic literature as is evident from the late writings in the Hebrew Bible, in the War Scroll at Qumran, and in the Apocalypse of the New Testament.[49]

Together with the prominence of the cosmic army in theophanies of the divine warrior and the evidence for Resheph and Deber as divine beings, mention should also be made of the terminology in Habakkuk 3. The verbs *hlk* and *yṣ'* describe the march of warriors into battle: *yṣ'* is a technical term for a military advance and is used also in v 13a for the advance of Yahweh himself. The positions of Deber and Resheph before (*lpnyw*) and behind (*lrglyw*) God picture the divine warrior flanked by his military entourage.[50] These facts all indicate that Deber and Resheph are to be understood in Habakkuk 3 as lesser divinities, members of God's cosmic army, who, as is common in Israel's ancient war songs, march with God into his holy war.

The Response to God's Appearance

The appearance of the divine warrior and his heavenly army is awe-some (vv 3–5). The response to it is sheer terror (vv 6–7). The entire world is shaken. Every colon of vv 6–7 has a word for it (*yndd*, *ytr*, *ytpṣṣw* , *šḥw*, *tḥt'n*, *yrgzwn*) except the last colon which has no verb.

This pervasive disruption of the cosmos is another element of Hab 3:3–7 which fits into the typology of the theophany of the divine warrior. Close parallels to the language of Hab 3:6–7 can be found in Israel's ancient war songs which describe the appearance of the divine warrior. Good examples are Judg 5:4–5 and Ps 68:9 in which the earth shakes (*'rṣ r'šh*) at God's appearance. Ps 18:8 in which the earth and the foundations of the mountains tremble (*tg'š tr'š 'rṣ/mwsdy hrym yrgzw*), and Exod 15:14–16 in which the peoples quake (*'mym yrgzwn*). Theophanic language of this kind is preserved in a number of hymns from the royal cult (Pss 46:7; 97:4–5; 144:5) but is used only rarely by the classical prophets (Amos 1:2; Mic 1:3–4; Nah 1:3–5; cf. Isa 6:1–4). It is reutilized in the proto-apocalyptic literature of the later prophets (e.g. Joel 2:10; Zech 14:4–5; Hag 2:6–7).[51]

The disruption of the cosmos in response to the appearance of the divine warrior is not unique to Israelite literature but, as Frank Cross has shown, has its roots in Canaanite mythology.[52] In the mythological texts from Ugarit, two patterns can be discerned in the theophany of Ba'l. In the first of these the divine warrior marches to battle and the cosmos convulses and nature languishes.[53] In the second pattern the divine warrior returns from battle and the cosmos returns to order and nature comes to life. Behind these two patterns is an archaic mythic scheme: the divine warrior goes out to battle the forces of chaos, convulsing nature; then, having subdued his foe, he returns to take up his kingship, bringing nature back to life. The cosmic disruption in Hab 3:6–7, as in Israel's ancient songs of the divine warrior mentioned above, clearly fits into the first pattern in this overall scheme. When the storm god appears to do battle, the entire cosmos is shaken.

As a result of the recent archaeological work at Kuntillet 'Ajrud, a pilgrimage site on the road to Elat and the east, a new text is available to illustrate this same pattern of the disruption of nature at the appearance of the divine warrior. Found in the debris which had fallen from the wall in the entrance from the bench room to the courtyard of the Western Building, the inscription in question was written on plaster in black ink in the Phoenician script of the late ninth century B.C.E.[54] Though the text is fragmentary and damaged, one can make out parallels to Hab 3:3–7. The context is the battle of the divine warrior. His appearance is accompanied by light (cf. Hab 3:4a), and the response to it is reflected in the convulsion of the cosmos: the mountains are melted and their peaks crushed.[55]

The response of the earth to God's appearance in Habakkuk 3 (v 6) is thus readily understandable. It is typical of the disruption of nature which results from the divine warrior's march into battle. But what of the response of the people (v 7)? How are the involvement of Kushan and Midian to be understood? Are they friend or foe? Do they shake because they are the enemy against whom the divine warrior goes into battle (cf. Exod 15:14–16)? Or are they shaken because they, like the poet (vv 2a, 16a), are friends of God overwhelmed by his appearance?

The former alternative which appears to be supported by the MT *(tḥt 'wn)* is immediately the more attractive one. Antipathy toward Midian is widespread in the Bible. Midian is remembered as an old enemy of Israel in the wilderness (Numbers 22, 25, 31), and during the league era (Judges 6–8), a memory which, as Gerhard von Rad has argued, survived in the writings of Isaiah of Jerusalem. When Isaiah referred to "the day of Midian" (9:3, 10:26), he did so to compare the new action of Yahweh against Israel's enemies, which he prophesied, to the sacral wars of the past in which Israel's ancient enemies had been defeated.[56] Many would like to include the author of Habakkuk 3 in the company of Isaiah at this point.[57]

But the opposite alternative, that Kushan and Midian were not the enemies of Israel's God, has much to be said for it. The accounts of apostasy and war with Midian in Numbers 25 and 31 are widely believed to come from the hand of the late Priestly editors of the Tetrateuch, and the animosity in them has been explained as part of a wider polemic by these Aaronid priestly editors against the Mushite priestly house and its ancient associations with Midian.[58] An ancient and close association of early or proto-Israel with Midian is indeed reflected in the epic traditions which describe Moses receiving instructions from a Midianite priest (Exodus 18), marrying a Midianite woman (Exodus 2; also identified as Kushite, Num 12:1), and encountering the mountain of God in the land of Midian (Exodus 3). This ancient association is still reflected later at Arad, where a family of Midianite priests settled among the Judahites and established an important Yahwistic shrine.[59]

This second alternative, that Kushan/Midian were associates of Israel and worshippers of Yahweh, may also be supported by internal evidence in Habakkuk 3. Part of this evidence is the use of the root *rgz*. The use of *rgz* to describe the response of Kushan/Midian to the theophany pictured in vv 3–7 might automatically be taken as descriptive of the trembling which seizes the enemies of the divine warrior (cf. Exod 15:14–16). But it should be noted that where this root occurs elsewhere in the poem, it is used to describe the poet's own response (v 16a) or that of his people (v 2) to God's appearance.[60] Since *rgz* is one of the keywords whose repetition links the entire poem together, the contextual situation should be taken seriously. Kushan and Midian, as the poet of Habakkuk 3, tremble with the entire cosmos at the appearance of the divine warrior.

Another part of this evidence is the presence of Kushan/Midian within the inclusion which frames vv 3–7. In this circular construction by which vv 3 and 7 have been linked through their identical poetic structure, Kushan/Midian (v 7) are associated with the mountain of God (v 3) where his theophany occurs. Could not this suggest the presence of Kushan/Midian among the Yahwists worshipping at the deity's sanctuary? Finally, it should be recalled that the negative remark about Kushan/Midian with which v 7 begins, *taḥat 'āwen*, is more than likely an old corruption of the text and does not represent the sentiments of the poet.

This evidence does not establish conclusively that Kushan/Midian were worshippers of Yahweh together with the poet who constructed this work. But it does suggest that this possibility, overlooked in the literature on Habakkuk, should be taken seriously. If Kushan/Midian are to be understood as sharing the poet's response of awe at God's appearance, this would suggest a very early date for the composition of this material. Had the poem been composed during the era of classical prophecy, Midian would certainly have played the symbolic role of God's archetypal enemy, as von Rad has shown. With a positive reference to Midian, however, this poem would have to be placed in the earliest days of the Israelite people, the era when proto-Israel still enjoyed friendly relationships with these peoples and before the hostilities, so vividly recalled in later traditions, had arisen.

Was your anger, Yahweh, against River?
The Battle with the Dragon (vv 8–15)

As can be seen from literary considerations, vv 8–15 of Habakkuk 3 form a distinct unit within the poem as a whole. The poetic analysis has shown that vv 8–15 are set off from the surrounding material by the technique of inclusion, the reference to God in the second person, the use of the divine name Yahweh, the introductory rhetorical question, and a special arsenal of poetic imagery which focuses on God's anger, his weapons, and the cosmic waters. At the same time, this stanza continues the narrative of the previous stanza. The divine warrior, whose departure from his sanctuary is described in the preceding stanza, prepares for war and marches into battle while the cosmos continues to quake. Finally, he attacks and subdues his foe.

The March to Battle and Cosmic Response

The description of the divine warrior's preparation for and march into battle in Stanza III includes some of the most vivid martial imagery for God in the Bible. Yahweh appears mounted on a horse-drawn chariot (v 8b). He carries a bow (v 9a), a quiver full of arrows (vv 9a, 11b), and a spear (v 11b). This imagery is drawn from the traditional picture of the storm god in Semitic mythology. The chariot is the storm cloud drawn by the wind, the arrows and the spear are bolts of lightning (*brq*, v 11b) hurled to earth from the cloud. The source of these images of Yahweh in Habakkuk 3 in the traditional imagery of the storm god in the ancient Near East may be briefly illustrated.

Closest at hand is Baʿl, storm god at Ugarit. Baʿl is described in the mythic texts as mounted on a cloud-chariot. One of his most common epithets is *rkb ʿrpt*, "rider of the clouds" (cf. *trkb* ... *mrkbt*, v 8b),[61] and in one text his chariot may be mentioned specifically.[62] Baʿl's weapon is the lightning bolt (*brq*), described as a spear in the mythic texts and pictured as such in his iconography.[63] Marduk, the god of Babylon, is similarly pictured. In *Enūma eliš*, when he prepares for battle with Tiamat, the primordial sea, Marduk mounts a horse-drawn storm-chariot, and takes into battle a bow and quiver with arrows of lightning.[64] Adad, a god of the storm popular among the West Semitic people who founded the kingdoms of Mari and Babylon at the beginning of the second millennium B.C.E., is also pictured with this imagery. When he brings the great deluge described in the Atrahasis and Gilgamesh epics, Adad appears riding the storm cloud, his divine chariot.[65] His weapon, described in literature and pictured in his iconography, is the lightning bolt.[66]

The response to the march of the divine warrior in this stanza of Habakkuk 3 is the same as the response in the preceding stanza (vv 3–7). The cosmos is shaken. The description of nature's response in Stanza III is contained in its second subsection, the three bicola in vv 9b–11a. This subsection lies between the description of Yahweh's preparation for battle (vv 8–9a) and his march (vv 11b–12). As in Stanza II, primordial and eternal realities crumble at the approach of the divine warrior. The foundations of the mountains, the zones of the cosmic waters, and the paths of the heavenly bodies are altered.

The predominant image in this description of nature's response is the agitation of cosmic waters. Three of the six cola in this subsection mention the waters. Subterranean rivers erupt (v 9b); water pours from the clouds (v 10a); and the deep roars (v 10b). Just as the ancient mountains, founded firmly on the waters at creation, are shaken (vv 6, 10a), so the cosmic waters, restrained at creation behind designated boundaries, break out.[67]

The waters erupt from below the earth (vv 9b, 10b) and storm down from above (v 10a), in an image which is reminiscent of the great deluge.[68]

This disturbance of the cosmic waters must be understood primarily as part of the typical pattern of a theophany. The appearance of God is accompanied by the convulsion of nature. In Ps 18:16, for example, the convulsion of nature includes the uncovering of the sources (springs) of the sea (cf. Hab 3:9b) as the foundations of the world tremble (cf. Hab 3:10a).[69] Some have suggested that these waters be viewed as the enemy of God.[70] I do not think this is their primary role here. God's enemy in this strophe is River/Sea, mentioned in the inclusive framework of the strophe and in the battle scene in vv 13b–14, as will be discussed in a moment. Furthermore, the convulsion of nature is expected as part of the theophanic pattern. But I would allow that the association of the enemy with the cosmic waters in vv 9–10 is not absent. It is certainly no accident that the poet has chosen to picture the response of nature to the appearance of God in this particular stanza, where God fights River/Sea, as a disturbance of the cosmic waters. In the cry of Tehom, there may be a distant echo of Tiamat's cry of fury when challenged by Marduk in battle.[71]

A puzzling occurrence at this point in the poem is the appearance of sun and moon. The significance of their involvement here has been widely debated. The most popular opinion by far is that sun and moon are described as being darkened in response to Yahweh's theophany.[72] But this opinion is unsatisfactory. It is not supported by the phraseology of the Hebrew text nor by the versions.[73] When the darkening of sun and moon is described in Hebrew literature, it is not expressed with the verbs *ʿāmad* and *nāśāʾ*. It is always expressed with such explicit terminology as *lōʾ-ʾôr/nāgah*, "not give light," *qādar*, "grow dim," or *ḥāšak*, "become dark."[74] If sun and moon are to be understood as involved together with the waters in the disruption of the cosmos of which the previous verses speak, then they must be seen not as losing their light but as being terror stricken by the appearance of God. Sun throws up his hands in fear, Moon is frozen in fright.

But a more promising approach may be found in pursuing the line of thinking of the old Jewish commentators (Tg, Rashi, Kimchi) who connected these lines with Josh 10:12, 13, their closest parallel in the Hebrew Bible. The phrase *yārēaḥ ʿāmad*, for example, appears in both texts. The old commentators considered Hab 3:11 a recollection of the event described in Joshua 10.[75] Though I do not agree with them that a specific historical allusion is involved here, I believe these commentators were on the right track in noting the similarities between the texts. The phrasing is strikingly alike and the holy war contexts are the same. An interpretation of either text should take these similarities seriously.

The two most attractive explanations for the role of Sun and Moon in Josh 10:12, 13 have been advanced by John Holladay and Patrick Miller. Holladay has shown that the appearance of Sun and Moon together in the morning sky at midmonth was a favorable omen in Semitic astrology and has suggested that Joshua's prayer was an appeal for this favorable astrological condition on the morning of the day of battle.[76] One could see a description of this astrological condition in Habakkuk 3 where Sun lifts his hands (rays) high at sunrise, while Moon stands (waits to set) in his place. In this case the recitation of the military victory in Habakkuk 3 would incorporate the memory of the favorable astrological conditions accompanying it.

While recognizing the strengths of Holladay's analysis Patrick Miller places more emphasis on the place of Sun and Moon in the heavenly armies of the divine warrior and their participation in the battle which is described in Josh 10:12, 13.[77] He has argued that Sun and Moon were part of the host gathered around Yahweh which commonly takes part in his sacral wars. This too is a plausible explanation for the role of Sun and Moon in Habakkuk 3. In the previous section of Habakkuk 3, God appears in the company of his cosmic warriors. In this stanza, where God's appearance is again described, it would not be unusual to see the motif of the cosmic hosts repeated.

I would not be surprised, in fact, to see elements of both of these explanations applicable to the place of Sun and Moon in Habakkuk 3. There may actually be a connection between them. Sun and Moon, members of the divine army, appear together in the sky in positions considered fortuitous astrologically, when the divine warrior goes into battle. As such they provide support for the attack (v 11b) launched by Yahweh.

The notion of the sun and moon being darkened at the appearance of the divine warrior is not found in archaic war songs where these celestial figures provide support for the divine warrior. It appears to arise only in later theophanies, particularly those in apocalyptic literature. Amos, who believed the divine warrior would fight against his people rather than for them, envisioned the theophany of God on the day of Yahweh accompanied by darkness rather than light (8:9). And this motif was picked up in later literature when God's final judgement of the nations was described (Joel 2:10; 3:4; 4:15; Isa 13:10).[78] A variation on this theme among the disciples of Second Isaiah was that the sun and moon would cease to shine in the last days because they would no longer be necessary when God himself would provide everlasting light (Isa 60:19, 20).

The Battle with the Dragon

All modern interpreters acknowledge connections between Habakkuk 3 and the ancient conflict myth in which the storm god goes out as a warrior to do battle with the sea. The description of Yahweh as a storm god warrior which has been summarized above, in which he appears with cloud-chariot and lightning arrows and spear, illustrates this connection clearly. Furthermore, connections between the adversary of the storm god in the conflict myth and in Habakkuk 3 have been noted. Umberto Cassuto and Theodor Gaster recognized soon after the Ugaritic texts became available the reflection of the enemy of Ba'l, Prince Sea/Judge River, in the parallelism of River/Sea in Hab 3:8a.[79] Cassuto, and later W. F. Albright, went so far as to say—on the basis of the Greek reading, *thanatos*, in Hab 3:13b— that the other great enemy of Ba'l, Death, is also mentioned in Habakkuk 3.[80]

Yet in spite of these widely acknowledged connections almost all have denied that the ancient battle between the storm god and the sea is actually described in Habakkuk 3. Even Cassuto and Gaster who first saw reflections of the ancient dragon of chaos in Habakkuk 3 believed that the actual enemy of God in this poem was a historical enemy of Israel. Wrote Cassuto: "The enemy whom YHWH defeats and destroys this time is not the primordial force of the waters, but the oppressor of Israel."[81]

A number of things can, at first glance, be advanced in favor of this position. First, there is the question in Hab 3:8a: "Did your anger burn, Yahweh, against River/Sea?" For a rhetorical question phrased in this way a negative answer is generally expected. To elicit a positive response, the negation *lō'* is usually added to the question. Indeed, there are those, like Sigmund Mowinckel, who have argued that this question clearly anticipates a negative answer. Mowinckel wrote: "Die Antwort is natürlich: Nein."[82]

This negative answer to the question in v 8a appears to be corroborated, as Mowinckel goes on to observe, by the fact that Yahweh's anger is later in the poem directed against the nations (v 12) on behalf of Israel (v 13a). I am not in complete disagreement with this common position that Yahweh's enemy in Habakkuk 3 is historical, but with the one-sided way in which it is stated. A great deal more can be said about the dragon.

In the first place, there are sound reasons for rejecting a negative response to the rhetorical question in v 8a. One is the link between vv 8a and 15 in this poem. Throughout the poem, the poet has used the literary device of inclusion to indicate stanzaic structure. Both major sections of the theophany, the appearance in the south (vv 3–7) and the battle with God's enemy (vv 8–15), are marked off by inclusion. V 8 opens the second section of God's theophany by juxtaposing the cosmic waters, River/Sea, with the storm god mounted on his horse-drawn chariot. V 15 concludes this section by again juxtaposing these same characters. Only here God's horses trample Sea, the cosmic waters. These two verses frame the action of vv 8–15 and make it clear that Yahweh's anger against River/Sea in v 8 culminates in his trampling of Sea in v 15. The climax described in v 15 necessitates an affirmative answer to the rhetorical question in v 8.

To this contextual evidence for an affirmative response to the rhetorical question in Habakkuk 3 can be added evidence from biblical usage. While it is customary to expect a negative answer for rhetorical questions like the one in Habakkuk 3, and a positive answer to rhetorical questions with the negation *lō'* added, this custom is not an absolute one. A number of examples can be given from biblical Hebrew in which the use of the interrogative differs from this custom. In these cases, questions like the one in Hab 3:8 serve to "express the conviction that the contents of the statement are well known to the hearer, and are unconditionally admitted by him" (e.g. Jer 31:10; Job 20:4; Gen 3:11).[83] This convention, together with the force of v 15, indicates that the answer to the question in v 8 must be yes, and that the enemy of God in this poem is in fact Sea, one of the names of the ancient dragon of chaos.

This conclusion derived from the inclusive framework of vv 8–15 is corroborated by a careful examination of the actual battle scene in vv 13b–14. Though the text has unfortunately suffered disruption at points, a clear picture emerges. Yahweh strikes (*māḥaṣtā*) first the back or trunk (*bāmat*) of his enemy's body, laying it bare, or exposing it (*ʿērîtā*), from one end to the other, from buttocks (*yĕsôd*) to neck (*ṣawwāʾr*). He pierces (*nāqabtā*) its head (*rōʾš*) with his arrows.

This scene is reminiscent of the slaying of the dragon of chaos in the ancient conflict myth. In the Ugaritic version of this myth, Baʿl strikes Sea/River with two blows, one on the back (*ktp*//*bn ydm*) and another on the head (*qdqd*//*bn ʿnm*), after which the joints of the enemy shake and its frame falls prostrate on the ground (*CTA* 2.4[68].16–26). The same verb which introduces the battle in Habakkuk 3, *māḥaṣ*, is also used in the story of Baʿl's battle with Sea/River (*CTA* 2.4[68].9; cf. 3[ʿnt].2.7 and 6[49].6.24). In the Babylonian version, Marduk strikes Tiamat's insides with an arrow, throws her slain carcass to the ground, stands on it, and splits her skull (*Enūma eliš* 4:97–104, 128–130). The part of the prostrate body of Tiamat on which Marduk stands is her buttocks (*išidsa*/*išdasa*), the same part of the enemy Yahweh exposes in Hab 3:13b. The subsequent action of Marduk is remarkably similar to the subsequent action of Yahweh. *ina miṭišu la padi ulatti muḫḫa*, "with his merciless shaft he split (her) head," it is said of Marduk (4:130); and of Yahweh it is said, *nāqabtā bĕmaṭṭêkā rōʾš*,"you pierced with your shafts (his) head" (v 14a). The parts of the body of the enemy are the same, the name of the weapon in Hebrew is cognate to its Akkadian parallel, and the verbs are similar in meaning.

These close parallels between the description of the slaying of the dragon of chaos in the Ugaritic and Babylonian conflict myths and the slaying of Yahweh's enemy in Habakkuk 3 suggest that Yahweh's enemy too was the ancient dragon. This of course fits perfectly into the inclusive framework for this section of the poem, in which Yahweh is pictured going into battle with River/Sea (v 8) and later treading on Sea (v 15; cf. Marduk treading on his vanquished foe, 4:104, 129). The enemy of Yahweh in

Habakkuk 3, whom he goes out to fight (v 8), whom he slays (vv 13–14), and whom he treads on in triumph (v 15) is River/Sea, alias "Many waters," the ancient dragon of chaos.

The corruptions in the versions and the interpretations of exegetes which reduce the enemy to a historical foe—MT: the leader from a wicked dynasty; LXX: wicked ones; Barb: arrogant men; and most commentators, following one of the versions or interpreting v 13b as the destruction of a building which serves as a metaphor for a historical foe[84]—I view as part of a subtle but powerful tendency over the passage of time to "historicize" mythical material in the Hebrew Bible and to lose in the process the original intent of certain texts. One can observe a growth of "historicism" in v 13b in the versions themselves, from the LXX's "wicked ones," to Barb's "arrogant men," to the MT's "leader from a wicked dynasty," to the Targum's "You destroyed before them kings and rulers: from their houses you drove the sinners."

M. Dahood has pointed out how in a text similar to Hab 3:13, Ps 68:22–23, the description of Yahweh's combat with the primordial monster was lost and replaced by a more "historical" understanding in the Masoretic vocalization.[85] It is true that vv 12 and 13a, which immediately precede the actual description of the battle in vv 13b–14, have a definite historical orientation in their mention of God's trampling the nations and going out to save his anointed, as will be discussed in a moment. But it should be recalled that God's victory over Israel's historical enemies is often predicated upon his victory over cosmic foes.[86] Perhaps these historical references helped bring about the loss of the consciousness of the cosmic enemy in vv 13b–14.

The remainder of v 14, following the first clear line in which Yahweh pierces the dragon's head, is severely damaged. Again the MT is awkward grammatically at a number of points, difficult to interpret, and not regular poetically. And the translations of the LXX and Barb are very different from the MT and from each other, suggesting an ancient disruption of the text. The final four words of the verse are confirmed by all the versions but are difficult to figure out. Wellhausen reacted to this text with fine understatement. "*przw*," he wrote, "gibt Anlass zu Bedenken, ebenso auch das was weiter folgt."[87]

I have not been able to progress substantially beyond Wellhausen. But I think v 14 must contain a description of the annihilation of the dragon. Of all the commentators on Habakkuk 3, William Irwin is the only one who has taken this possibility seriously, and I think he is right to do so.[88] The annihilation of the dragon is an important part of the ancient mythic scheme describing the battle between the storm god and the dragon of chaos. After the dragon is defeated its body is destroyed. This is true at Ugarit where Ba'l, after killing Sea/River, drinks (*yšt*) his adversary, completely disposing (*ykly*) of it. In another text 'Anat annihilates the body of Mot by cleaving (*bq'*), scattering (*dry*) burning (*šrp*) grinding (*ṭḥn*), and scattering/sowing (*dr'*) his remains. Elsewhere 'Anat scatters the remains on the sea.[89] Whether 'Anat's act is to be understood as representing the imitative magic of Canaanite fertility rites or as "the ritual destruction of a hostile deity," the defeat of the enemy is in any case followed by his annihilation.[90]

The annihilation of the dragon is also present in the Babylonian myth. Marduk, after splitting Tiamat's skull with his shaft (cf. Hab 3:14a), cuts through her carcass so that her blood flows, and he causes his winds to carry it to an unknown place.[91] Even in Egyptian mythology, the tales of the destruction of the serpent monster describe the dismemberment of the dragon after his death.[92]

In the places where God's battle with the dragon has survived in biblical literature, this same pattern emerges. In Ps 74:13–14, after God smashes the heads of Tanin/Leviathan, he gives the body of the dragon as food (*m'kl*) to the animals in the desert (? *l'm lṣyym*). In Ezek 29:3–5 and 32:6, where the king of Egypt is pictured as the primordial monster of the seas, the dragon is killed and then the dragon's carcass is thrown into the wilderness, its flesh strewn about as food for the birds and the beasts.

A number of the elements in the description of the annihilation of the dragon in cognate literature are present in Hab 3:14. The wind (*s'r*) is there with which Marduk scattered Tiamat's blood. The scattering is there (*lhpyṣny*, perhaps *prz* > *pzr*) which is characteristic of the dispersing of the dragon in a number of accounts. And the act of devouring (*l'kl*) is also there, paralleling the image of feasting on the body of the slain monster in the parallel contexts. It is difficult to put these clues together into a coherent text, but the disruption in all of the versions may indicate that the original text is no longer recoverable.

Having given the dragon its due it is now necessary to return to vv 12–13a where the war of Yahweh appears to be placed in a more historical context. It is clear from these verses that Yahweh's battle with the dragon is not viewed as purely mythical or cosmic but as a battle for the salvation of God's people in which the nations are trampled down. The realm of history clearly surfaces here within the highly mythological language of this stanza (vv 8–15).

The mention of the *ʿam yahweh* in v 13a relates Yahweh's cosmic war to the historical arena in which God's people were participants. And one can be even more specific than this. Study of the designation *ʿam yahweh* has indicated that it derives from the context of tribal confederation where unity is provided by kinship relationships among tribes and by obligation to the god of the confederation.[93] Furthermore, *ʿam yahweh* can be used in a more limited sense—and this may have been its ultimate origin—to identify the militia of the tribal confederation, the warriors of the tribes who united in the battle camp under the banner of their god to fight a common foe.[94] This is how the designation was used in the old war songs from the Israelite league (Judg 5:2, 11, 13; Deut 33:3, 29; Ps 68:8).

The literary context of *ʿam yahweh* in Habakkuk 3, a hymn about holy war, suggests that *ʿam yahweh* was used here in its more limited sense as a reference to the tribal militia. This is confirmed by the use of the verb *yṣʾ* in the bicolon within which *ʿammekā* occurs. *yṣʾ* is often used as a technical military term denoting the attack of an army, its advance into battle.[95] This is certainly the sense of *yṣʾ* here. The picture is one of the divine warrior leading his armies into battle. And these armies include not only his heavenly hosts (vv 5, 10-11) but his earthly hosts, the army (*ʿam*) of Israel as well. The combination of heavenly and earthly forces in the army of the divine warrior is a typical motif in the war songs of the Israelite league.[96] In Habakkuk 3, as in these ancient songs, the battle is not purely mythic. Its aim is victory in a war waged by the people of God.

Exodus 15, on the surface, provides something of an exception to the typical participation of God's people in holy war. Here the battle seems to be God's alone. This should not be taken, however, as Millard Lind has done, as a direct sentiment against human participation in divine warfare.[97] In the first place, a common custom throughout the ancient Near East was to downplay the contribution of human agents in order to emphasize the decisive role of the divinity, not to counsel against human armies.[98] In the case of Exodus 15, the inability of this group of refugees to defend itself only added power to the experience of God's presence for them. Secondly, the absence of an army in Exodus 15 may be purely circumstantial if the setting of the poem—a group of slaves on the run, a storm at sea—is accepted as genuine. Finally, the image of Yahweh as a warrior, so central to Exodus 15 and Israel's other old poems, is difficult to reconcile with pacificism at the human level.

The presence of the *mĕšîaḥ yahweh* (*mĕšîḥekā*) beside the *'am yahweh* (*'ammekā*) within this same bicolon, need not, contrary to first impressions, contradict this league context. Though most frequently applied in the Hebrew Bible to the reigning king in the monarchic era, the title *mĕšîaḥ* is a broader term designating the bearer of a sacred office. It was also applied to the high priest, for example (Lev 4:3, 5, 16; 6:15); and there is evidence that it was applied in the premonarchic era to the military commander of the league militia. Key texts are 1 Sam 9:16 and 10:1, from the older source describing Saul's appointment, in which Saul is anointed a *nāgîd* to lead Israel's armies against the Philistines. These events, as Wolfgang Richter has pointed out in his study of the *nāgîd*, are based on authentic customs from the era of the Israelite league. The term *nāgîd*, argues Richter, referred to the military commander of the league militia, and his installation to this office by anointment is to be seen as one of the initial acts in the ritual of holy war as it was conducted by the tribes in the premonarchic era.[99] It should be noted that Saul is anointed *nāgîd* over (*'al*) the *'am yahweh* (*'ammî*). It would be reasonable on this basis to consider *mĕšîaḥ* in Hab 3:13 the title for the military commander of the league militia, the *'am yahweh*, with which he is paired in this bicolon.

The poet appears to have little interest in singling out a specific political enemy in this hymn. Of the two designations in v 12 which might be taken to identify a historical foe, one, *'ereṣ*, is cosmic in its connotations, the other, *gôyim*, is extremely general. These two terms are moreover a stereotypical parallel pair (cf. v 6) hardly selected by the poet for exact historical reasons.

The historical character of the enemy may, ironically, be

alluded to more specifically in the battle with the dragon in vv 13–14 than in the bicolon in v 12. Frank Cross has recognized a relationship between the mythic enemy of the divine warrior, Sea/River, and the symbolic events chosen by Israelite poets for epic recital, the escape at the Reed Sea and the crossing of the Jordan River at the conquest of Canaan. Cross has suggested that the event at the Reed Sea, where the Egyptians were defeated, was chosen as symbolic of Israel's redemption and creation as a community specifically because it involved a familiar symbol, Sea, which retained for Israel the power and meaning it evoked as the primeval enemy of God in the old mythic cycle. Cross has suggested further that in the reenactment of Israel's ancient traditions in the cult of the league, the crossing of the Jordan River in cultic procession became associated with the crossing of the Reed Sea in Egypt. "Exodus and entrance, the sea-crossing from Egypt and the river-crossing of the Conquest," writes Cross, "were ritually fused" in the recitation and dramatic reenactment of these events in Israel's early league cultus (cf. Psalm 114; Josh 2:9–10; 5:1; Ps 66:6).[100] Thus the poet who composed Habakkuk 3, by referring to Yahweh's primordial enemy as River/Sea, may also have evoked in the mind of his listeners the victory of God for his people at the Reed Sea and its reenactment at the Jordan River.

It is now possible to return to the larger question of God's enemy in Habakkuk 3 with which this discussion began. As described in the framework (vv 8, 15) of this section of Habakkuk 3 as well as in the actual battle scene which provides the climax to the poem (vv 13b–14), the enemy is a cosmic one. It is the ancient dragon of chaos, River/Sea, slain to ensure order in heaven and on earth. But this cosmic battle is recited to celebrate God's victory in earthly wars, the archetypal wars of exodus and conquest by proto-Israel. No single historical battle or enemy is singled out by the poet as is the case, for example, in Judges 5. The hymn of triumph celebrates, as do Deut 33:2–3, 26–29 and Psalm 68, the wars of conquest as a whole. One can only become more particular than this by suggesting that the defeat of the cosmic enemy, the dragon River/Sea, evoked in the mind of the listeners the defeat of their primal historical enemies, the Egyptians at the Reed Sea and the Canaanities at the Jordan River.

This blending of the cosmic and historical realms in Habakkuk 3 is a key element in the form, setting, and aim of the poem as a whole. It may be best elaborated following a discussion of the rest of the poem, the framework of the entire composition found in v 2 and vv 16–19.

The Literary Framework (vv 2, 16–19)

The account of the appearance of the divine warrior and his battle is enclosed within a literary framework (vv 2, 16–19) which provides the introduction and conclusion for the poem as a whole. The ways in which the opening and closing sections of Habakkuk 3 are linked by literary devices have been discussed in the poetic analysis.[101] Because of this intentional connection between the introduction and conclusion, these two sections of Habakkuk 3 can be most clearly understood if analyzed together.

Yahweh, I heard the account of you

The first important fact which the inclusive framework reveals is that the poem has been composed as a recitation of God's deeds. This can be seen in the first line of the introduction (v 2) and in the first two lines of the conclusion (v 16). The key word is *šāmaʿtî*, which opens both the introduction and the conclusion. This verb indicates at the outset that the information which the poet communicates here (vv 3–15) has been received through the medium of the spoken word. This is corroborated by the nouns associated with *šāmaʿtî*: *šēmaʿ* and *qôl*. *šēmaʿ*, the cognate accusative of *šāmaʿtî* in the first line of the introduction, refers to a report or account. *qôl*, which is parallel to *šāmaʿtî* in the first bicolon of the conclusion and semantically though not grammatically its object, means "voice" or "words." Though usually rendered by modern translators with the general term "sound," *qôl* more often means "voice" or what is spoken by the voice.

The poem as a whole clearly reveals that the source of this spoken word heard by the poet is human rather than divine. This is indicated by the fact that the divine subject of the account is addressed in the third and second persons throughout the poem. The 2ms suffix on *šēmaʿ* in the opening line of the introduction is to be understood, as all modern commentators acknowledge, as an objective genitive rather than a subjective genitive (as *KJV*). The narrative of Habakkuk 3 is the poet's account about Yahweh, not Yahweh's account to the poet. The poem is not God's speech but an account about God's deeds which the poet has heard and which he in turn recites.

The poet thus locates himself within the milieu of recital. He has heard the account of God's saving deeds and has taken his own place among those preserving these traditions by his recitation, his re-counting of these events. The fact that Habakkuk 3 is a recitation of God's deeds means that it is not an audition in which the poet, as prophets and others, received the word of God. In auditions, like the ones which were experienced by the prophet Habakkuk for example (see 1:5), God typically speaks of himself in the first person.

The fact that Habakkuk 3 is a recitation of God's deeds also means that it is not a vision. This interpretation of Habakkuk 3, though it cannot be supported by a careful examination of the text, has been popular from the time of the translation of the Septuagint down to the current day. The vision interpretation can already be clearly seen in the LXX.[102] It remains perhaps the most common modern interpretation. The two apparent occurrences of *rā'â* in the poem (vv 2, 7) which might suggest a visionary experience are both problematic. The first is a variant reading for *yārē'*. It was to be found originally in only one of the Greek versions, probably Barb. and may safely be dismissed for good text critical reasons. The second occurrence of *rā'â* is more difficult to explain. It is found in a section of the text which was misunderstood by the Masoretes and appears to be expansionistic. It may be an explanatory gloss. Probably neither instance of *rā'â* was original.[103]

The distinctions which have just been made among recitation, audition, and vision are in one sense too clear cut. No hard and fast distinction was made, of course, by Hebrew poets between words and visions. *šāmaʿ* and *rā'â* are a common parallel pair in Hebrew poetry, and in prophetic contexts the line between audition and vision is often not clearly defined. But these distinctions are necessary at this point to indicate the problems with the traditional interpretation of Habakkuk 3 as a prophetic audition/vision and to disclose the original *Sitz im Leben* from which this poem comes. When the text is excised of secondary elements and the original vocabulary is taken seriously, the poem clearly exhibits features of the recitation of religious traditions and lacks the typical features of the prophetic audition or vision.

The recognition that Habakkuk 3 is a recitation helps to clarify the tricolon which concludes the introducton. This tricolon, usually understood as a prayer, is better considered a continuation of the recollection of God's deeds found in the opening bicolon (*po'olĕkā*). The deeds of God are recalled in general terms in the opening bicolon and the tricolon which follows as an introduction to the more specific recital of the saving events themselves in vv 3–15.

This necessitates an entirely different understanding of the verbs in this tricolon from that of the Masoretes, who took them to be an imperative followed by two jussives, indicating a request for God's future help. The Masoretic interpretation of these verbs, though, finds little support in the versions. In the Greek translations (LXX, Barb; cf. OL) the first verb is read as a noun, the second two in the future tense. In the Tg the first verb is a perfect, the second two imperfects. Jerome (Vg) reads an imperative followed by two verbs in the future tense. The prevailing understanding among the versions is to take the last two verbs as future. The variety among the versions' readings of the initial verb (noun, perfect, imperative) points to a textual corruption.[104]

If the original reading of the initial verb was the 2ms perfect form, as I have suggested, then the verb pattern in this tricolon reflects the verb pattern in the narrative recital in the body of the poem, where perfect is paired with the old preterit (a prefix conjugation later understood as imperfect) for the composition of past narrative. The fact that the versions later understood the final two verbs as future or jussive indicates that here, as in the remainder of the poem, they no longer understood this archaic feature of the Hebrew verbal system.[105]

If the verbs are read in the past tense and understood as a recollection of God's deeds, then an enigmatic feature of this tricolon may be solved, the phrase *bĕqereb šānîm*. As has been noted in the textual analysis, *bĕqereb* is used here, elsewhere in Hebrew poetry, and in Ugaritic poetry as a ballast variant of *bĕ*, meaning simply "in." The translation "In the years," if understood more idiomatically as "through the years" or "in the past," fits its context well. By this phrase the poet simply places the actual occurrence of the events he is reciting within the history of his people and reminds his audience that his is a recitation of these events.

The bicolon and tricolon which open the poem thus provide an appropriate introduction for the body of the poem which makes up the main recitation. The account (*šēma*ʿ) which the poet has heard is the one he recreates in vv 3–15. The acts (*pōʿal*) of God are those narrated there. The self-disclosure (*tiwwāda*ʿ) of God to which the poet refers is the theophany of vv 3–15. The turmoil (*rōgez*) mentioned by the poet is the agitation within the world which results from this theophany(cf. vv 6–7, 9–10). The life (**ḥayyit*) mentioned by the poet is the survival of his people because of victory in battle which God has granted (cf. Pss 118:17; 18:5–6, 17–18). The mercy (*raḥēm tizkôr*) which the poet recalls introduces the divine act of salvation in v 13 which is the climax of the poem and provided the motivation for its composition and recitation.

I am in awe, Yahweh, of your work

In addition to identifying the character of the poem as recitation, the poetic framework also expresses the response of the poet to the recollection of God's act of salvation. This response includes two emotions which on the surface appear to be contradictory: fear and exultation.

On the one hand is the poet's fear. This is the most immediate reaction to the recollection of God's appearance. Hearing of God's appearance instantly instills fear. The verb which comes on the heels of *šāmaʿtî* in the opening bicolon of the introduction is *yārēʾtî*. The verb which follows *šāmaʿtî* in the opening bicolon of the conclusion is *tirgaz*. The first two bicola of the conclusion are, in fact, a detailed development of this motif. The physical symptoms of the emotion of fear are described in vivid detail—the stomach churns, the lips quiver, the body weakens, the legs shake—indicating the depth of the emotional response.

By responding in this manner the poet is in no sense abnormal, unique, or peculiarly psychic. He is not describing an ecstatic response to a private vision or trance, as many have suggested.[106] He is simply responding, together with the whole cosmos, with the typical reaction to a theophany. Just as the ancient mountains are shattered (v 6) and the primeval waters disrupted (vv 9–10), just as the tents of Midian and Kushan are shaken when God appears (v 7), so too the poet trembles at the recollection of these events. The connection between the response to God's appearance described in the theophany itself and the poet's own response is underscored by the repetition of the key word *rgz*. It is used first in the introduction (v 2b) to describe in general terms the trembling accompanying God's self-disclosure (*twd'*, v 2a), then in the body of the poem (v 7) to describe the trembling of the tents of Midian and Kushan at God's appearance, and finally twice in the first two bicola of the conclusion (v 16a) to describe the trembling of the poet himself upon recalling God's appearance.

This fear is not the fear of the enemy against whom God moves, nor the fear of Israel that it is the object of God's punishment, but the deep dread of the worshiper of Yahweh at the recognition of his awful power. The intensity of this response in Habakkuk 3 may be related to the manifestation of God in the thunderstorm. Anyone who has witnessed the devastating effects of the winds, lightning, hail, and cloudbursts which accompany a severe thunderstorm has also felt the emotions the poet has described in v 16.

It is within this same context, the devastating effect of the appearance of the storm god, that v 17, the second subsection of the conclusion, may be understood. This verse has remained a particular problem in the poem. It has been understood as a description of drought, or the results of some other crisis—disease, the long dry summer—which has rendered nature infertile. As such it does not seem to fit its context, a hymn focusing on political affairs: the victory of God in battle against Israel's enemies. Moreover, a description of distress appears out of place at the end of the poem, when the victory of God has already been described. Consequently, many have decided that v 17 was not part of the original poem, added later perhaps to adapt a hymn celebrating political victories for use in an agricultural liturgy.[107]

Of all sections of Habakkuk 3, v 17 is most vulnerable to the charge of being a later addition to the poem. These three bicola stand apart from the context by focusing on nature in the middle of a description of the poet's response and by exhibiting a parallelistic structure, unique in the poem as a whole, in which the parallelism transcends individual bicola. One is tempted to follow the lead of those who have removed it from the poem.

Enough archaic characteristics are present in v 17, however, to make the decision, in my judgment, in favor of its genuineness. The archaic pattern of verb tenses, where prefix and suffix forms alternate to express past narrative, which is characteristic of the poem as a whole, is present in v 17. The practice of extending parallelistic structure beyond individual bicola, though rare elsewhere in Habakkuk 3, is an archaic phenomenon.[108] And the chiastic patterns in these bicola are found elsewhere in Habakkuk 3. Furthermore, the presence of such old linguistic features as an internal Qal passive (*gzr*) argue for the age of v 17.[109]

The incongruity of introducing an agricultural scene at this point in the poem may be removed if the languishing of nature described here is not considered a drought but one of the effects of the theophany of the storm god. The languishing of nature is in fact an element within the disruption of the cosmos which accompanies the appearance of the divine warrior. This can be seen in the archaic mythic scheme in Canaanite mythology. When Baʿl attacked the primeval dragon "the heavens withered (and) drooped/ Like the loops of (his) garment."[110] This same motif appears in biblical theophanies, of which Isaiah 34 is a good example. Here, in an apocalyptic war song, when the divine warrior appears to do battle with his enemies, "the heavens roll up like a scroll/ And all their hosts wither/ As the leaves of the vine (*gepen*) wither/ And as the fig tree (*tĕʾēnâ*) withers" (Isa 34:4). Other examples of this motif can be seen in Amos and Nahum. When Yahweh thunders from Jerusalem "the pastures of the shepherds languish/ The top of Carmel withers" (Amos 1:2). At Yahweh's appearance in the theophany which begins the book of Nahum, "Bashan and Carmel languish/ The blossom (*peraḥ*) of Lebanon languishes" (Nah 1:4).

This image of the devastation of nature at the appearance of the storm god to do battle may have its origin, just as the dread of the poet, in the destructive power of the thunderstorm. The devastating effect of the thunderstorm on nature can be seen in hymnic (Pss 105:32,33; 78:47) and epic (Exod 4:13–35) descriptions of the storm which struck the Egyptians before the exodus. Vines (*gĕpānîm*) and fig trees (*tĕʾēnâ*) were destroyed together with their produce (*yābûl*),[111] all of the plants and animals out in the open field were struck down, and the flax and barley, which had already budded, were ruined. This is not to say that the poet was describing an ordinary thunderstorm. The poet was rather drawing from a reservoir of imagery, which often exceeds normal experience (e.g. vv 6, 9–10), to picture the power of Yahweh's presence.[112]

Even when v 17 is understood in this way, the devastation of nature before the theophany may seem out of place here surrounded by the description of the poet's response. The recoiling of nature would be more appropriate, according to the mythic pattern, as the divine warrior marches out to battle (cf. vv 6, 9–12), not after the battle has been won (v 15). But this difficulty may be overcome if this scene were considered part of an "imagistic" style in which the poet does not feel constrained to follow exact chronological sequences but overlaps descriptions of events which have taken place.[113] Returning at this point in the poem to the motif of the disruption of the cosmos at God's appearance is another way of linking the poet's response (v 16) to that of the entire cosmos. The poet is part of the entire creation which shudders at the appearance of the divine warrior.

Fear is not the only response to the recollection of God's acts of salvation to which the poet gives expression within the framework of Habakkuk 3. The other response is exultation. This response, described primarily at the conclusion of the poem, arises from the result of God's appearance, his triumph over his (and the poet's) enemies. The poet ends the hymn by describing God's victory over his enemies as his own victory. This inspires in the poet praise, courage, and security.

The triumph of God is identified as the triumph of the poet and his people in the final bicolon and tricolon of the poem. This is accomplished by the use of the term *yiš'ī*. Previously in the poem this term has been used to describe God's victory. It was used to describe God's chariot as a chariot of victory (v 8) and to describe God's victory in his divine warfare as a victory for his people (v 13). Now the poet uses the term for the third time to identify God's victory as his own.

Another term with which the poet identifies God's victory with his own is *ḥêlî*. Since the focus of the poem has been on the exploits of the divine warrior and his heavenly hosts (vv 5, 11) who have won the victory for the poet and his people, the sense of *ḥayyil* as "army" would be as prominent in the ear of the listener as "strength," if not more so. The poet acknowledges that the armies which have delivered the victory for him and his people have been God and his cosmic hosts.

A third expression uniting God's triumph and the poet's

is the final line of the poem *ʿal bāmôti yadrikēni*. This is the ultimate and final image of victory: the triumphant warrior with his feet on the back of the conquered foe. It is an image which is widespread in ancient Near Eastern art commemorating military achievements and common in biblical and other ancient Near Eastern literature.[114] It is the same image with which the poet concluded the account of God's victory. After slaying the dragon (vv 13-14), Yahweh trampled on it in a gesture of triumph (v 15). The same verb used of Yahweh, *dārak*, is now used of the poet. Just as God stands astride his conquered foe at the conclusion of his battle, so he has caused the poet to do likewise. If *bāmat* is the original reading for the body of the dragon struck by Yahweh in v 13, then the conquest of God is also linked to the poet's by the repetition of this term. This very image concludes the old war hymn in Deut 33:2–5, 26–29 (v 29b: *weʾattâ ʿal-bāmôtêmô tidrōk*). It is also employed in Judges 5: *tdrky npšy ʿz*. "You shall trample the throat of the mighty."

The customary translation of this final phrase, "on my/the heights he made me tread," pays no regard to the common image of conquest in the ancient Near East, to the appropriate use of this image at the conclusion of a war hymn, to the parallel use of *dārak* in v 15, to the original meaning of *bāmôt* or to the parallel use of this image in Israel's ancient songs of victory. It seems to be dictated, however, by the preceding cola: "he made my feet like the hinds'." If the final phrase of the poem completes the image of the hind, it appears to describe the poet as a surefooted hind climbing over the hills. But the final line of the poem probably does not complete the simile in the previous line at all. It is likely a second image linked to the previous one because both have to do with the feet of the victorious warrior. The feet of the triumphal warrior are as surefooted as the hinds' in battle, they tread on the enemy in conquest. This interpretation of these two lines has been challenged on the basis of the context in which these same two lines occur in Ps 18:34 (=2 Sam 22:34). There the equipment of the warrior, rather than his battle, appears to be the topic.[115] But the royal hymn in Ps 18:32–51 describes both the equipment of the warrior (vv 34–36, including surefootedness) and his conquest of his enemy (vv 37–42, in which the enemy falls under his feet). These two lines could well provide an introduction for the two motifs of equipping and victory in the narrative which follows.

The poem thus concludes on a note of triumph, courage, joy, and praise. The juxtaposition of these emotions with those of fear and terror with which the conclusion began has been observed by commentators and explained in various ways. The incongruity has been interpreted as the combination of visionary ecstasy and hope for the fulfillment of the vision, or as a radical reversal on the part of the poet who moves from a mood of sorrow brought on by the suffering of his people to one of joy in anticipation of an end to the suffering. Neither of these interpretations describes the case here. The combination of these responses—awe and exultation—is to be understood rather as characteristic of profound religious experience.

Rudolf Otto has called attention to the fact that religious experience is characterized by what appear to be contradictory feelings: a deep dread at the tremendous mystery and power of the holy, and a rapture at the gracious intent of the deity. "The qualitative *content* of the numinous experience, to which 'the mysterious' stands as *form*," writes Otto, "is in one of its aspects the element of daunting 'awefulness' and 'majesty:'... but it is clear that it has at the same time another aspect, in which it shows itself as something uniquely attractive and *fascinating*. These two qualities, the daunting and the fascinating, now combine in a strange harmony of contrasts, and the resultant dual character of the numinous consciousness ... is at once the strangest and most noteworthy phenomenon in the whole history of religion."[116]

This "harmony of contrasts" in the poet's emotional response which is the focus of the conclusion to the poem is already alluded to in the introduction. There, in the last line of the introduction, the poet joins in a single phrase the two feelings which will be developed more fully in the conclusion. The awfulness (*rōgez*) and the merciful character (*raḥēm tizkôr*) of the divine self-disclosure are placed side by side as inseparable elements of a single experience.

It is this fundamental religious experience, this "strange harmony of contrasts," to which Habakkuk 3 gives expression. The same power at whose manifestation the entire cosmos (vv 6, 9–10), nature (v 17), the peoples (v 7), and the poet himself (vv 2,16) tremble in awe discloses itself as merciful (v 2), as a source of joy and occasion for praise (v 18), and as deliverer of salvation to the cosmos (vv 13–15), to his people (v 13), and to the poet himself (v 19).

Conclusions

Form

The form of Habakkuk 3 may best be identified as a song of victory, a song celebrating an Israelite military victory as a triumph of Yahweh, the divine warrior. It opens with a brief introduction in which the poet identifies the events he is about to describe as events which have been preserved by oral recitation and in which he provides a short summary of these events. The body of the poem follows, a lengthy recital of the war of Yahweh and his victory. The poem closes with the poet's expression of his and his people's response to Yahweh's war: awe at his power and joy at his victory.

The song of victory is structured according to an ancient mythic scheme found in the mythic cycle of Baʿl at Ugarit and in the Akkadian cosmogony *Enūma eliš*. According to this scheme the divine warrior leaves his holy mountain, advances into battle with his weapons, which causes the convulsion of the cosmos, makes war on the ancient dragon of chaos, and conquers it. Victorious, he returns to his holy mountain to claim his kingship, which results in the fertility of nature and a great feast establishing his rule in heaven and on earth. The second half of this scheme, the return of the victorious warrior from battle, is not brought into the purview of the song of victory in Habakkuk 3. But the first part of the scheme—the march, battle, and victory of the divine warrior—is clearly the pattern from which the account of sacral war in Habakkuk 3 derives.

The element which sets the song of victory apart from the ancient myth from which it draws its shape is its historical mooring. The narrative within the song of victory is epic rather than mythic. I use the term epic here in the sense in which it has been used by Frank Cross. He has employed it as a designation for the form in which Israel's early traditions were cast. Noting that Israel's traditions are neither mythic, taking place entirely in the divine arena, nor historical, taking place entirely in the human arena, Cross has defended "epic" as a more appropriate designation for literature "in which acts of god(s) and men form a double level of action."[117] The double level of action can be seen clearly in Habakkuk 3 where the divine warrior fights for his people. His armies are made up of cosmic and human forces, his enemy is at once the primeval enemy of God, River/Sea, and the primeval enemies of his people, the Egyptians at the Reed Sea and the Canaanites at the Jordan River.

This same genre is reflected in a number of songs which have been preserved from Israel's early history. Exodus 15:1–18, Judges 5, Deuteronomy 33:2–5, 26–29, and Psalm 68 are the finest examples.[118] All celebrate the victory of the divine warrior over Israel's primal enemies and the salvation of his people. They are structured according to the same ancient mythic scheme evident in Habakkuk 3 and are composed in epic narrative which commemorates Yahweh's early victories for Israel. Most have the same introduction-body-conclusion form which characterizes Habakkuk 3, and two, Exodus 15 and Judges 5, are composed in the first person singular perspective of Habakkuk 3.[119]

The song of victory has some similarities with the genre of the hymn or psalm of praise in the Psalter.[120] The intent in each is to praise God for his glorious deeds. The song of victory usually begins, as does the hymn, with the expression of the intention or call to praise God (Exod 15:1–2b; Judg 5:2–3; Ps 68:3–4; cf. Hab 3:2a), continues with the motive for praise, the battle and victory of Yahweh, in the body of the poem, and concludes with a final exclamation of praise (Exod 15:18; Judge 5:31; Ps 68:32–35) of which Hab 3:16–19 is the fullest example.

This point of view represents a direct challenge to the most common form critical judgment made about Habakkuk 3 by modern commentators, that it is a lament.[121] This judgment is based on understanding the tricolon which concludes v 2 as a prayer (accepting the MT's interpretation of these verbs), vv 3–15 as an expression of confidence, vv 16–17 as a description of distress, vv 18–19 as certainty of hearing or vow of praise, and the title (v 1) as an accurate and original designation for this poem. But this would indeed be a strange example of a lament. A lament ordinarily begins with a cry of despair, which is not present here. The description of distress normally comes at the outset, not at the end where scholars have located it in Habakkuk 3. The expression of confidence is usually brief, not an elaborate theophany which makes up the entire body of the poem. And the prayer for help normally comes at the end of the lament on the heels of the description of distress, not at the beginning where scholars have located it in this poem. As a lament, Habakkuk 3 would stretch the form almost beyond comprehension. Furthermore, titles, like the one given to this poem, must always be regarded with suspicion. Their redactional character—in the Psalms, in the Prophets—is widely recognized, and the burden of proof lies as much with those who would defend a title's authenticity as with those who would question it. More will be said about the title of Habakkuk 3 in the following chapter.

Setting

The setting for this song of victory within Israelite history and religious life which fits all of the evidence best is the cultus of the Israelite or proto-Israelite league. The literary form, the poetic style, the linguistic features, the historical allusions, the mythological imagery, and the religious concerns, all point to the premonarchic era. Apparent in all of these aspects of Habakkuk 3 is the archaic character of the poem as a whole. The evidence, which has been presented in this and the previous chapters, may be reviewed briefly.

On the basis of linguistic evidence alone, David Robertson has concluded that Habakkuk 3:3–15 is early poetry, composed sometime between the thirteenth and tenth centuries B.C.E.[122] This is a rather remarkable conclusion, since it places Habakkuk 3 among a very small group of poems, including Exodus 15 and Judges 5, whose linguistic usage is consistent enough to make their early date reasonably certain. This dissertation confirms and strengthens Robertson's conclusions. On the one hand it has shown that vv 3–15 are even more consistently archaic than Robertson recognized. The three verbal forms in this section (prefix forms with the conjunction parallel to suffix forms) which fail to harmonize with the archaic verbal pattern, for example, may be regarded on the basis of textual considerations as secondary or on the basis of internal evidence as coordinate rather than converted forms. In addition, this study has also shown that the archaic features Robertson recognized in vv 3–15—for example, the alternation of prefix and suffix forms of the verb for past narrative—are present as well in the framework of the poem, vv 2, 16–19. These conclusions indicate a date for the composition of Habakkuk 3 as a whole in premonarchic Israel, the era in which early poetic Hebrew had not yet given way to standard poetic Hebrew.

On the basis of poetic style as well, Habakkuk 3 gives evidence of originating in the era of Israel's earliest literary conventions. Although Habakkuk 3 contains some parallelistic patterns in use throughout Israelite history, it contains a unique pattern, climactic parallelism (vv 2, 8, 12), which appears to be limited to archaic poetry, being replaced in the classical Hebrew poetry of monarchic Israel by assonance and paronomasia.[123] The meter of Habakkuk 3 consists of patterns which are among the most frequent in early Hebrew meter (l:l, l:l:l).[124] And the presence of old formulaic language, for example word pairs such as *yām/nāhār* and *harĕrê ʿad/gibʿôt ʿôlām*, suggests an archaic composition as well.

The historical allusions in Habakkuk 3, though not extensive, are significant and together with the linguistic features and poetic style reflect the premonarchic era of Israelite history. The first of these historical data is the location of Yahweh's sanctuary in the southeastern mountains: *têmān*, *har pāʾrān*. This is the earliest Yahwistic sanctuary to which biblical traditions refer, predating even the sanctuaries of the league in the land of Canaan following the conquest. The mention of a sanctuary of Yahweh in southern Transjordan during the Late Bronze Age in Egyptian texts reinforces these biblical traditions. This southern sanctuary retained its importance, because of its associations with the origins of Yahwism, during the days of the Israelite league in Canaan, as the poetry from the time of the league clearly shows (Judg 5:4–5; Deut 33:2–3; Exod 15:13; Ps 68:8–9). The establishment of Zion at the inception of the monarchy as the principal Yahwistic sanctuary, as has been noted, reduced the importance of the old sanctuaries of the era of the league, including the ancient one in the southeast. In the monarchic era, Zion thus replaced the southern shrine as the location of Yahweh's theophany in both psalmody and prophetic literature. Of course the historical memory of Israel's origin at a sanctuary in the southern mountains was preserved in the epic sources throughout Israelite history; but following the establishment of Jerusalem and the temple of Yahweh there, living hymnic and prophetic literature no longer identified the theophany of Yahweh with the southern mountains but with Mt. Zion.

This southern sanctuary of Yahweh apparently retained its prominence at least into the ninth century among the northern Israelites who preserved old league traditions in the political and cultic structures of their monarchy. Elijah's pilgrimage to the southern mountain of God in the traditions relating to the era of the Omrid dynasty suggests this, as does the recent evidence from Kuntillet ʿAjrud, a pilgrim station in the Negeb on the road to the southern sanctuary. The artifacts from Kuntillet ʿAjrud, dating to the end of the ninth century, reveal many traces of northern influences—Syro-Phoenician artistic motifs, Phoenician script traits, the mention of *šmrn*, etc.—combined with references to the southern sanctuary of Yahweh, *yhwh tmn* (cf. Hab 3:3).[125] One of the inscriptions contains a theophanic hymn with motifs similar to those in Habakkuk 3.

It is reasonable to conclude that the poem in Habakkuk 3 was related to this southern sanctuary. Celebrating the archetypal victory of the God of this southern sanctuary over both cosmic and earthly enemies, this hymn may have arisen within the cultic recitation of the *magnalia dei* at this ancient shrine. The continued prominence of the southern sanctuary and its traditions among the northern Israelites, who stopped at Kuntillet ʿAjrud on pilgrimmage to it, at least as late as the ninth century, may well account for the preservation of Habakkuk 3 in later Israel. The similarities between the traditions preserved in Habakkuk 3 and at Kuntillet ʿAjrud—the identification of Yahweh with Teman, the theophany in which 'El shines forth in the day of battle and the mountains tremble—suggest a continuing life for these traditions in the same northern circles.

The second important historical allusion in Habakkuk 3 is the mention of Kushan and Midian (v 7). This datum conforms nicely with the connection between Habakkuk 3 and the old southern sanctuary of Yahweh which has just been made. The territory of Midian and Kushan is to be located in the same area, the southern part of the Transjordan, as *têmān*//*har pā'rān*, the designation for Yahweh's sanctuary. Furthermore close cultural and religious relationships between proto-Israel and the Midianites/Kushites have been preserved in the epic traditions about Moses. The Midianites and Kushites are probably to be seen in Habakkuk 3 as among the people of Yahweh who worshiped at his southern sanctuary. The similarity between the Midianite and Kushite response to Yahweh's theophany and that of the poet himself would certainly appear to indicate a close relationship between them and the author of the poem. The negative assessment of Kushan and Midian in some of the versions (MT, OG, Tg, Vg; but not Barb) and in most modern commentaries stems from later strained relationships between Israel and Midian and from the misreading of a corrupt text (v 7).

The designations *ʿam yahweh* (*ʿammekā*) and *mĕšîaḥ yahweh* (*mĕšîḥekā*) in v 13 ought also to be mentioned here. As has been shown, both properly fit the premonarchic era in which the league militia (*ʿam*) was led by a military commander installed by anointment (*mĕšîaḥ*). Here too the terminology points to the period of the league as the appropriate setting for the song of victory in Habakkuk 3.

The manner in which mythological language is employed in Habakkuk 3 also fits appropriately into the early days of Israel. The vivid parallels between the Ugaritic myth in which the storm god Baʿl fights *zbl ym*/*šptˌ nhr* and Habakkuk 3 in which the storm god Yahweh fights *nāhār-m*/*yām* suggest a setting in Israel's early religious life when its own religion was emerging from its Canaanite context. Of course, the battle of the divine warrior and other ancient mythological motifs are not absent from other periods of Israelite history. They are present in hymns of the royal cult and in the archaizing hymns composed by the followers of Second Isaiah in the postexilic period.[126] But the plain personification of divine beings who represent Yahweh's entourage (*rešep*, *deber*, *šemeš*, *yārēaḥ*) and enemy (*nāhār-m*, *yām*) together with the detailed use of storm imagery to describe Yahweh are especially characteristic of Israel's early religious thought. The appearance of Yahweh the divine warrior in the thunderstorm was largely repudiated by the epic tradents and classical prophets of the monarchic era, who, as Frank Cross has shown, chose to describe the revelation of Yahweh rather as a word or decree issued by the divine judge.[127] It is hardly conceivable, furthermore, that the prophet Habakkuk, who must have been distressed as was his contemporary Jeremiah with the worship of *Šemeš*, *Yārēaḥ*, and the hosts of heaven (Jer 8:2; 2 Kgs 23:11; cf. Hab 2:18–19), would have personified these heavenly figures with the elaborate detail found in Habakkuk 3.

When the image of the divine warrior in the thunderstorm accompanied by heavenly armies was revived in proto-apocalyptic literature, it was transformed. Explicit language of lightning and thunder was deemphasized while other motifs—the new creation, divine kingship and the feast on Zion—became more prominent.[128] Sun, moon, and stars played an entirely different role. In archaic hymns they participated with the divine warrior in battle (Judg 5:20; Josh 10:12–13; Hab 3:10–11); in apocalyptic literature they dissolve together with the rest of the cosmos at the close of the age when divine judgment is rendered (Joel 2:10–11; 3:3–4; 4:14–15; cf. Isa 34:4, 60:19).

Finally, the literary character of Habakkuk 3 fits well into what can be reconstructed of the cultus of the league, where the *magnalia dei* were recounted as part of the ritual of covenant renewal. As has been noted, Habakkuk 3 derives from the context of recital. The poet, having heard the account of God's deeds, recounts them in his song, thus taking his place among the bards and singers who preserved Israel's traditions. The epic character of the narrative in the song, in which God's victory over his people's enemies is celebrated within the ancient mythic scheme of divine combat, is exactly the type of literature which was employed within the liturgy of the league cultus, as the old hymns from the era of the league demonstrate (e.g. Exod 15:1–18; Judges 5).

Significance for Israelite Religion

As a song of victory from the cultus of the Israelite league, Habakkuk 3 has a number of contributions to make to our understanding of Israelite religion. The first of these contributions is a clearer perception of the relationship between myth and history in early Israelite thought. On the one hand, Habakkuk 3 is dependent on an ancient mythic scheme of divine combat reflected in the Baʿl cycle from Ugarit and in *Enūma eliš* from Babylon. This dependence on myth includes the imagery of Yahweh as a divine warrior manifested in the thunderstorm; the structure of Habakkuk 3 in which the divine warrior leaves his holy mountain, arms himself for battle, advances to battle as nature quakes and quails before him, conquers his foe, and stands astride his enemy in triumph; and, finally, the identity of Yahweh's foe as River/Sea, the primeval dragon of chaos. On the other hand, Habakkuk 3 commemorates historical events. Yahweh's abode is identified with a particular southern shrine, his theophany is witnessed by actual people, the Kushites/Midianites, his holy war is fought against the nations on behalf of his people and his anointed one.

There is here a fusion between the mythic and historical realms, a fusion which has already been identified in literary categories as epic narrative. Cosmic conflict is combined with earthly conflict in this war song, and this is so at every point in the poem. The mountain from which God marches out is at once an actual mountain and a representation of God's heavenly abode. The response to Yahweh's theophany occurs within the primeval mountains and waters as well as within actual people. The divine entourage is made up of a combined force of cosmic and earthly armies. And the enemy is at once the primeval Sea and the nations.

The religious significance of this fusion of myth and history in the epic recitation in Israel's early cultus may be seen in two dimensions. In one sense, myth is grounded in history. The cosmic conflict of the divine warrior is identified with the wars of a people which take place in earthly time and space. And the victory of Yahweh over his primeval foe is identified with the victory of his people over their historical enemies. The focus of the early Israelite cultus, if this ancient song of victory is typical of its character, was a celebration of historical and not only mythical events. At the heart of the ancient cult, beside the affirmation that God had brought order to the cosmos, was the affirmation that God had brought order to history. This is evidence that the celebration of mythic events, common in the religious festivals of Israel's neighbors, was superceded in Israel by the celebration of the historical events which had brought the community into being.

In another sense, however, Habakkuk 3 indicates that for ancient Israel history was grounded in myth. The victory in Israel's wars was won not by the militia of the league or by the genius of its military commander but by the divine warrior, who marched out for his people (v 13). And the foe is not purely, or even prominently, historical, but mythic. The victory which Habakkuk 3 commemorates is not only a particular historical one, but a victory over the primeval forces of chaos. The order which Israel had experienced in the formative events in its history was grounded in the order which Yahweh had established in the cosmos as a whole. To express this Israel drew on the familiar cosmogonic myths within its cultural milieu. In so doing it reflected its affinity with its neighbors. Like them, and with similar language, Israel affirmed the defeat of chaos and establishment of order in all realms of life.

The picture which emerges is that the mythic and historical dimensions of experience for the ancient Israelite were part of the single fabric of existence. The experience of order within the cosmos and within the politics of earthly life was the result of the victory of Yahweh over unruly elements in every sphere of life. "The war god who establishes the order of the cosmos," writes Frank Cross, "also establishes the political-historical order thereby. Kingship in heaven and kingship on earth belong to the 'orders of creation.'"[129]

The matter which makes Habakkuk 3 unique among Israel's other ancient war songs, which contain this same fusion of mythic and historical elements, is its high mythology. This can be seen in the extended theophany, in the detailed description of the divine warrior and his weaponry, in the vivid personification of the divine beings in Yahweh's entourage, and, particularly, in the identification of Yahweh's foe as the primeval dragon of chaos. In Exod 15:1-18 and Judges 5 for example the mythic foe of the divine warrior has been replaced by historical enemies, the Egyptians and the Canaanites. Though the nations are trampled under by Yahweh in Habakkuk 3, his real battle is joined with River/Sea, the mythical monster. The mention of River and Sea must have recalled for ancient Israelites their historical experiences at the Sea of Reeds and the Jordan River (the exodus and conquest). But the mythic River/Sea is in the foreground and the geographical ones in the background, not the other way around, as in Exodus 15.

This association of the defeat of Israel's enemies with the defeat of the primeval dragon, however, is not absolutely unique to Habakkuk 3. It is also to be seen in Psalm 68, an ancient hymn which also appears to be a celebration of military victories in the era of the Israelite league.[130] There too, when the battle of the divine warrior is described (vv 22–24), the enemy is the ancient mythic dragon (*bšn/mṣlwt ym*). Furthermore, in his study of the cosmic connotations of the phrase *mayim rabbîm* (cf. Hab 3:15), Herbert May has shown how widespread the practice became among Israelite poets of linking Israel's enemies with Yahweh's primeval enemy. The enemies of Israel, declares May, were "manifestations of the intransigent elements which had to be quelled by Yahweh before creation could begin, and which must ever be defeated by him as he continues his activity in history. The enemy defeated by Yahweh is something more than just the enemy of Israel or of an individual Israelite: he is the enemy of Yahweh and identified with the corporate whole of Yahweh's antagonists. ... In this sense," concludes May, "Yahweh's conquest over the enemies of Israel ... is a victory over cosmic evil and wickedness, over the demonic, or more properly the dragonic."[131]

The highly mythological language of Habakkuk 3 is a reminder of the indebtedness of early Israelite religious thought to the religious milieu from which it emerged. Of course Israel gave unique epic shape to the ancient mythic themes which it appropriated, but its early poets also placed themselves solidly within the ancient mythic traditions. Using the language, imagery, and myths of the ancient Near East, the poet of Habakkuk 3 affirmed, with his neighbors, that the primal forces of chaos which threatened himself and his people had been overcome.

Another contribution which Habakkuk 3 has to make to our understanding of Israelite religion is a better perception of the nature of theophany in the Bible. Since Habakkuk 3 is the most detailed example of this genre, it is an extremely significant text for comprehending the character of this form. Based on the evidence presented here, the theophany of Yahweh must be understood to have its roots in the ancient mythic scheme of the battle between the storm god and the dragon of chaos.[132] Failure to recognize this has led Jörg Jeremias in his study of theophany to limit the theophanic pattern to two elements—appearance and the resultant agitation in nature—and to make the unusual suggestion that the battle scene in Hab 3:12–15, certainly the climax of Habakkuk 3, is not integral and may have been a later addition.[133]

Furthermore, Habakkuk 3 indicates that the primary context of theophany in Israelite life is to be seen in the setting of holy war rather than in the enthronement liturgy of the New Year festival.[134] The appearance of the divine warrior in Habakkuk 3 is identified as the determinative factor contributing to the victory of the league militia. This coincides with the witness of other ancient war songs from the era of the league in which the divine warrior appears to fight for his people. The time did come at a later date, however, when Habakkuk 3 was understood as an account of God's appearance in the temple. This interpretation of the poem, which can be seen more clearly in the Septuagint, is in all respects secondary, as will be pointed out in the following chapter.

Finally, Habakkuk 3 contributes to our recognition of the central place holy war had in early Israelite religion. The song of victory in Habakkuk 3, as well as those in other ancient hymns (Exodus 15, Judges 5, Deuteronomy 33, Psalm 68) are celebrations of triumph in warfare. The image of God which dominates is that of the divine warrior who acts to defeat Israel's foes. Of early Israel Julius Wellhausen wrote: "At that time and for centuries afterwards, the highwater marks of history were indicated by the wars it recorded. The (war) camp was, so to speak, at once the cradle in which the nation was nursed and the smithy in which it was welded into unity; it was also the primitive sanctuary."[135] The life of the league was absolutely dependent on military victory and the activity of the divine warrior. This concern was carried in Israelite religion until it broke out again in vivid colors in the literature of the apocalypse. As Patrick Miller has recognized, no interpretation of Israelite religion, no theology of the Old Testament, will be ultimately satisfactory which does not start out from the ancient songs of victory which celebrate Israel's wars and offer praise to God as the divine warrior.[136]

CHAPTER 4

Incorporation of the Hymn into the Habakkuk Corpus

The thesis which has just been presented, that Habakkuk 3 is an ancient hymn of triumph from the period of the Israelite league, raises important questions about its current context among the oracles of the seventh century prophet Habakkuk. For what reason was such an ancient poem included with the words of a prophet of the late seventh century? At what time, in what sort of setting, and by what process was it included? These questions are valid ones and deserve some explanation in light of the proposal that Habakkuk 3 is much older than the canonical context in which it has been preserved.

The purpose of this chapter is to treat these questions and in so doing describe the relationship of Habakkuk 3 to the rest of the Habakkuk corpus. The problems which lie in the current consensus on the original unity of Habakkuk will be examined first. Then a proposal will be made for the setting in which Habakkuk 3 was added to the prophecies of Habakkuk, the reasons for its addition, and the process by which this addition took place. Finally, the reinterpretations of Habakkuk 3 to which its its new canonical position gave rise will be discussed.

Problems with the Unity of Habakkuk

As has been mentioned, a consensus has emerged among recent commentators that Habakkuk is a unity, that Habakkuk 3 was composed by the same figure who composed Chapters 1 and 2. Whereas an earlier generation of scholars was prone to question the authenticity of Habakkuk's authorship of Chapter 3, the present generation on the whole accepts it.[1]

One fact on which the current consensus about the unity of Habakkuk rests is the attribution of Chapter 3 to "Habakkuk, the prophet" in the title of the poem (v 1; Barb and some LXX mss. omit "the prophet"). The authenticity of the superscription is usually assumed with little defense or examination. J. H. Eaton refers to the significance of tradition in his discussion of the title and then states that "the burden of proof is accordingly upon those who do not accept this testimony."[2] Given the problems with the historicity of titles attributing authorship to literature throughout the Hebrew Scriptures, the burden of proof lies rather with those who would defend a title's authenticity.

Titles attributing authorship to poems which have been preserved in the Psalter, for example, have for the last century almost universally been regarded as unreliable witnesses to authorship. They are frequently anachronistic and inappropriate for the content of the psalm; and they vary significantly in the versions and manuscripts.[3] These titles do not reflect authentic historical memory but are derived, as B. S. Childs has pointed out, from a later exegesis of the text itself. This is important information, given the psalmic character of Habakkuk 3. In his discussion of psalm titles, Childs makes a statement which must be taken seriously when considering the function of the title in Habakkuk 3: "The titles represent an early reflection of how the Psalms as a collection of sacred literature were to be understood. The titles established a secondary setting which became normative for the canonical tradition. In this sense the titles form an important link in the history of exegesis."[4] It should be noted, again with Habakkuk 3 in mind, that it was not uncommon in this exegetical process to attribute psalms to prophetic figures. Titles in the LXX attribute four psalms (Psalms 145–148) to Haggai and Zechariah.

The same problems with the authenticity of titles of poems preserved in the Psalter is apparent in titles of poems preserved in narrative contexts. Some poetry fits its narrative context well, as the Song of Deborah (Judges 5) illustrates, though this poem was composed about her, not by her. Other poems are related to figures who would not have authored them. The Song of Moses (Exod 15:1–18) was likely composed later at a sanctuary in Canaan (see vv 13–18) and secondarily placed on the lips of Moses and Miriam at the Sea.[5] The present context of the Song of Hannah reflects a clear reinterpretation of an Israelite poem. A royal psalm (v 10), because of a passing reference to the barren baring children, is placed on the lips of a woman in premonarchic Israel.

Titles in the prophets might be considered at the outset more reliable than those in the Psalter and in narrative contexts. There can be no doubt that titles introducing the prophetic books can be accepted to a certain extent as reliable attestations of authorship. But here too the situation is very complex. The redaction of prophetic books has introduced much material which cannot be attributed to the prophet identified in the title of the book. Isaiah, for example, accounts for only a part of the literature in the scroll which bears his name. And later redactors have used his name directly in a title of a poem he did not compose (Isa 13:1). The same can be said of Jeremiah (Jer 41:6) and others, like Jonah, where the author has placed an ancient poem on the lips of a later prophet (Jon 2:1).[6]

All of this evidence illustrates the conclusion that titles are redactional elements in Israelite literature and more often than not reflect, as Childs has observed, "a secondary setting which became normative for the canonical tradition." Titles are not *prima facie* evidence for the original setting of a poem. When the character of a poem conflicts with the interpretation of it given in its title, as the previous chapter has shown to be the case with Habakkuk 3, the authenticity of the title must be questioned and the possibility that the title might be a later interpretation, a "link in the history of exegesis," must be examined.

A second fact on which the recent consensus on the unity of Habakkuk rests is the cultic character of the psalm.[7] The cultic nature of this poem can be seen in the first place in the musical notations accompanying it. The term *selâ* occurs three times in the poem, following vv 3a, 9a, and 13. And the poem is followed by the subscription *lamnaṣṣēaḥ bingînôt*, "for the chief musician, with stringed instruments."[8] The Piel participle, *mĕnaṣṣēaḥ*, accompanying fifty-five psalms, is admittedly somewhat obscure but its root *nāṣaḥ*, "be preeminent," and use of the Piel verb by the Chronicler to indicate oversight or supervision (1 Chr 15:21; 23:4; 2 Chr 2:1; 34:12) suggest a translation like "chief musician, director, choirmaster."[9] The term *selâ*, occurring 71 times in 39 psalms, is probably impenetrable. It may have provided some liturgical direction for the rendition of the poem or its musical accompaniment.[10]

The cultic character of Habakkuk 3 is also indicated for most recent commentators by their understanding of its literary form as a lament (vv 2, 16–19) containing a hymn (vv 3–15), a hybrid form or a combination of forms typical of the cultic poetry of the Psalter. This analysis of the form of Habakkuk 3 is usually related to an acceptance of the term *tĕpillâ* in the title, a term usually identifying laments in the Psalter, as an authentic description of the genre in which the poem was originally composed. Furthermore, the vocabulary of Habakkuk 3 has been linked with remarkable detail and rigor by P. Humbert to the vocabulary of the poetry of the Psalter.[11]

This evidence is then linked to the cultic elements of Habakkuk 1–2 to establish the unity of the whole. In Chapters 1 and 2 psalm forms are also employed, especially the lament (1:1–4; 1:12–17). There too the vocabulary representative of the psalms has been employed. The conclusion reached on the basis of these parallels is that all three chapters are the work of a cultic prophet, a figure from the prophetic tradition responsible also for public worship in the cult. P. Humbert has gone so far as to claim that the entire book of Habakkuk was in fact constructed as a cult liturgy.[12]

Cult prophets in Israel are not inherently improbable. A great deal of evidence in Israel and outside of Israel—at Mari, for example—can be produced which links prophets with the cult.[13] But exactly what the nature of this cultic role was and to what extent this role can be established for a single author behind the book of Habakkuk is another matter. At each level where the unity of Habakkuk is defended by attributing the whole to a cult prophet serious difficulties exist.

On the level of vocabulary, P. Humbert's work, though unmatched in thoroughness, is methodologically problematic. Humbert has attempted to establish the unity of Habakkuk by showing that all three chapters contain a similar mixture of vocabulary representative of the cultic poetry of the Psalter and of the prophets of the last quarter of the seventh century B.C.E. He succeeds in linking the majority of terms in Habakkuk 3 with the vocabulary of the Psalter. But he is unsuccessful in establishing at the same time a connection between the vocabulary of Habakkuk 3 and the prophetic usage of the late seventh century which is characteristic of Chapters 1 and 2.[14]

Humbert concludes, after surveying the biblical usage of every significant term in Habakkuk 3, that only a single term, the verb *sāʿar*, can be judged without doubt to have a specifically prophetic provenance. Five other terms, though more frequent in the prophets, can also be found in the psalms. One problem here is the questionable practice of limiting the inquiry to the specific form of a root found in Habakkuk 3. *sāʿar* as a noun, for example, is common outside of the prophets in Job and the Psalter (e.g. Pss 55:9; 83:16; 107:25). But a far more serious problem is the meagerness of the evidence. The evidence is so marginal in fact that it more properly argues that Habakkuk 3 is unrelated to prophetic speech. Furthermore, as Humbert admits, many vocabulary items in Habakkuk 3 are to be found nowhere in the prophets.

Humbert recognizes that he can find only a few possible links with prophetic language, but he believes that he can link the usage of Habakkuk 3 much more substantially to biblical language of the last quarter of the seventh century. In this cause, he enlists a collection of twenty or more terms from Habakkuk 3 which he believes occur in no period earlier than the seventh century, or which seem to come into vogue at the end of the seventh century. When he identifies terms in Habakkuk 3 which were not in use before the end of the seventh century, Humbert is simply mistaken at many points, since he did not have available more recent evidence for the age of such biblical poems as Exodus 15, Judges 5, and Psalm 68. He considers *tĕhillâ* (Hab 3:3; cf. Exod 15:11!), for example, nonexistent in biblical Hebrew before the end of the seventh century. When he identifies terms in vogue in the late seventh century, Humbert pushes the matter of probability, a matter which continually plagues this study, to unacceptable lengths. Humbert disregards the psalms since they are difficult to date, and this often leaves a minority of the occurrences of a term with which to establish date. Of the 92 occurrences of *ḥārâ* (Hab 3:8) in the Old Testament, for example, Humbert considers its two occurrences in Jeremiah (12:5; 22:15) important evidence for its popularity in the seventh century.

Humbert's work, though monumental, is no longer able to provide unexamined conclusions about the literary unity of Habakkuk based on its vocabulary. Humbert's study, especially his analysis of the vocabulary of Habakkuk 3, is now in need of substantial revision.

On the level of literary genre, recent analyses face major difficulties as well. The problems with identifying Habakkuk 3 as a lament encompassing a vision have been described in the previous chapter where it was concluded rather that this poem is formally a hymn of triumph celebrating the victories of the divine warrior. Understood as a vision within a lament, Habakkuk 3 could easily be linked with the elements of lament in Chapter 1 (vv 1–4, 12–17) and with the visionary expectations in Chapter 2 (vv 1–5). But understood as a hymn of triumph, Habakkuk 3 no longer fits its context. Hymns of the divine warrior such as this were typical of Israel's earliest years as a league, were preserved later in the royal cult, and flourish again in the proto-apocalyptic literature of the postexilic era. They are atypical of classical prophecy.[15]

With respect to its musical notations Habakkuk 3 again appears more distinct from its canonical setting than a part of it. These notations could conceivably reflect the liturgical purpose of a prophetic composition. But it is remarkable that in all of the Hebrew literature which has been preserved these notations never appear, except in this case, outside the Psalter. Furthermore, the question can legitimately be raised why Habakkuk employed liturgical notes here but not with other pieces in Chapters 1 and 2 which reflect cultic forms and vocabulary. This evidence was considered by a whole generation of scholars to be significant enough to suggest that Habakkuk 3 existed originally as part of a collection of psalms independent of its current location with the prophecies of Habakkuk.[16] The failure to deal with this issue by recent commentators is an unwarranted oversight.

A third element in the current consensus about the unity of Habakkuk is a perceived connection between the content of Habakkuk 3 and that of the first two chapters. Chapter 3 is understood to provide the logical resolution for the problems raised in Chapters 1 and 2. Just as Habakkuk questions God's justice in allowing the wicked to flourish (Chapters 1 and 2), so God answers by arriving to destroy the wicked (Chapter 3). This is a very appealing pattern, but there are numerous indications that it is a secondary pattern, not a development constructed by the seventh century prophet responsible for Chapters 1 and 2.

One of these indications is the mention of the salvation of Yahweh's *měšîaḥ* in 3:13a as a goal of Yahweh's battle. Had this been composed by Habakkuk the only referent for *měšîaḥ* would have been the reigning king, Jehoiakim (609–598 B.C.E.) or Zedekiah (597-587 B.C.E.), in one or both of whose reigns most scholars would place Habakkuk. This desire on the part of the poet for the salvation of the *měšîaḥ* comes into direct conflict with a common interpretation of Hab 1:1–4 where wickedness, violence, and the impotence of the Torah are understood to be the result of the corrupt leadership of Judah. Even apart from this particular interpretation of Hab 1:1–4, what is known elsewhere about the character of these two men does nothing to alleviate the problem of the positive reference to the *měšîaḥ* in Habakkuk 3.

Another indication of the secondary character of the connection between Habakkuk 3 and the first two chapters is treatment of the enemy. The Babylonians and their ruthless practices, described in great detail, are the enemy posing the central threat to Israel in Chapters 1 and 2. But there is no specific reference to the Babylonians or their particular cruelties in Chapter 3.[17] Indeed, as has been described in Chapter 3 of this dissertation, the enemy in Habakkuk 3 is best understood as the dragon of chaos. And the historical events which lie in the background are the early victories of Yahweh at the Sea and at the (Jordan) River, not events in the seventh and sixth centuries.

Finally, on close examination Habakkuk 3 does not provide an entirely appropriate resolution to the Babylonian crisis described in Chapters 1 and 2. A resolution to the problem raised in Chapter 1 is already offered in Chapter 2. This resolution has two elements: a command to be faithful regardless of the circumstances (2:4), and an expectation of the demise of the Babylonians by the natural retribution which overtakes the despot when his own power wanes and those he has oppressed rise up against him (2:6–17). Furthermore, these resolutions have an entirely different character, a more narrowly historical cast, than the direct intervention of God in a cosmic theophany like that described in Habakkuk 3.[18]

Problems with the current consensus on the unity of Habakkuk thus exist at all levels of form and content. These problems, together with the archaic character of Habakkuk 3 demonstrated in Chapter 3 of this dissertation, support the thesis that Habakkuk 3 originally existed independently of its present canonical context in the book of Habakkuk. The present consensus, in the light of this information, appears to be a step backward rather than forward in the history of Habakkuk scholarship. The previous generation of scholars who questioned the authenticity of Habakkuk 3 often made the mistake of placing it later than the prophet Habakkuk, but their inclinations about the discontinuity between Habakkuk 3 and the rest of the Habakkuk corpus were right; and their reasons for placing Habakkuk 3 later than the seventh century prophet were, as will be seen in a moment, in a certain sense legitimate.

The Incorporation of Habakkuk 3

The archaic hymn of triumph in Habakkuk 3 stands in tension in almost every respect with the classical prophecy with which it has been related in the canon. Only a radical turn of events in the history of prophecy in Israel could account for the addition of this old poem to the prophetic corpus in which it is now found. Such a turn of events occurred immediately after Habakkuk's career with the fall of Jerusalem and the Babylonian captivity which brought an end to classical prophecy for all intents and purposes. The exile and the attempts at restoration following Cyrus' edict of liberation substantially reshaped the prophetic movement and created a climate within this movement which led to the combination of the old ode in Habakkuk 3 with the corpus of Habakkuk.

The developments in Israel's prophetic movement which occurred during the exile and early postexilic period have been fully documented by Paul Hanson in his work on the origins of apocalyptic in Israel.[19] Hanson has described in detail the loss of classical prophetic eschatology in which divine activity was viewed within the political and historical realm of everyday life and the consequent rise of apocalyptic eschatology in which divine activity was to a greater and greater extent identified with the cosmic realm. He finds the development adumbrated in the great prophet of the exile, Second Isaiah, but initiated in actuality in the early postexilic period within an alliance of visionaries made up of the followers of Second Isaiah and disenfranchised Levites.

These visionaries, at odds with the postexilic hierocracy of the Zadokites and increasingly excluded from the cult, lost the optimism of the classical prophets that restoration would occur within the politico-religious structures of their community. They turned instead to a new vision of restoration in a cosmic context. And to express the vision they reappropriated the literature in their past which most forcefully described God's cosmic activity, the old hymnic literature which was full of mythological patterns, motifs, and images; and they recast this material to express their own expectations of cosmic restoration.

A key element of the literary heritage which the visionaries reappropriated was the Divine Warrior Hymn, as Hanson refers to it. These hymns, characteristic of the era of the league (e.g. Exodus 15, Judges 5) and later of the royal cult (e.g. Psalms 29, 89b, 110), were a natural choice for the visionaries. "What form better portrayed Yahweh acting alone against humanly impossible odds to save his people than the archaic Divine Warrior Hymn?" Moreover, for a people engaged in a conflict with the Zadokites over the true Israel, the "use of that archaic form served well the purpose of demonstrating their solidarity with early Israel."[20]

The disciples of Second Isaiah took this old form and recast it to meet the needs of their postexilic community, to express the hope of God's cosmic victory on their behalf. These new hymns of the victory of the divine warrior can be found in Isa 59:15b–20; 63:1–6; 63:19–64:2; 66:14b–16; and in Zech 9:1–17; 10:1–12; 12:1–13:6; and 14:1–21.[21] In some of these Yahweh does battle with the nations which threaten Israel (Isa 63:1–6, Zech 9:1–17), as was characteristic of the ancient divine warrior hymns, but in the majority the intracommunity polemic has reshaped the form so that unrighteous Israel has become the divine warrior's enemy.

These hymns, together with the other compositions of the disciples of Second Isaiah, were then added to the writings of Isaiah and Zechariah to give them an apocalyptic conclusion. The claim which this redactional work made was that the expectations of Isaiah Second Isaiah and of Zechariah were to be ultimately fulfilled in the apocalyptic act of Yahweh which the postexilic visionary redactors expected. For these postexilic disciples of Isaiah the cosmic victory of the divine warrior was believed to be the true culmination of the hopes of Isaiah and Zechariah.

The addition of Habakkuk 3 to the writings of Habakkuk is to be understood as having occurred in just such a setting.[22] Among the disciples of the prophets, including those preserving the writings of Habakkuk, arose the apocalyptic fervor of the late sixth and early fifth centuries. This led to a new understanding of the way in which the expectations of the classical prophets would be fulfilled; and this in turn led to a redaction of their writings to include material which reflected this new understanding. In the case of Habakkuk, this new understanding was not expressed by the inclusion of a new divine warrior hymn which recast old hymnic traditions to describe God's future cosmic victory. Rather, a genuinely archaic hymn of triumph was appropriated. This hymn was then understood eschatologically rather than historically. It was interpreted as an expression of the expectation of Yahweh's future activity rather than as the recital of Yahweh's past activity for which it was originally composed.

That a composition originally composed as a recital of God's activity in the past could be reinterpreted as an expectation of God's activity in the future may on the surface appear improbable. But a number of characteristics of Habakkuk 3 made this reinterpretation a relatively easy process. One of these characteristics is the poem's mythic character, in particular its focus on cosmic conflict. U. Cassuto, in his comparison of Habakkuk 3 with the mythological texts from Ugarit, has observed that in Israel traditions of cosmic conflict "polarize in two different directions. On the one hand, they appear before us as memories of events that took place in remote antiquity ... On the other hand, they are treated as events projected into the distant future—the End of Days—when the victory of God will be renewed and endure forever."[23] A major hermeneutical leap would not have been necessary to take a hymn reflecting the memory of God's cosmic victory and reread it as an affirmation of his ultimate victory.

This *Urzeit-Endzeit* characteristic of myth in Israel has long been noted. It was discussed in the last century by H. Gunkel in his *Schöpfung und Chaos in Urzeit und Endzeit*.[24] More recently F. M. Cross, in his study of the development of Israelite religion, has spoken of the "recrudescence of mythic themes" with the rise of apocalyptic literature in the sixth century B.C.E.[25] And P. Hanson has shown in detail, as has just been noted, how specific archaic forms focusing on cosmic conflict, such as the divine warrior hymn, were reappropriated in postexilic Israel for eschatological purposes. A circle of visionaries who were reappropriating ancient myths of cosmic conflict to express future hopes would hardly have found it difficult to reinterpret an archaic hymn of the victory of the divine warrior as a vision of God's future triumph.

Another characteristic of Habakkuk 3 which facilitated its reinterpretation is its theophanic nature. In his work on theophanic literature, J. Jeremias has noted that theophanies are not always clearly distinguishable from visions.[26] This phenomenon allows for the natural transposition of an ancient theophanic hymn into the arena of prophetic visionary experience. An old hymn celebrating the historical victory of God in highly mythological dress now becomes a prophetic glimpse of the cosmic realm and the activity of the divine warrior there. The tremor of the poet which accompanies the appearance of God as the customary response to a theophany is reinterpreted as the prophetic ecstasy which accompanied the visionary experiences of the prophets. More will be said about this transposition in relation to the discussion of the reinterpretation of Habakkuk 3 as a vision in the final section of this chapter.

A third characteristic of Habakkuk 3 which allowed for a natural reorientation toward the future is its martial nature. In his discussion, "The Origin of the Concept of the Day of Yahweh," G. von Rad has pointed out that the future military victory of Yahweh envisioned by the prophets as the "Day of Yahweh" had its roots in the ancient traditions of Yahweh's holy wars.[27] The imagery with which the prophets describe the decisive divine victory to come on the Day of Yahweh is taken from the ancient traditions celebrating his victories against Israel's first enemies. A major effort would not have been necessary to connect a genuine record of Yahweh's ancient holy wars with the concept of the Day of Yahweh as it was developed by the later prophets.

Finally, a peculiar grammatical feature of Habakkuk 3, its archaic verbal system, provided a linguistic vehicle for this future reorientation. According to archaic conventions, past narrative was expressed by the alternation of prefix (the old preterit) and suffix (the perfect) forms of the verb.[28] With the shift to standard Hebrew in the era of the classical prophets, this old convention fell out of use and prefix forms of the verb not preceded by a conjunction signified only incomplete action. Hence the prefix forms in Habakkuk 3 came to be understood as imperfect verbs, referring not to the past but to the future. The suffix forms were then understood in light of the prefix forms, rather than the other way around. Reference to the past in the poem was simply tied to the future, the real orientation of the poem. God's coming acts would recreate the victories he had once accomplished.

The question may be raised at this point whether Habakkuk 3 was not actually a new poem, like the other divine warrior hymns composed by the visionaries of the late sixth and early fifth centuries, which drew as the new divine warrior hymns did on archaic motifs and expressed them in archaizing style. Might not Habakkuk 3 be understood as a precursor of the visionary literature which would follow it rather than as an old hymn which was later reinterpreted?

One objection to this proposal is the consistently archaic character of Habakkuk 3 which has been documented in the first three chapters of this study. But one can also point to significant differences between Habakkuk 3 and new divine warrior hymns composed in the sixth and fifth centuries to illustrate the age of Habakkuk 3. In many of these new hymns there is specific reference to Zion as the sanctuary of Yahweh (e.g. Isa 59:20; Zech 9:9, 13; 12:2ff.; 14:2ff.), a practice consistent in literature written after the establishment of Zion in the monarchy. In Habakkuk 3 Yahweh is still related to the ancient southern shrine.

Further differences may be noted: 1) A number of these new hymns clearly reflect the restoration setting of the postexilic era rather than the period of the league reflected in Habakkuk 3. This can be seen in their reference to the return of the exiles (Zech 9:8, 11; 10:6–10) and in their polemic against the hierocratic party by the visionaries of this era (e.g. Isa 59:15b–20; Zech 10:1–12). 2) Specific storm imagery of lightning and thunder, so characteristic of the appearance of the divine warrior in Habakkuk 3 and other ancient hymns, is almost entirely absent in the newer divine warrior hymns.[29] 3) New divine warrior hymns are composed in the standard Hebrew of the prophetic era and do not reflect the archaic linguistic features characteristic of Habakkuk 3. 4) No effort is made in the new hymns to relate the intervention of Yahweh to events in the political order as was characteristic of ancient hymns, including Habakkuk 3. Even Zechariah 9, which contains so many political allusions, refers not to historical places and events but presents a symbolic description of the ideal kingdom won by the cosmic conquest of the divine warrior.[30]

The reinterpretation of old material for eschatological purposes which I am suggesting for Habakkuk 3 to explain its inclusion with the Habakkuk corpus ought not to be viewed as an unusual phenomenon. The rereading of old literature as having a future orientation appears to have been common in postexilic Israel. B. S. Childs provides one example in his discussion of the Psalter. He has shown how the royal psalms, written originally for a reigning king, were later reinterpreted as messianic and given their present canonical position in the Psalter on the basis of this messianic understanding. The entire Psalter in fact, according to Childs, though comprised of hymns originally written for Israel's cult, was later valued for a different reason. It was considered a witness to Yahweh's eschatological salvation.[31]

Having described in general terms the postexilic setting within which an old hymn was included in the Habakkuk corpus, as well as the futuristic reinterpretation of the hymn to which its new canonical setting gave rise, the process by which this took place may be described in more detail.

After originating in the league or proto-league period within the setting of Yahweh's ancient sanctuary in the mountains of southern Transjordan, Habakkuk 3 was likely preserved in northern circles.[32] Following the fall of the North, it would have found a natural home within the hymnic literature of Jerusalem's royal cult. The reference to Yahweh's *mĕšîaḥ* (v 13) would automatically have placed this poem among the royal psalms.

The musical directions accompanying Habakkuk 3 attest to its presence at one time in a collection of psalms associated with the cult. The precise age of these notations is hard to determine. but there is some evidence for their antiquity.[33] The use of musical instruments in early Israel, though once questioned, has now been extensively demonstrated by archaeologists.[34] The fact that the Greek translators no longer understood these musical notations argues for their age. This misunderstanding is clear in the Greek translation of Habakkuk 3, particularly at the conclusion of the poem. The musical notations in the subscription are understood as part of the text of the hymn itself. *lamnaṣṣēaḥ bingînôt* is rendered as the concluding phrase of the final colon of v 19: "(on the heights he puts me) to conquer in his song" (*tou nikēsai en tę̄ ǫdę̄ autou*). *selâ* is rendered *diapsalma*, as is customary in the psalms. This interpretation of *selâ* as an interlude does not appear to be based on a clear knowledge of the term, at least if one expects interludes to be associated with the stanzaic structure of psalms. In the psalms, as in Habakkuk 3, *selâ* has little relationship with stanzaic structure.

A peculiar feature of the musical directions in Habakkuk 3 may argue further for their antiquity. That feature is the position of *lamnaṣṣēaḥ bingînôt* at the end of the poem. H. M. I. Gevaryahu has argued, on the basis of a comparative study of Akkadian literature, that biblical colophons were originally written at the end of the text and later transferred to the beginning.[35] He finds evidence for this in biblical literature in the position of *halĕlû-yâ* at the end of Psalms 104, 105 and 115 (transferred to the beginning in the LXX) and in the position of biographical data at the end of the LXX version of Job and in the original ending of Ben Sira, 50:27–29. The colophon at the end of Habakkuk 3 may represent, in Gevaryahu's opinion, an archaic practice of which only traces still remain in the canonical text.

Finally, the presence of liturgical notes in Habakkuk 3 can hardly be accounted for subsequent to its attachment to Habakkuk in the sixth or fifth centuries B.C.E. A copy of this poem circulating separately after this time might have attracted notes, but hardly the poem which was now regarded as part of the text of the Habakkuk corpus. It is more reasonable to assume that these notations had become so firmly fixed as part of the text of this poem that they could not be disregarded when the poem was added to the writings of Habakkuk.

This ancient hymn of triumph, preserved as a psalm, was, as has already been argued, added in the postexilic era to the collection of Habakkuk's writings. Freed from its most recent location in the royal cult by the fall of the Davidic dynasty, this hymn was reinterpreted, by disciples of the prophets who were caught up in the apocalyptic fervor of the postexilic era, as an expression of the future cosmic act of the divine warrior to restore the fortunes of the righteous. A specific suggestion may at this point be made about the group responsible for this redactional activity.

Evidence exists which may link the circle responsible for including the old hymn in Habakkuk 3 in the Habakkuk corpus together with the same visionaries who edited Isaiah and Zechariah. A common interest in the old divine warrior hymns is present, of course, in both cases. Beyond this, the editorial colophons used in Habakkuk are notably similar to those used in the books of Isaiah and Zechariah. H. W. Wolff has suggested that similarities in editorial headings of prophetic books may be indications of a common editorial group. Noting, for example, that *dābār yhwh* with *hāyâ* and *'el* occurs in the Deuteronomistic History and in the headings of Jeremiah, Ezekiel, Hosea, Micah, and Zephaniah, Wolff sees in these books traces of a circle of Deuteronomistic theologians who edited a series of the preexilic prophetic writings during the exile.[36]

Similar kinds of correspondences can be seen between the superscriptions of Habakkuk and those in Isaiah and Zechariah. The prophecy of Habakkuk is identified by the term *maśśā'* (Hab

1:1), a term used only elsewhere in superscriptions by the editors of Isaiah (13:1; 15:1; 17:1; 19:1; etc.), Zechariah (9:1; 12:1; Mal 1:1), and Nahum.[37] Furthermore, the identification of Habakkuk as a *nābî'* in the superscriptions of Habakkuk (1:1; 3:1) is paralleled only in Zechariah and Haggai. Finally, the verb *ḥāzâ* is used to describe the reception of Habakkuk's prophecy (1:1). This root is preferred also by the editors of Isaiah (1:1; 2:1; 13:1), Nahum (1:1) and Obadiah (v 1).[38] All of this may point to the very visionaries P. Hanson has described as the circle within which the book of Habakkuk was given its present shape.

It is my judgment that the title of Habakkuk 3 was added to the poem at the time the old hymn was placed among the writings of Habakkuk. Scholars in the past generation thought that the title attributing this poem to Habakkuk already existed when the poem was part of a collection of psalms and that this provided the motivation for its inclusion in the Habakkuk corpus.[39] But it is more likely that the title was added when the poem was appended to Habakkuk.

In the first place, the attribution of authorship to a text has all the marks of being a late phenomenon. H. M. I. Gevaryahu has concluded that the biographical information—the name of the author, the identification of his family, occupation, or residence—is the last information included in biblical colophons in the prophets and Psalter alike, and that the addition of this information only began with the exile and continued into the postexilic era.[40] Secondly, it is unnecessary to posit the prior attribution of this psalm to Habakkuk in order to explain its eventual association with the Habakkuk corpus. As has been argued in detail above, it was the content and character of the poem itself which led to its selection by the editors of Habakkuk for inclusion in this prophetic corpus. This psalm, reinterpreted as an eschatological work, suitably expressed the expectations of the postexilic editors of Habakkuk that Yahweh would soon achieve cosmic salvation for his people. It is reasonable to assume that both colophons in the Habakkuk corpus, the title of Chapters 1 and 2 (1:1) and the title of Chapter 3 (3:1; with the possible exception of the final term *'al šigyōnôt*), were both added by the visionaries who edited Habakkuk in the postexilic era and who were responsible for its present canonical shape.[41]

The Reinterpretations of Habakkuk 3

The transformation in the interpretation of Habakkuk 3 which occurred when this old poem was included in the Habakkuk corpus has already been described in general terms. A poem composed as a historical recital was reread as an eschatological vision. Its past orientation became a future orientation. It is possible now to be even more precise than this about the new understandings of Habakkuk 3 which accompanied its connection with Habakkuk.

One way in which Habakkuk 3 was identified with the future was by understanding it as a prayer. The term *tĕpillâ* which identifies the nature of Habakkuk 3 in its title does indeed mean, as recent commentators have pointed out, a prayer of supplication. *tĕpillâ* is frequently used in the titles of laments in the Psalter. This designation is not to be understood, however, as recent commentators have argued, as an accurate identification of the genre in which Habakkuk 3 was originally composed. It is rather an indication of the new interpretation given this old poem by its visionary editors who were responsible for the title (3:1).

This new understanding of Habakkuk 3 as a prayer of the prophet Habakkuk, in which he asks Yahweh to renew his ancient deeds and come to the aid of his people, can be seen not only in the title given the poem but also in textual alterations and later translations. The major textual change to which this new interpretation gave rise is the form *ḥayyêhû* in the MT (v 2a). As has been pointed out, the imperative form of *ḥiyyâ* (Piel) with the 3ms suffix is supported by none of the versions and does not commend itself as the original reading. Once present, however, it automatically determined a jussive interpretation for the following two verbs in its tricolon, *tôdîa‘* and *tizkôr*. This single textual corruption transformed the entire tricolon in which it appears into a supplication for Yahweh's future salvation and provided the context within which the reader now had to understand the picture of Yahweh's activity which immediately followed (vv 3–15). The prefix conjugation verbs in this following section (vv 3–15) were understood, in light of the conventions of standard Hebrew, as imperfect forms expressing the expectation that the supplication just made (v 2) would be answered.

The understanding of Habakkuk 3 as a prayer is also reflected in the LXX. The Hebrew term *tĕpillâ* is translated "prayer" (*proseuchē*). Furthermore, the term *ṣālălû* in v 16a is rendered "prayer" as well. This latter instance is apparently a mistranslation of the Hebrew text on the basis of the Aramaic root *ṣl'*, "pray."[42] It reveals that the activity of the poet in the concluding section of the poem, as in the introductory section, was understood as a prayer by the Greek translators.

This interpretation of Habakkuk 3 tied it in nicely to the Habakkuk corpus. The prophecy of Habakkuk opens with a prayer (1:2–4) in which the prophet laments God's inactivity and continues with another (1:12–17) in which the lament is carried further. That the prophecy should end with a prayer in which the laments of the initial prayers were resolved would seem entirely appropriate.

When recent commentators interpret Habakkuk 3 as a prayer of lamentation, they are correct in one sense. That is how the poem was once understood. But they fail to see that this is only a secondary understanding of the poem. The indications that Habakkuk 3 is a prayer are remarkably few and all secondary elements in the text. The title is best understood as an editorial addition, the term *ḥayyêhû* in v 2 is a corruption of the text, and the translation *proseuchēs* in v 16 of the LXX is inaccurate. Without these features, nothing in the poem would lead a modern exegete to judge it a prayer. The power of the canonical level of interpretation, however tenuous, to eclipse the original character of a text is remarkable.

Another way in which Habakkuk 3 was identified with the future once it was attached to the corpus of Habakkuk was by understanding it as a vision. This particular transformation in the interpretation of Habakkuk 3 is clearest in the LXX, where a series of readings reflect this reinterpretation. The most important of these readings appears in the opening line of the first tricolon in Habakkuk 3 (v 2a), the same line in which the crucial corruption *ḥayyêhû* appears in the MT. For *bqrb šnym ḥyy(t)*, where MT reads "in the midst of years renew it" (*bqrb šanîm ḥayyēyhû*), LXX reads "in the midst of two living beings" (*en mesǭ duo zǭōn* = *bqrb šĕnayim ḥayyôt*).[43]

The referent for this image in the minds of the Greek translators must have been the cherubim throne in the temple where God came to be present on earth. The two living beings would be the two cherubim which made up Yahweh's throne (*šnym krbym*:

Exod 25:18; 2 Chr 3:10). The term *ḥayyâ* and its plural *ḥayyôt* are employed regularly for the throne cherubim in Ezekiel's visions (Chaps. 1, 3, 10). That the midst of the two beings represented the location of God's presence is indicated by the conclusion of this phrase in the LXX with *gnōsthēsē*: "(in the midst of two living beings) you will be known." One is reminded immediately of the temple vision of Isaiah (Chap. 6).

A second reading with the same orientation is found in the line preceding the one just analyzed. For "I feared (*yr'ty*), O Yahweh, your deed," the LXX contains the variant "I observed (*katenoēsa* = *r'yty*) your deed." A similar reading occurs in the first word of the conclusion of the poem which immediately follows the theophany in vv 3–15. The conclusion opens in the LXX with "I watched" (*ephylaxamēn* = *šmrty*) in place of "I heard" (MT: *šm'ty*). These readings in the introduction (v 2) and conclusion (v 16) of the poem provided a framework for the theophany in vv 3–15 and indicated that this theophany was understood as a vision of God's activity seen by the prophet in the temple.

Two readings within the theophany itself seem to have arisen from this orientation. The translators of the LXX understood *dbr* in v 5 as "word" (*dābār*) rather than as Deber, a mythological figure parallel to Resheph, and translated, "before his (Yahweh's) face a word will proceed." In v 9 the divine name has been added to the end of the first colon which ends in MT with *'mr*, itself a problematic reading. The result is the phrase "said Yahweh." Both of these readings give the impression that the information in vv 3–15 was communicated by God himself directly to the poet as part of a prophetic visionary experience.

The interpretation of Habakkuk 3 as a vision, like the interpretation of it as a prayer, tied this poem in well with the Habakkuk corpus. Following his initial dialogue with God (Chap. 1), the prophet waits for a vision (2:1). And Chapter 3 has been widely understood to be the vision for which the prophet waited. Habakkuk 3 thus provides the conclusion which the reader has been led to expect in Chapter 2.

When recent commentators interpret the theophany in Habakkuk 3 as a vision, they are correct in the sense that this is how this poem was once understood. But in this interpretation too, as with the interpretation of Habakkuk 3 as a prayer, they fail to see that this is only a secondary understanding of the poem associated with its inclusion in the Habakkuk corpus. Each of the readings just discussed which reflect the understanding of Habakkuk 3 as a temple vision can be shown on textual grounds to be based on corruptions or misinterpretations of the original text (see the textual study in Chapter 1). When they are removed from consideration, the setting of recitation of the *magnalia dei* in which this poem was originally composed becomes plain. Also to be noted here is the fact that Chapter 3 does not provide an entirely appropriate response to the vision anticipated in Hab 2:1 as has been alleged. In Hab 2:1 the prophet has taken up his watch on the city's fortifications (*'al-mišmartî//'al-māṣôr*) not in the temple. And in Chapter 2 the prophet already receives a response from Yahweh which he is told to record (2:2–5).

This exegetical activity reinterpreting Habakkuk 3 as an expectation of God's future action can be seen to continue in the minds of later translators of the poem. It is evident, for example, in the Aramaic translation of Habakkuk 3. The translators of the Targum appear to have understood Habakkuk 3 as both prayer and vision directed toward the future. Their rendition of the title (1:1) reveals both interpretations: "The prayer which Habakkuk the prophet prayed when it was revealed to him concerning the length (of time) which he gave to the wicked ..." But the Aramaic translators go much further. They understand the poem to have been addressed specifically to their own historical setting. Vv 16 and 17 make the connection explicit. These verses are understood to predict judgment against the evil kingdoms which oppressed the Jews following the fall of Jerusalem. After identifying the distress (of the poet) in v 16 as Babylon's anguish under God's judgment, v 17 continues:

> For the kingdom of Babylon will not endure,
> and it will not administer rule over Israel.
> The kings of Media will be killed,
> and the heroes of Greece will not prosper.
> The Romans will be consumed,
> and they shall not gather rakings from Jerusalem.[44]

In one respect, however, the Targum comes close to reflecting the original character of Habakkuk 3. The entire theophany (vv 3–15) is treated as a historical account of God's deeds. All the verbs in this section, suffix and prefix forms alike, are rendered in the past tense. Vv 3–15 are presented as a recitation of God's deeds for his people. But a major change has occurred. The whole theophany has been "demythologized." It has been interpreted as a summary of Israelite experience on a narrowly historical plain. The mythological images have disappeared. In the minds of the Aramaic translators the images in Habakkuk 3 recall the creation of the world (v 4), the great flood (v 6), the tower of Babel (v 6), the exploits of Gideon against the Midianites (v 7), the exodus from Egypt (vv 8, 14, 15), the presentation of the law at Mt. Sinai (v 10), and Joshua's battle in the plain of Gibeon when the sun and moon stood still (v 11).

For Jerome, to cite a final example of the transformation in the interpretation of Habakkuk 3, the poem also pointed to the future. But for Jerome, translating now from a Christian context, the expectations in Habakkuk 3 had been fulfilled in the Christ event. He renders *měšîaḥ* (v 13) not with a form of *ungo* or *unctito* but with *christo*, and he reads *'et* as the preposition "with" instead of as the sign of the direct object to avoid a reference to the salvation of Christ. Jerome noted with satisfaction that even Aquila, who had replaced the LXX *christos* elsewhere with *ēleimmenos*, because of its Christian connotations, had retained it in the present text: *Iudaeus Aquila interpretatus est ut Christianus*.[45] Jerome's Christological reading of Habakkuk 3 is further apparent in his rendering of *yiš'î* in v 18 as a proper name, *Iesu meo*, "my Jesus."

For the majority of recent commentators these secondary interpretations of Habakkuk 3 have retained their power and have been decisive in their exegesis of the poem. These commentators have, one might say, continued the work of the early editors and translators of Habakkuk 3. The interpretations of Habakkuk 3 as the prayer of the prophet Habakkuk and/or as the prophet's vision are particularly common in contemporary literature on Habakkuk.

These interpretations were once given to Habakkuk 3 and they are therefore important and valid, particularly in discussions of the canonical position of Habakkuk 3. But they are at the same time secondary interpretations. And they should not be allowed to obscure the original setting, form, and character of this ancient hymn. These transformations in the interpretation of this old poem should not be permitted, as they have in both historical and modern scholarship, to conceal the fact that Habakkuk 3 contains an ancient hymn of triumph which ultimately provides a vivid portrait of the religious thought of earliest Israel.

NOTES

Notes to Chapter 1

[1]B. Margulis, for example, has almost rewritten the poem, as the title of his study indicates ("The Psalm of Habakkuk: A Reconstruction and Interpretation" [1970]). Other important recent studies of the text of Habakkuk 3 include the following: W. Rudolph, *Micha, Nahum, Habakkuk, Zephanja* (1975); J. Jeremias, *Theophanie* (1965) 38–43; J. H. Eaton, "The Origin and Meaning of Habakkuk 3" (1964); E. M. Good, "The Text and Versions of Habakkuk 3: a study in textual history" (1958); S. Mowinckel, "Zum Psalm des Habakuk" (1953); W. F. Albright, "The Psalm of Habakkuk" (1950); P. Humbert, *Problèmes du livre d'Habacuc* (1944); W. A. Irwin, "The Psalm of Habakkuk" (1942); J. Lachmann, *Das Buch Habbakuk: Eine Textkritische Studie* (1932). Also to be noted are the following older studies: S. R. Driver, *The Minor Prophets*, II (1906); B. Duhm, *Das Buch Habakuk* (1906); J. Wellhausen, *Die Kleinen Propheten* (1898); R. Sinker, *The Psalm of Habakkuk* (1890); F. Delitzsch, *Der Prophet Habakuk* (1843).

[2]A. E. Housman characterized textual criticism as "the science of discovering error in texts and the art of removing it" (*Selected Prose* [1962] 131).

[3]Published in *Discoveries in the Judean Desert II* (1961), edited by P. Benoit, J. T. Milik, and R. de Vaux. In spite of the fact that P. Skehan has mentioned the presence of Habakkuk 3 among Qumran manuscripts ("Texts and Versions" [1968] 565), I have been unable to verify this. The pesher on Habakkuk at Qumran dealt only with Chapters 1 and 2.

[4]The information available for the reconstruction of the Old Greek translation of Habakkuk 3 can be found in the Göttingen Septuagint (Joseph Ziegler, ed., *Duodecim Prophetae* [1943]). Ziegler's text has been followed here except in cases where I have noted and explained my disagreement with his reconstruction. The OG is useful in certain instances in reconstructing the text of Habakkuk 3, though its usefulness is limited by the fact that it represents a textual tradition closely related to the proto-rabbinic text represented by the MT.

[5]D. Barthélemy, *Les Devanciers d'Aquila* (1963).

[6]M. L. Margolis, "The Character of the Anonymous Greek Version of Habakkuk, Chapter 3" (1908).

[7]H. St. J. Thackeray, "Primitive Lectionary Notes in the Psalm of Habakkuk" (1911) 192–193; E. M. Good, "The Barberini Greek Version of Habakkuk III" (1959); Compare also D. H. Bévenot's comments on Barberini in "Le Cantique d'Habacuc" (1933).

[8]E.g. Albright, 11, 13; Humbert, 58; Rudolph, 233.

[9]Barb has *eulabēthēn* instead of the LXX *ephobēthēn*, its only departure.

[10]For similar expressions of Yahweh sustaining life with the verb *ḥiyyâ*, see Deut 32:29 and 1 Sam 2:6.

[11]Good, "Text and Versions," 10–11.

[12]The two possible exceptions to this usage (1 Chr 11:18; 9:16) appear in the late prose of the Chronicler.

[13]See Ezek 1:5. 13. 15; 3:13. Cf Good. "Text and Versions," 93, and Humbert, 58–59.

[14]Rudolph, 233.

[15]Good, "Text and Versions," 10.

[16]This suggestion was made by Wellhausen (36, 171).

[17]D. A. Robertson. *Linguistic Evidence in Dating Early Hebrew Poetry* (1972) 7–55. esp. pp 33–34: cf. F. M. Cross and D. N. Freedman. *Studies in Ancient Yahwistic Poetry* (1950; reprint, 1975) 28–29; and C. H. Gordon, *Ugaritic Textbook* (1965) no. 9.4.

[18]The former occurrence of Teman is discussed by John Emerton in "New Light on Israelite Religion: The Implications of the Inscriptions from Kuntillet 'Ajrud," (1982) 3, 9–10, 13. The latter was communicated in a private communication with F. M. Cross which he based on readings by Patrick Miller. The occurrence of Samaria is discussed by Ze'ev Meshel in "Did Yahweh Have a Consort" ([1979] 30–31).

[19]Cross and Freedman, (1975) 126–127, 161–168; Y. T. Radday, in his studies of Hebrew particles, has shown that in poetry in general the conjunction is less frequent than in prose ("AND in Isaiah" [1974]).

[20]For a similar explanation, see Sinker, 44–46.

[21]Several instances in the LXX where names of mountains are expressed adjectively are *Itabyrion* for the usual *Thabōr* in Hos

5:1 and Jer 26:18, and *Karmēlion* for the usual *Karmēlon* in 1 Kgs 18:19; 2 Kgs 2:25; and 2 Kgs 4:25. See H. St. J. Thackeray, *A Grammar of the Old Testament in Greek* (1909) 170-171.

[22]Duhm, 77.

[23]Y. T. Radday and H. Shore have shown that the definite article, like the conjunction, is in general less frequent in Hebrew poetry than in prose ("The Definite Article: A Type- and/or Author-Specifying Discriminant in the Hebrew Bible" [1976]).

[24]The ideas for rereading this term and the following ones in this line were suggested to me by F. M. Cross. W. R. Arnold ("The Interpretation of *qrnym mydw lw*, Hab 3:4" [1905] 168) and Irwin (20) have also suggested reading the verb *nāgah* here.

[25]See BDB, 902.

[26]All the versions reflect this understanding, none of them interpreting *qrnym* as "rays of light" here.

[27]This view has been defended by William H. Propp in an unpublished study, "The Skin of Moses' Face."

[28]Albright, 11, 12.

[29]ʿAnat: *CTA* 10[76].2.21; Baʿl: *UG* 5.1.1.20 (or another divine being); *UG* 5.3.1.6; 2001.2.10 (?); Yariḫ: *CTA* 18[3 Aqht].4.-10. M. Dahood is hardly correct in interpreting *qrn* in *CTA* 10[76].-2.21, 22 and in Hab 3:4 as "wings" ("Ugaritic Lexicography" [1964] 95). Both contexts fail to support his view. Ugaritic texts are cited in this study by their numbering in *Corpus des tablettes en cunéiformes alphabétiques* (ed. Andrée Herdner [1963]). In brackets is the corresponding numbering from C. H. Gordon's *Ugaritic Textbook*.

[30]Albright, 11, 14.

[31]See Chap. 3.

[32]Good, "Text and Versions," 63–64; Lachmann, 70. J. Ziegler thinks *en pedilois* original; but had it been, the translator would have used one of the customary words for "sandal" (e.g. *hypodēma* or *sandalion*). *pedilois* occurs only here in the LXX and was probably a misreading of *pedia* based on the influence of *hoi podes autou (rglyw)*.

[33]Duhm, 80; Humbert, 60.

[34]Driver, 89.

[35]Wellhausen, 171.

[36]Good, "Text and Versions," 100.

[37]G. R. Driver, "Hebrew Notes" (1934) 54–55.

[38] Margolis, 138; Albright, 14.

[39] Good, "Text and Versions," 101.

[40] U. Cassuto, "Chapter iii of Habakkuk and the Ras Shamra Texts" (1975) 10.

[41] Rudolph, 234. Good suggests the translator interpreted *'d* according to Talmudic *'wd*, "strong" ("Text and Versions," 100–102).

[42] Good suggests that *thrausthēsetai* renders *ytrṣṣ* (cf. Deut 28:33; Isa 42:4; 58:6), a corruption of *ytpṣṣ*, and omits *'d* ("Barberini," 14).

[43] Albright, 14, note t.

[44] Lachmann, 72.

[45] Albright, 11, 14–15.

[46] T. H. Gaster, "On Habakkuk 3.4" (1943) 346; G. R. Driver, "Critical Note on Habakkuk 3.7" (1943) 121; Mowinckel, 14; Jeremias, 40.

[47] See Chap. 4.

[48] Duhm, 81–82.

[49] Humbert, 60.

[50] Albright, 15. For an argument against the presence of the enclitic *mem* here, see Robertson, 100.

[51] This possibility has been suggested to me by F. M. Cross.

[52] W. L. Moran, "Some Remarks on the Song of Moses" (1962) 323–327; W. B. Barrick, "The Meaning and Usage of RKB in Biblical Hebrew" (1982). For a contrasting position, see S. Mowinckel, "Drive and/or Ride in the OT" (1962).

[53] Humbert, 61.

[54] Y. Yadin, *The Art of Warfare in Biblical Lands* (1963) 4–5, 39–40, 88–89, 199, 212, 214–215, 240–241.

[55] Delitzsch, 165.

[56] Thackeray, "Primitive Lexionary Notes," 191–213, esp. pp. 195–202.

[57] M. Dahood, "Ugaritic-Hebrew Parallel Pairs" (1972) 1.-258; F. M. Cross, *Canaanite Myth and Hebrew Epic* (1973) 23, note 59.

[58] Dahood, "Parallel Pairs," 1.258.

[59] Ziegler, 270; Good, "Text And Versions," 66, 103.

[60] See also Deut 32:42 where Yahweh makes his arrows (*ḥṣym*) drunk (*škr*) with blood.

[61] Cross, 23.

[62]Cross, 23, note 59; J. C. de Moor, Review of *The Violent Goddess* (1969) 226.

[63]Cassuto, 11; for the interpretation *ʾay-ymr*, see Cross's comments (115).

[64]The possible *Vorlagen* for *pharetras autou* are *ʾšptw*, *tlyw*, and *ytrw*. *BHS* opts for the latter, "bowstring."

[65]Cf. Good, "Text and Versions," 104.

[66]GKC, no. 118m–r; see Deut 2:9; 4:11; and Isa 57:2 for similar constructions.

[67]See textual note 4.

[68]Margolis, 136; Good, "Barberini," 16, note 1.

[69]Margolis describes the OG as "haggadic" (139).

[70]Eaton, 152.

[71]E.g. Wellhausen, 172; Duhm, 88; Lachmann, 77; Humbert, 63; Rudolph, 236; Albright, 11, 16.

[72]E.g. Wellhausen, 172; Duhm, 89; Humbert, 63–64; Rudolph, 236; Margulis, 422–425; Albright, 11–12.

[73]Rudolph, 236.

[74]See H. Gressmann, *Altorientalische Bilder zum Alten Testament* (1927) nos. 310, 332; and A. Erman, *Die Religion der Ägypter* (1934) 111.

[75]Albright, 12, 16; for *yrḫ* with *zbl* in Ugaritic literature, see *CTA* 15 (128).2.4 and 18 (3 Aqht).4.8.

[76]E.g. Albright, 12; Eaton, 145.

[77]Humbert (64) and Jeremias (43) have suggested sun and moon as subjects. Mowinckel ("Zum Psalm des Habakuk," 17) and Irwin (27) have suggested cosmic enemies as subjects. Bévenot has suggested the cosmic waters as subject (509). And Margulis has suggested the divine procession as subject (436).

[78]Duhm, 90.

[79]GKC, no. 52f.

[80]BDB, 516.

[81]Lachmann, 78, 79.

[82]BDB, 516.

[83]M. Dahood, "Ugaritic-Hebrew Parallel Pairs," 2.18.

[84]Sinker, 53; Margolis, 140; Good, "Text and Versions," 107.

[85]Lachmann, 79.

[86]Lachmann (79) suggests *tsʿr*; cf. Jonah 1:11, 13 where *exegeirein* = *sʿr*. Sinker (54) and Good ("Barberini," 16) suggest

t'wr; cf. Hab 3:9; Ps 107 (108):2; and Joel 3(4):2, etc. where *exegeirein* = *'wr*. Margolis (140) believes Barb is reading *ṣ'd* with the MT.

[87]Good believes the *Vorlage* of the OG to have read *trwš*, the translator understanding it as a form of *ršš*, "beat down" ("Text and Versions," 107).

[88]Sinker, 54.

[89]C. North, *The Second Isaiah* (1964) 88, 125; J. Jeremias, "Theophany in the OT" (1976) 898.

[90]Barthélemy has shown that the seventh column of the Hexapla contains this recension (267).

[91]The OL (and Th) reads the 2ms imperfect preceded by *ut*. This may simply be an attempt to make the purposive quality of the infinitive more explicit.

[92]Wellhausen, 172; cf. Duhm, 91; Lachmann, 79; Humbert, 64; Margulis, 426; Rudolph, 237; Albright, 11, 16; and G. A. Smith, *The Book of the Twelve Prophets*, II (1928) 156.

[93]To ease this difficulty Wellhausen suggested reading the apocopated form *lwšy'* which would be closer to the MT (172).

[94]Eaton has suggested that *'t* was used in the second line of this bicolon for rhythmical balance (154).

[95]Albright, 16–17; F. Horst, *Die Zwölf Kleinen Propheten* (1938).

[96]Cross and Freedman, 28; Albright, 16; Margulis, 425.

[97]Albright, 16–17.

[98]Suggested to me by F. M. Cross.

[99]Eaton, 154. Elsewhere the OG consistently uses the singular for this term. Even here some Greek mss. contain the singular form, though Good ("Text and Versions," 69) and Ziegler (271) consider these readings accommodations to the Hebrew.

[100]Margolis, 135; Good, "Barberini," 17. Or it may simply be a choice of terminology with no doctrinal implications. The vocabulary of Barb is frequently quite different from that of the OG.

[101]Margolis, 135; but cf. Ps 131(132):10 where Aq uses *christos*.

[102]Duhm, 92; Lachmann, 79.

[103]Sinker, 34, 55; Eaton, 154.

[104]Humbert, 65; Margulis, 425.

[105]Cassuto, 13; Albright, 11, 13, 17.

[106]*CTA* 2.4[68].4, 15, 17, etc.; 5[67].2.8, 14, etc.

[107]Paul Hanson has brought to my attention the image in Zech 5:4 in which Yahweh promises the destruction of the house of an evil man, the thief. This image may have had some influence in bringing about the corruption in the MT and the modern interpretations of the "house" type (see below).

[108]Note Yahweh's treading on the back of the Sea (*bmwty ym*) in Job 9:8.

[109]*CTA* 4[68].16–17, 24–25.

[110]F. J. Stephens, "The Babylonian Dragon Myth in Habakkuk 3" (1924) 290–293.

[111]It has been called to my attention by F. M. Cross that *běhēmôt* does not designate the primordial Sea in biblical literature. Compare M. Pope's discussion of the term in his study on *Job* ([1965] 320–322). He allows that *běhēmôt* might have mythological connotations in Job 40:15 but identifies it as a bovine creature.

[112]Delitzsch, 182–183; Duhm, 92–93; S. R. Driver, 93; Smith, 156; Rudolph, 237.

[113]Delitzsch, 182–183.

[114]See textual note 59.

[115]M. Held, "*mhṣ* / **mhš* in Ugaritic and other Semitic Languages" (1959) 169–176.

[116]*māḥaṣ* occurs almost exclusively in archaic poetry. In addition to Ps 68:22 and Job 26:12, it occurs in Num 24:8, 17; Deut 32:29; 33:11; Judg 5:26; Ps 18:39 = 2 Sam 22:39; Ps 110:5, 6.

[117]Cross and Freedman, 121–122, note 93.

[118]Pope, 67, 69–70. Pope also suggests that where Yahweh tramples (*drk*) the *bmwty 'rṣ* (Amos 4:13; Mic 1:3) he is treading on the backs of the wicked of the earth and not on earth's high places (cf. Isa 63:3).

[119]Delitzsch, 183; Duhm, 92; Mowinckel, 18; Rudolph, 237; Eaton, 154; Albright, 17; GKC nos. 75n, 75aa, 113h.

[120]See also Job 41:5 where Leviathan is described as being laid bare (*my-glh pny lbwšw*, "who can reveal [strip off] his outer garment"). Cf. Job 26:6 where Sheol and Abbadon are naked before God.

[121]Dahood thinks *yswd* in this text means "foundation" and "buttocks" at the same time, the poet comparing Jerusalem to a woman: *'rw 'rw 'd hyswd bh*, "strip (her), strip (her) to her buttocks/foundation" (*Psalms*, 3.268, 273).

[122] Albright, 13, 17.

[123] LSJ cites its use for a coin with a hole drilled in it (see *diakoptō*).

[124] Eaton, 155.

[125] Margolis, 141: Good, "Barberini," 17.

[126] From Egyptian literature compare the image of the deity piercing the head of the serpent in "The Book of Overthrowing 'APEP" (R. O. Faulkner, "The Bremner-Rhind Papyrus: The Book of Overthrowing 'APEP" [1937–1938]).

[127] Note the mention of Yahweh's weapon (a sword) when he slays the dragon in Isa 27:1.

[128] Eaton, 155.

[129] Rudolph, 237.

[130] Good, "Text and Versions," 109.

[131] K. A. Vollers, *Das Dodekapropheton der Alexandriner* (1880) 35.

[132] Margolis, 135–136: cf. Good, "Barberini," 17; Sinker, 61; Eaton, 155. Vollers believes it represents *'ōz* (35).

[133] Duhm, 93; S. R. Driver, 94; Mowinckel, 18–20; Humbert, 66; cf. the *NEB* and *NAB*. Eaton is quite insistent, on the other hand, that the 3ms suffix, the *lectio difficilior*, should be read, and he cites texts in the Bible (Pss 9:16; 10:2; 35:8; 37:14–15; 2 Chr 20:23) and in Babylonian literature (*Enuma eliš* 4.104ff.) in which the weapons of the enemy are turned against them.

[134] Lachmann, 81; Barthélemy cites Zeph 1:4 as an analogous situation (194); cf. Ps 68:22.

[135] M. Dahood believes the form to be singular but the meaning collective, an archaic feature he sees reflected also in Pss 110:6; 140:10, and Job 22:12 and in Ugaritic literature (*CTA* 3['nt].2.9–10; *Ugaritic-Hebrew Philology* [1965] 37; *Psalms* [1968] 2.144). Compare Gordon's comments on this phenomenon (no. 13.16).

[136] Albright, 11; Rudolph, 237; Mowinckel, 18–20; Duhm, 93; G. R. Driver, "Linguistic and Textual Problems: Minor Prophets, III" (1938) 397–398; cf. the *NEB*.

[137] Wellhausen put it: "*przw* gibt Anlass zu Bedenken, ebenso auch das was weiter folgt" (172).

[138] Lachmann, 81; Rudolph, 237.

[139] Good, "Text and Versions," 109–110; Humbert, 66.

[140] Margolis, 141. Compare Aq for Ezek 18:10.

[141]It was understood in this way also by Rashi and Kimchi (Sinker, 36–37). Albright thinks these may be the villagers who make up the army of the evil foe, a possibility that deserves serious consideration (11, 17; cf. the Vg).

[142]Cf. the metathesis of *reš* and *zayin* in *prz* in Est 9:19 (cf. Ps 89:11).

[143]Lachmann thinks *r'š* was in the textual base of the OG.

[144]Noted by Sinker (59) and Humbert (66–67); cf. *exekinēthē*, "stirred, agitated," for *ys'r* in 2 Kgs 6:11.

[145]The choice of Sym, *epelthonta*, "approaching," may represent an interpretation similar to that in the Vg.

[146]Margolis, 142.

[147]On Job 26:13, see Pope, 166; cf. also Ps 18:11; Exod 15:10; Gen 8:1 (and Dan 7:1 ?). Note Marduk's winds in *Enūma eliš* 4.45–48, 96–99, 132.

[148]Taking *ypṣw* from *pṣh*, "open, part;" Sinker, 59; Good, "Text and Versions," 110. Eaton postulates *yipṣūn* (155).

[149]Margolis, 142; Good, "Barberini," 14; Humbert, 66.

[150]In Isa 41:16 *pwṣ* is also used with *s'rh*: *s'rh tpyṣ 'wtm*, "the storm wind scattered them (i.e. the mountains/hills which were crushed)." Cf. Jer 13:24 and 18:7 for the use of *pwṣ* with wind (*rwḥ*).

[151]The translator of the OG seems to derive this term in Zech 14:20 and Hab 3:14 from *ṣll*, "tingle," and to understand it as a bell laden bridle for horses (cf. Good, "Text and Versions," 110; Sinker, 60; Lachmann, 82–83; Vollers, 35). That the equipment in question is for horses is indicated by Zech 14:20 (*mṣlwt hsws*) and by the translation of Hab 3:14 in the Achmimic version where *autōn* is replaced by "of the horses."

[152]Good, "Barberini," 17–18; Eaton, 155; Humbert suggests *'l yṣrm* as a possibility (66–67).

[153]Eaton, 155.

[154]Albright, 11, 17. The nominal form of *'lṣ* occurs only here in the Hebrew Bible. Compare the gods' rejoicing after Marduk's victory (*Enūma eliš* 4.133).

[155]For *mṣlt ym* as the name of Yahweh's adversary, see Ps 68:23 (cf. Dahood, *Psalms*, 2.144–146). Elsewhere *mṣlt ym* stands in parallelism with *ym* (Job 41:23), *thwm* (Exod 15:5), *nhr* and *lbb ymym* (Jonah 2:4). Compare also Mic 7:19 and Ps 107:24. Could

the difficult phrase at the end of Ps 74:14 *l'm lṣyym*, also be a corruption of *mṣlt ym*?

[156]Margolis, 142; Good, "Barberini," 17–18, "Text and Versions," 310; Humbert considers *kmw* a gloss (67).

[157]Lachmann, 83.

[158]Barb appears to read *'nyym* (*tous ptōchous*).

[159]Albright, 17.

[160]Cassuto, 13; Irwin, 31–32.

[161]Irwin, 30–32.

[162]*CTA* 4.128–132.

[163]*CTA* 6[49].2.30–37.

[164]*CTA* 6[49].5.19.

[165]Faulkner, "The Bremner-Rhind Papyrus: The Book of Overthrowing 'APEP" and A. M. Blackman and H. W. Fairman, "The Myth of Horus at Edfu-II" (1944).

[166]Compare the destruction of the Golden Calf in Exod 32:20, a remarkable parallel with the Ugaritic literature in which 'Anat disposes of Mot.

[167]Albright, 11, 17; Humbert, 67–68; Lachmann, 83; Margolis, 140. For *epibibazō* for *drk*, see v 19 in the OG and Barb. The usual referent for *epibibazō*, *rkb*, would be entirely out of context in this phrase. R's *eneteines* . . . is unusual, since in the LXX it renders *drk* only in its technical meaning of stepping on a bow to bend and string it.

[168]GKC, no. 144l (cf. Ps 17:13: *plṭh npšy mrš' ḥrbk*, "deliver my life from the wicked with your sword"). Cf. also Eaton, 156.

[169]See Pope, 69.

[170]On Deut 33:29, see Cross and Freedman, 121–122, note 93; on Judg 5:21, see R. G. Boling, *Judges* (1975) 113; on Amos 4:13 and Mic 1:3 see Pope, 69.

[171]Good, "Text and Versions," 111; "Barberini," 18.

[172]See H. G. May, "Some Cosmic Connotations of *Mayim Rabbîm*, 'Many Waters'" (1955).

[173]Duhm, 94; Wellhausen, 172; S. R. Driver, 95; Margulis, 428.

[174]The poem in Ps 77:17–20, which has remarkable similarities with Hab 3:8–15, also concludes with the parallel pair *ym*//*mym rbym*, though used differently.

[175]This is the consistent practice of the translator of the Minor Prophets (17 times) and the customary practice in the LXX as a whole. The two instances in the LXX where *phylassein* represents *šm'* (3 Kgs 11:38; Prov 19:27) may represent the same *'ayin/reš* confusion as here. Cf. Sinker, 62.

[176]A haplography of *'ayin*: cf. Margolis, 142, and Good, "Barberini," 18. *tassein* usually represents a form of *śym* in the Minor Prophets (10 times in 14 occurrences, including Hab 1:12; 2:9; and 3:19) and in the LXX as a whole.

[177]Aramaic *ṣlw*, "prayer" (with the haplography of *l* ?). Cf. Sinker, 62–63; Lachmann, 83; Rudolph, 238; Good, "Text and Versions," 112. In Ezra 6:10 and Dan 6:11, *proseuchesthai* represents *ṣl'*.

[178]Barb's *eisedy* may represent *b'* or *yb'*; the Tg *'ḥd* is an interpretive rendering and likely represents the MT (the Tg translates all the verbs in this poem in the past tense).

[179]Good, "Text and Versions," 112; Eaton, 157; cf. the similar phrase in Ps 55:6: *yr'h wr'd yb' by*, "fear and trembling came on/into me."

[180]Lachmann, 83; Humbert, 68.

[181]Duhm, 96–97.

[182]Note the similar expression *ṣ'dy tḥty*, "my steps under me," in Ps 18:37.

[183]Smith, 157.

[184]GKC, no. 114n.

[185]Albright, 17. Cross and Freedman have called attention to the old *t*-form of the verb used with duals and collectives as a characteristic of archaic Israelite poetry (27).

[186]Gordon, no. 9.15.

[187]Good, "Barberini," 18.

[188]Wellhausen, 172; Duhm, 96–97; Smith, 157; Humbert, 68; Mowinckel, 19; Albright, 17; Eaton, 157; Rudolph, 238.

[189]*hexis* translates such terms as *bry'* (Dan 1:15), *gbh* (1 Kgs 16:7), *gwyh* (Judg 14:9), and *gw* (Dan 7:15).

[190]The translator of the OG may have bypassed the usual translation for *'šwr*, *diabēma* (cf. Pss 17:5; 37:31; 40:3; 73:2), in order to capture the more pervasive bodily distress described here. The OG carries a figurative translation for *'šwr* in Job 23:11 (*entalma*).

[191]Elsewhere *ischys* is used to translate *mtnym* (Isa 45:1) and *grwn* (Isa 58:1).

[192]Compare the expression *ṣʿdy tḥty* in Ps 18:37.

[193]The only exception the Masoretes make is in Job 31:7.

[194]S. R. Driver, 96–97.

[195]Cf. Lachmann, 84–85.

[196]Margolis thinks Barb's reading may represent *tnyḥ*.

[197]Duhm, 97; Margulis, 431. Cf. G. R. Driver, "Studies in the Vocabulary of the Old Testament VI" (1933) 377; Humbert, 68; Eaton, 157.

[198]Albright, 17.

[199]Gordon, no. 9.11; Cross and Freedman, 27.

[200]Cross and Freedman, 88, note 67.

[201]The Tg may have a conflate text with both the OG and MT readings: *lʿdn ʾsqʾ glwt ʿmyh mny ytbrynny*, "at the time of the bringing out of the exiled community of his people from me he will break me." *glwt ʿmyh mny* = the OG *Vorlage mgwry* and *ytbrynny* = *ygwdny* (with the confusion of *y*, *w*).

[202]Though *karpophorēsei* translates *prh* in the LXX only here, it renders a synonym of *prh* (*nwb*) in Sym in Ps 61(62):11 and Ps 91(92):15.

[203]Albright 12, 13, 17; Rudolph, 238; Humbert, 69.

[204]Lachmann, 85; Gordon believes this to be a possibility for the Ugaritic cognate *šdmt* (no. 2388).

[205]M. R. Lehmann, "A New Interpretation of the term *šdmwt*" (1954); J. S. Croatto and J. A. Soggin appear to be in substantial agreement with Lehmann ("Die Bedeutung von *šdmwt* im Alten Testament" [1962]). Cf. Margulis, 433.

[206]Communicated in seminar discussions at Harvard University.

[207]L. E. Stager, "The Archaeology of the East Slope of Jerusalem and the Terraces of the Kidron" (1982). This is now the translation used for *šdmt* in Gibson's revised version of G. R. Driver's *Canaanite Myths and Legends* ([1978] 123).

[208]Wellhausen, 172; cf. Duhm, 100; Lachmann, 85; Smith, 157; Humbert, 69.

[209]This solution has been proposed by Dahood (*Ugaritic-Hebrew Philology*, 21–22; cf. GKC, nos. 52e, 53u). Other proposals which have been made include the passive participle *gāzūr* (Albright, 12, 13, 18) and the unusual suggestion by L. Delekat

that *gzr* is a mistake for a hitherto unidentified root in Hebrew, *grz*, "to disappear" ("Zum Hebräischen Wörterbuch" [1964] 11–13).

[210]Good, "Text and Versions," 113; Lachmann, 85; Rudolph, 239; Vollers, 35.

[211]Perhaps the translator of the OG was influenced here by Joel 1:15–20 (esp. vv 16, 18).

[212]Duhm, 100; Rudolph, 239; Margulis, 433; cf. BDB, 476; and GKC, no. 23a, e.

[213]Sinker (64) and Good ("Text and Versions," 72) have suggested that the alternate readings *exilaseōs* and *exelaseōs* are inner Greek corruptions of *ex iaseōs*.

[214]Lachmann, 86; Rudolph, 239.

[215]GKC, no. 135q and note 2.

[216]Sinker, 65; cf. Job 26:10. For similar suggestions, see Good, "Text and Versions," 114; Rudolph, 239; Eaton, 158; and Lachmann, 86.

[217]Margolis, 136.

[218]For some attempts, see Sinker, 65; Good, "Barberini," 19; and Rudolph, 239.

[219]Rudolph, 239; Albright restores *ym*, "Sea" (12, 13, 19); Cross and Freedman, in a similar text in Ps 18:34 (= 2 Sam 22:34), restore *mt*, "Death" (152–153, note 78).

[220]On the survival of the genitive case ending in archaic poetry, see Cross and Freedman, 160, note 40, and 229, note 53.

Notes to Chapter 2

[1]M. O'Connor (*Hebrew Verse Structure* [1980]) has provided a massive, useful catalogue of the types of lines and varieties of tropes employed in Hebrew verse structure. My reservations about his study arise when he suggests that larger units of Hebrew verse are marked primarily by shifts in troping and line type. I grant that literary variation creates the boundaries of larger units, but I do not agree that the literary variation that marks units in Hebrew poetry is primarily of the tropological and typological kind that O'Connor proposes. O'Connor's study of gross structure overlooks a variety of literary devices which can be employed to mark larger structures: inclusion, shifts in person of verb forms and suffixes, shifts in meter, repetition of key words, special struc-

tures like particles and rhetorical questions, and other patterning devices like series of similar verb forms or identical suffixes. Finally, O'Connor's analysis suffers in my judgment from a lack of cohesion between form and content in Hebrew poetry. The attempt to provide an "objective" literary analysis based solely on structure is laudable, but larger structures are signaled as much by the content which fills the structures as by the structures themselves. As a result of its specific focus on shifts in tropes and line types, O'Connor's analysis obscures, in my judgment, a whole variety of thematic and literary structures which are also operative in this poem and significant in establishing its structure. The attempt to find Greek literary forms in Hebrew poetry such as that of A. Condamin ("La forme chorale du ch. III d'Habacuc" [1899]) is no longer in fashion and properly so. Other literary studies of Habakkuk 3 which may be compared with these two are those of F. T. Kelley ("The Strophic Structure of Habakkuk" [1902] 113–119) and D. H. Bévenot ("Le cantique d'Habacuc" [1933]).

[2]A survey of the early scholarship on this issue can be found in C. F. Kraft's *The Strophic Structure of Hebrew Poetry* (1938).

[3]Two recent discussions of strophic structure are those of J. Muilenberg ("Form Criticism and Beyond" [1969]) and D. N. Freedman (Prolegomenon to *The Forms of Hebrew Verse* [1972]).

[4]Good treatments of inclusion are found in the discussions of Muilenberg and Freedman above, as well as in an essay by M. Dahood ("Poetry, Hebrew" [1976]).

[5]F. M. Cross has suggested that the basic building blocks of biblical Hebrew poetry are long (*longum*) and short (*breve*) cola (*Canaanite Myth and Hebrew Epic* [1973] 115, note 14; "Studies in the Structure of Hebrew Verse: The Prosody of the Psalm of Jonah" [1983] 159). This system has the advantage of leaving open the question of auditory rhythm, whether identified by stress or by the exact quantity of syllables in a line. According to this system, lines of six and seven syllables provide the general boundary between long and short cola. In Habakkuk 3, lines of six and seven syllables, on the basis of their relationship to their context, are best described as long (l). Lines of six and seven syllables appear together with lines of eight and nine syllables without suggesting, by any clear pattern or alternation, a shift in meter from these clearly long cola.

[6]Reading the short form of the 2ms suffix, *śim'ak*, and counting two syllables. F. M. Cross and D. N. Freedman have noted the distinction between short (*-k*) and long (*-kh*) forms of the 2ms suffix in preexilic Hebrew, a distinction obscured by the Masoretes who indicated the long form by their vowel points in all cases (*Early Hebrew Orthography* [1952] 53, 65–67). Cross and Freedman state that the long form was common in elevated speech and literary works, and it may thus have been employed (selectively ?) by the author of Habakkuk 3 for metrical purposes, adding a syllable to the line in which it is used. However, since long forms are not indicated by the orthography of Habakkuk 3, I have for the sake of consistency read the short form in all cases.

[7]Vocalizing *baqirb* and counting two syllables. Segholation is a late phenomenon unattested for the most part in the transliterations of Origen's Hexapla.

[8]Reading the short form of the 2ms perfect, *ḥayyît*, and counting two syllables. The remarks in endnote 6 above apply also to the 2ms perfect verbal form (see Cross and Freedman, 55, 67). Again, in spite of the fact that the poet may have selectively used both long and short forms, I have followed the orthography of the received text and consistently read short forms.

[9]S. A. Geller, *Parallelism in Early Biblical Poetry* (1979) 236.

[10]Repetitive or climactic parallelism was first noted by S. R. Driver (*Introduction to the Literature of the Old Testament* [1914] 363–364), popularized by C. F. Burney (*The Book of Judges* [1918; reprint 1970] 169–171), recognized as present in Ugaritic as well as Hebrew poetry by H. L. Ginsberg ("The Rebellion and Death of Ba'lu" [1936]), and discussed by many since, including J. H. Patton (*Canaanite Parallels in the Book of Psalms* [1944] esp. pp. 8–9), W. F. Albright ("The Psalm of Habakkuk" [1950] 1–18), and F. M. Cross and D. N. Freedman (*Studies in Ancient Yahwistic Poetry* [1950; reprint 1975] 11).

[11]S. Mowinckel is suspicious of isolated tricola in Hebrew poetry as a whole (*Real and Apparent Tricola in Hebrew Psalm Poetry* [1957]) and in Habakkuk 3 in particular ("Zum Psalm des Habakuk" [1953]). Others who attempt to remove tricola from Habakkuk 3 for literary reasons include W. A. Irwin ("The Psalm of Habakkuk" [1942] esp. p. 18), J. Lachmann (*Das Buch Habbakuk* [1932]), and P. Humbert (*Problèmes du livre d'Habacuc* [1944]).

Compare the bias of the translators of the *NEB* and *JB*.

[12]Some of the first to recognize the significance of the isolated tricolon in Ugaritic poetry for a more proper understanding of Hebrew poetry were H. L. Ginsberg (161-198) and W. F. Albright ("The Furniture of El in Canaanite Mythology" [1943] esp. p. 43; and "The Old Testament and Canaanite Language and Literature" [1945] esp. p. 21).

[13]Evidence for the use of climactic parallelism in Ugaritic and ancient Hebrew poetry has been compiled by W. F. Albright ("The Psalm of Habakkuk," esp. pp. 3–8; and *Yahweh and the Gods of Canaan* [1968] 4–28). See also B. Margulis, "The Psalm of Habakkuk: A Reconstruction and Interpretation" (1970) 425.

[14]See Exod 15:3, 6, 11, 16; Judg 5:3, 5, 6, 7, 11, 12, 19, 21, 23, 27, 30; Pss 18:45–46; 29:1, 2, 4, 5, 8, 10; 77:17; 93:3.

[15]Vocalizing *bagapanīm* and counting four syllables. The rule of shewa resulting in the reduction of a syllable is a late phenomenon unattested in the transliterations of Origen's Hexapla.

[16]Vocalizing *ma'śê* and counting two syllables. Artificial vowels added to assist in the pronunciation of gutturals should not be included in the assessment of line length (GKC 22m, 26k, 28c).

[17]See Chap. 3.

[18]Geller, 14.

[19]See textual note 88 in Chapter 1.

[20]Vocalizing *'ilōh* and counting two syllables. The *pataḥ* furtive is taken as an artificial vowel to assist in the pronunciation of gutturals and omitted in the syllable count.

[21]Vocalizing *šamaym* and counting two syllables. The helping vowel in dual forms is taken, like segholation, to be a late development to assist in the pronunciation of doubly closed syllables.

[22]See Chap. 3.

[23]See textual note 25 in Chapter 1.

[24]Vocalizing *tu'ar* and counting two syllables. The short form of 3rd weak verbs, still attested in the *waw* consecutive and jussive forms of classical Hebrew, was likely the old preterit form used in past narrative as here. See textual note 35 in Chapter 1.

[25]Muilenberg, 16.

[26]See Chap. 3

[27]See Chap. 3.

[28]M. Dahood (*Psalms* [1966–1970]) and L. J. Liebreich ("Psalms 34 and 145 in Light of Their Key Words" [1956]) have discussed the use of inclusion in the Psalms; L. J. Liebreich ("The Compilation of the Book of Isaiah" [1956]) in Isaiah; J. R. Lundbom (*Jeremiah: A Study of Ancient Hebrew Rhetoric* [1975]) in Jeremiah; F. Landsberger ("Poetic Units Within the Song of Songs" [1954] esp. pp. 213–214) in the Song of Songs; and N. Lohfink (*Lectures in Deuteronomy* [1968]) in Deuteronomy. Compare the comments on inclusion of R. G. Moulton (*The Literary Criticism of the Bible* [1899]) in the last century.

[29]M. Coogan, "A Structural and Literary Analysis of the Song of Deborah" (1978) 151–158.

[30]Cross, "The Psalm of Jonah."

[31]W. Rudolph, *Micha, Nahum, Habakuk, Zephanja* (1975) 241.

[32]J. H. Eaton, "The Origin and Meaning of Habakkuk 3" (1964) 164–165.

[33]E. M. Good, "The Text and Versions of Habakkuk 3: a study in textual history" (1958) 11–13.

[34]D. A. Robertson, *Linguistic Evidence in Dating Early Hebrew Poetry* (1972) 7–55.

[35]Robertson has pointed out that this form is ambiguous (8, 33). The consonantal text could be interpreted also as a *waw* + suffix form. In initial weak verbs, the 3ms prefix and suffix forms are indistinguishable without the Masoretic vocalization.

[36]The Alexandrian mss. which contain the conjunction represent an accommodation to the MT (J. Ziegler, *Duodecim Prophetae* [1943] 269; Good, 64).

[37]Robertson, 43.

[38]See Chap. 3.

Notes to Chapter 3

[1]U. Cassuto, "Chapter iii of Habakkuk and the Ras Shamra Texts" (1973) 3.

[2]W. A. Irwin, "The Psalm of Habakkuk" (1942) 10.

[3]Cassuto (9) and B. Margulis ("The Psalm of Habakkuk: A Reconstruction and Interpretation" [1970] 437–440) have questioned the interpretation of vv 3–15 as a vision; Irwin (36–39) is almost alone among contemporary scholars in denying Chapter 3

to Habakkuk.

[4]See Chapters 1 and 4.

[5]W. F. Albright ("The Psalm of Habakkuk" [1950] 9) and R. H. Pfeiffer (*Introduction to the Old Testament* [1949] 632) have called the author of Habakkuk 3 archaizing. Others, such as G. G. V. Stonehouse (*The Book of Habakkuk* [1911] 126) and Margulis (437–439), have noted the appropriation of older texts.

[6]E.g. Exodus 15, 1 Samuel 2, the psalms of David, Jonah 2, Malachi.

[7]See the poetic analysis in Chapter 2.

[8]Shôbak has been accepted as a possible site for biblical Teman by such geographers as F. M. Abel (*Géographie de la Palestine* [1938] 479–480) and J. Simons (*The Geographical and Topographical Texts of the Old Testament* [1959] 90). A. Musil (*The Northern Hedjaz* [1926] 249–251) identified Teman with Kh. eth-Thuwâneh, an identification accepted as a possibility by E. Kraeling (*Rand McNally Bible Atlas* [1956] p. 373, map V).

[9]N. Glueck, *Explorations in Eastern Palestine*, II (1935) 82–83. Glueck's view has been accepted as likely by such scholars as G. E. Wright and F. V. Filson (eds., *The Westminster Historical Atlas to the Bible* [1956] maps 5, 6, 7, 10), H. G. May (ed., *Oxford Bible Atlas* [1962] pp. 59, 75), Y. Aharoni (*The Land of the Bible* [1967] pp. 37, 52, 384, maps 14, 21, 28), and V. R. Gold ("Teman" [1962] 533–534).

[10]C.-M. Bennett, "Ṭawilân (Jordanie)" (1969) 390. Bennett's discussion of her excavations at Ṭawilân can be found under this title in *RB* 76 (1969) 386–390 and in *RB* 77 (1970) 371–374; and under the heading "Edom" in the *IDBSup*, 251–252.

[11]R. de Vaux, "Téman, ville ou région d'Edom?" (1969) 379–385.

[12]Z. Meshel, *Kuntillet ʿAjrud: A Religious Centre from the Time of the Judean Monarchy on the Border of Sinai* (1978); "Did Yahweh Have a Consort?" (1979) 24–35; Z. Meshel and C. Meyers, "The Name of God in the Wilderness of Zin" (1976) 6–10. For the occurrence of *yhwh tmn* at Kuntillet ʿAjrud, see textual note 7 in Chapter 1.

[13]Later tradition appears to have identified Teman with the site of Tema in northwestern Arabia about 250 miles southeast of Aqaba. The "Prayer of Nabonidus" from Qumran places the Babylonian king in Teman (*tymn*; J. T. Milik, "'Prière de

Nabonide' et autres écrits d'un cycle de Daniel, fragments de Qumran 4" [1956] 407–411), certainly to be identified as Tema, the Arabian site known from Assyrian (*ANET*, 283–284) and Babylonian (*ANET*, 306) historical records, from Old Aramiac inscriptions of the 5th and 6th centuries B.C.E. (*tym'*: *KAI*, Nos. 228–230), and from biblical references (Isa 21:14; Jer 25:23).

[14]E.g. May, 59; Wright and Filson, 42; J. L. Mihelic, "Paran" (1962) 657; and BDB, 803. Cf. Simons, 256.

[15]W. F. Albright, "The Historical Background of Genesis XIV" (1926) 231–269; E. A. Speiser, *Genesis* (1964) 99–109. Albright, relying on traditional identifications, considers the itinerary in v 6 "improbable" since it would involve a swing through Sinai (261). But the campaign was probably directed south through the Transjordan with the return along the same route and not through Sinai at all.

[16]BDB connects El-paran with modern Eilat (803).

[17]F. M. Cross, *Canaanite Myth and Hebrew Epic* (1973) 293–325, esp. 308–309, 314–315; Cf. M. Noth, *Numbers* (1968) 76, 101, 106.

[18]R. Cohen, "Did I Excavate Kadesh-Barnea?" (1981) 20–33; I. Beit-Arieh, "Sinai Survey 1978–79" (1979) 256–257. H. Bar-Deroma ("Kadesh-Barne'a" 1964 101–134) has pointed out at length the problems with locating Kadesh-Barnea in the Negev and has marshalled evidence for placing it east of the Arabah.

[19]W. L. Moran, "Deuteronomy" (1969) 225. Moran considers vv 1b–2 intrusive with the original introduction to this address including vv 1a, 4–5.

[20]P. K. McCarter, Jr. (*I Samuel* [1980] 338) reads with LXX^B against MT, "the wilderness of Maon."

[21]J. A. Montgomery, *The Books of Kings* (1951) 238–239. Montgomery considers 1 Kgs 11:14–25 an old historical source, the biography of an Edomite prince, which came into the hands of the Israelite archivists.

[22]For the references to this ancient city and an analysis of them, see W. Dumbrell ("Midian—A Land or a League" 1975 330) and G. M. Landes ("Midian" 1962 375).

[23]B. Rothenberg and J. Glass, "Midianite Pottery" (1981) 85–114; P. J. Parr, G. L. Harding, and J. E. Dayton, "Preliminary Survey in N. W. Arabia, 1968" (1968–69) 193–241.

[24]Cf. e.g. the opinion of Y. Aharoni (*The Archaeology of*

the Land of Israel [1978] 137–139, 166) with those of F. M. Cross, T. Dothan, and B. Mazar in the discussion of Mazar's paper "Yahweh Came out from Sinai" (1981) 8–9. See also P. Parr, "Contacts between North West Arabia and Jordan in the Late Bronze Ages," 127–133.

[25]Dumbrell, 323–337; see also his unpublished dissertation ("The Midianites and their Transjordanian Successors" [1970]). Compare the discussions of W. F. Albright ("Midianite Donkey Caravans" [1970]), O. Eissfeldt ("Protektorat der Midianiter über ihrer Nachbarn im letzten Viertel des 2. Jahrtausends v. Chr." [1968] 383–393), and Ernst A. Knauf ("Midianites and Ishmaelites" [1983]).

[26]In the other occurrence of *'ereṣ midyān* in the Bible, Exod 2:15 (epic tradition), it is also clear that the Midianites—here Moses' in-laws—were a nomadic folk tending flocks.

[27]M. Coogan has called my attention to the fact that similar misidentifications have been made of the Israelite store cities of the Exodus, Pithom and Raamses, both within later biblical traditions and in the versions. Later tradents and translators identified these sites with cities which were occupied in their day and with which they were familiar. This kind of geographical revisionism seems to be common in the handing down of old traditions.

[28]W. F. Albright, "The Land of Damascus between 1850–1750 B.C." (1941) 34, note 8; *Archaeology and the Religion of Israel* (1942) 110, 205 note 49. Cf. G. Posener, "Syria and Palestine, c. 2160–1780 B.C." (1971) 554; and Simons, 20.

[29]G. Posener, *Princes et pays d'Asie et de Nubie* (1940) 88–89.

[30]Posener ("Syria and Palestine," 554–555) believes that *Kwšw* is a country or region, but notes that the designation "great men of the tribes of *Kwšw*" may be a sign of a nomadic type of organization.

[31]Compare the comments of Cross (204) and Mazar (8).

[32]Musil, 249–251, 278–296.

[33]R. Giveon, "Toponymes ouest-asiatiques à Soleb" (1964) 244.

[34]R. Giveon, "'The Cities of our God' (2 Sam 10:12)" (1964) 415–416. M. C. Astour disagrees with this analysis. He has argued that the toponym Yahwe in these Egyptian lists refers to a place in central Syria ("Yahweh in Egyptian Topographic Lists"

[1979]; "Yahwe" [1976] 971).

[35]This identification was proposed by Jarvis and has been championed by Mazar (5–6).

[36]Note, for example, Cohen's failure to find evidence of Late Bronze occupation at Ein el-Qudeirat, the traditional site of Kadesh-Barnea in the Sinai ("Did I Excavate Kadesh-Barnea?" 20–33). See also Beit-Arieh ("Sinai Survey").

[37]R. Giveon, *Les Bedoins Shosou des documents égyptiens* (1971).

[38]See R. Clifford, *The Cosmic Mountain in Canaan and the Old Testament* (1972) 98–160, esp. pp. 120–121 note 26, and 154–155; and H. Schmid, "Jahwe und die Kulttraditionen von Jerusalem" (1955) 189–190.

[39]For *māqôm* in Mic 1:3 as a technical term describing the dais of the god within his temple, cf. 1 Sam 5:3.

[40]W. J. Fulco (*The Canaanite God Rešep* [1976]) has collected all of the Egyptian and Semitic evidence on Resheph. Fulco's footnotes provide a comprehensive bibliography of the work done on Resheph to date.

[41]For the appearance of Resheph at Ebla, see G. Pettinato (*The Archives of Ebla* [1981] 44, 58, 143, 247, etc.); note also M. Dahood's comments in the "Afterward" (296).

[42]Resheph is associated with Nergal in the god lists in Ugaritica V. See Laroche, "Notes sur le panthéon hourrite de Ras Shamra" (1969) 150. In addition to Fulco's discussion of the character of the deity Resheph, see also W. F. Albright's comments ("The Egypto-Canaanite Deity Ḥaurôn" [1941] 11–12; *Archaeology and the Religion of Israel*, 79; *Yahweh and the Gods of Canaan* [1968] 139–140) and those of M. Coogan in his review of Fulco's monograph ([1978] 111).

[43]A number of commentators including A. Caquot ("Sur quelques démons de l'Ancien Testament: Reshep, Qeṭeb, Deber" [1956] 61) and Fulco (59–60) have proposed reading *dbr* with Symmachus against MT *brd* in Ps 78:48. On the mythological character of Ps 91:56 see M. Dahood's discussion (*Psalms* [1968] 2.331–332). On Deber as a divine figure note Caquot's comments in *Semitica* 6.

[44]Pettinato, 245, 247; note Dahood's comments in the "Afterward" (296). F. M. Cross has suggested in a personal communication that the vocalization *dabir* may indicate the reading, "holy

place/sanctuary (Hebrew: *dĕbîr*) of the god of Ebla" (cf. *bêt 'ēl* as the name of a sanctuary [Gen 29:19] and the deity [Jer 48:13]).

[45]P. Miller, *The Divine Warrior in Early Israel* (1973) 8–63. Miller's study deals also with the prominence of the cosmic armies in the biblical literature mentioned below. J. Day has suggested that in the famous *b'l. ḫẓ. ršp* text at Ugarit (*PRU* 2.1.3; Gordon, 1001) Resheph the archer is accompanying Ba'l in his battle with the dragon, just as Resheph accompanies Yahweh in Hab 3:5 ("New Light on the Mythological Background of the Allusion to Resheph in Habakkuk III 5" [1979] 353–354).

[46]For Adad, see Tablet 11: 96–100 in the Epic of Gilgamesh (*ANET*, 94); for Tiamat, see Tablet 3 of *Enūma eliš* where she prepares for war with Marduk; for Marduk, see J. Hehn (*Hymnen und Gebete an Marduk* 1905) p. 314, 11:4–5).

[47]Cross defends this interpretation for Yahweh Sabaoth and argues that it was originally an epithet of 'El. See his discussion of this term in *Canaanite Myth and Hebrew Epic* (60–71). Cf. Miller, 151–155.

[48]See the analysis of Josh 10:12–13, where Sun and Moon are involved, and the early prose traditions (Josh 5:13–15; Gen 32:2–3; 2 Sam 5:22–25; 2 Kgs 6:15 19; 7:6) by Miller (123–135).

[49]In late Hebrew literature: e.g. Isa 40:26; 45:12; Zech 14:5; in the War Scroll from Qumran: 1QM 1:9–11, etc.; in the Apocalypse: Rev 19:14. Miller discusses some of these and other texts in *The Divine Warrior* (135–144).

[50]Cf. 2 Sam 5:24, *yāṣā' yhwh lĕpānêkā*.

[51]J. Jeremias has discussed this element in the theophany of the divine warrior at length. He sees the theophanic pattern as two-fold: 1) the going forth of Yahweh, and 2) the resultant agitation of nature. See *Theophanie* (1965) and "Theophany in the OT" (1976) 896–898.

[52]Cross, 147–163.

[53]Examples from Canaanite literature which may be cited include *CTA* 5[67].1.1–5; and *EA* 147.13–15 which describes the cry of Ba'l (Addu) in the heavens shaking the whole land. Cf. *CTA* 4[51].7.29–35.

[54]Meshel, *Kuntillet 'Ajrud*; "Did Yahweh Have a Consort?" 29–30.

[55]Based on a photograph and communicated in a personal conversation by F. M. Cross.

[56]G. von Rad, "The Origin of the Concept of the Day of Yahweh" (1959) 106-107. Cf. Ps 83:10, 12.

[57]Miller, 119.

[58]Cross, 195–215.

[59]Judg 1:16: "And the descendents of the Kenite, Moses' father-in-law, went up with the people of Judah from the city of palms into the wilderness of Judah which lies in the Negeb near Arad; and they went and settled with the people" (*RSV*). See B. Mazar, "The Sanctuary of Arad and the Family of Hobab the Kenite" (1965) 297–303; Y. Aharoni, "Arad: Its Inscriptions and Temple" (1968) 27–28; "Arad," in *The Encyclopedia of Archaeological Excavations in the Holy Land*, 88–89; Cross, 200–201.

[60]See the discussion of v 16 below.

[61]See e.g. *CTA* 4[51].3.11,18; 5[67].2.7.

[62]*CTA* 5[67].5.7; Cassuto (11) and J. Day ("Echoes of Baal's Seven Thunders and Lightnings in Psalm XXIX and Habakkuk III 9 and the Identity of the Seraphim in Isaiah VI" (1979) 147, note 18) have proposed reading "your chariot/chariot team" for *mdlk* (from *mdl*, "to harness").

[63]'*ṣ brq* in *UG* 5.3(*RS* 24.245).3–4; cf. *CTA* 4[51].5.70–71. For Ba'l's iconography see *ANEP*, no. 490. On the relation between these texts and this iconography, see L. R. Fisher and F. B. Knutson ("An Enthronement Ritual at Ugarit" [1969] 159, note 10).

[64]*Enūma eliš* 4:35–54 (*ANET*, 66).

[65]Atraḫasis, fragment E (reverse), 4–10 (*ANET*, 514); The Epic of Gilgamesh, 11:96–100 (*ANET*, 94).

[66]T. Jacobsen, *The Treasures of Darkness* (1976) 233; *ANEP*, nos. 501, 537, 538.

[67]Job 38:8–11; Judg 5:22.

[68]E.g. F. Delitzsch, *Der Prophet Habakuk* (1843) 174.

[69]F. M. Cross and D. N. Freedman, *Studies in Ancient Yahwistic Poetry* (1975) 147, note 41.

[70]W. A. Irwin, 14–15, 25–27; D. H. Bévenot, "Le Cantique d'Habacuc" (1933) 509.

[71]*Enūma eliš* 4:89 (*ANET*, 67); M. Coogan has called my attention to the fact that *tĕhôm* never occurs in biblical literature with the article, an indication that the term never became a common noun. The personification of *tĕhôm* here in Hab 3:10 is vivid.

[72]E.g. Delitzsch, 175; W. Rudolph, *Micha, Nahum, Habakuk, Zephanja* (1975) 236.

[73]See Chap. 1.

[74]Isa 60:19; 13:10; Joel 2:10; Eccl 12:2; neither *ʿāmad* nor *nāśāʾ* is ever used to mean "darken."

[75]See R. Sinker, *The Psalm of Habakkuk* (1890) 29–31.

[76]J. S. Holladay, "The Day(s) the Moon Stood Still" (1968) 166–178.

[77]Miller, 123–128.

[78]A similar use of darkness as divine punishment has been noted by Jo Ann Hackett in her study of the new texts from Deir ʿAllā (*The Balaam Text from Deir ʿAllā* [1984] 41–42, 75–89).

[79]Cassuto, 11–14; T. H. Gaster, "The Battle of the Rain and the Sea" (1937) 26.

[80]Cassuto, 13; Albright, "The Psalm of Habakkuk," 11, 17.

[81]Cassuto, 11.

[82]S. Mowinckel, "Zum Psalm des Habakuk" (1953) 14.

[83]GKC 150e; BDB (210) cites examples of this convention where the interrogative "is used in questions which, by seeming to make doubtful what cannot be denied, have the force of an impassioned or indignant affirmation."

[84]See Chap. 1.

[85]M. Dahood, *Psalms*, 2.145–146; "MIŠMĀR, 'Muzzle' in Job 7:12" (1961) 270–271. Dahood follows S. Loewenstamm ("The Muzzling of Tannin in Ugaritic Myth" 1959 260–261) in his understanding of *šbm*. See also P. Miller, "Two Critical Notes on Psalm 68 and Deuteronomy 33" (1964) 240–243. Compare the usual definition given *prr* in Ps 74:13 for a modern example of "historicizing."

[86]H. G. May, "Some Cosmic Connotations of *Mayim Rabbîm*, 'Many Waters'" (1955) 9–21. See, for example, Psalms 89 and 74.

[87]J. Wellhausen, *Die Kleinen Propheten* (1898) 172.

[88]Irwin, 30–33.

[89]*CTA* 2.4[68].27; 6[49].2.30–37; 6[49].5.19.

[90]Compare the comments of Cross (*Canaanite Myth and Hebrew Epic*, 117–118), P. L. Watson ("The Death of 'Death' in the Ugaritic Texts" [1972] 60–64), and S. E. Loewenstamm ("The Killing of Mot in Ugaritic Myth" [1972] 378–382).

[91] *Enūma eliš* 4:130–133.

[92] R. O. Faulkner, "The Bremner-Rhind Papyrus: The Book of Overthrowing 'APEP" (1937) 166–185 and (1938) 41– 53 in *ANET*, 6–7; A. M. Blackman and H. W. Fairman, "The Myth of Horus at Edfu-II" (1944) 5–22.

[93] E. A. Speiser, "'People' and 'Nation' of Israel" (1960) 157–163; F. M. Cross, "The Epic Traditions of Early Israel: Epic Narrative and the Reconstruction of Early Israelite Institutions" (1983) 35–38; cf. *'am kĕmôš* in Num 21:29.

[94] See 1 Sam 4:3, 4, for example, and the comments of G. von Rad (*Der Heilige Krieg im alten Israel* [1958] 7), C. U. Wolf ("Terminology of Israel's Tribal Organization" (1946) 45–49), and Miller (*The Divine Warrior*, 80, 85, 92, 159–160).

[95] See Chap. 1.

[96] E.g. Judg 5:2, 12, 13, 23; Deut 33:2, 3, 29; Ps 68:8, 9; see Miller's comments (*The Divine Warrior*, 156–162).

[97] M. Lind, *Yahweh is a Warrior* (1980).

[98] This can be seen in the Exodus narrative itself when the epic tradition states specifically that the people need only be still and watch God fight (Exod 14:14) and when the later Priestly tradents glorified God's acts even more by the introduction of walls of water. Judg 5:19–21 and Josh 10:11, and the Gideon stories, are other examples of cases in which the writer sought to attribute victory to God in wars which Israel fought. This same interest is present in Habakkuk 3 when the poet describes Yahweh marching out for the victory of his people (vv 13, 18). The emphasis here is certainly on Yahweh's crucial involvement. This same emphasis on divine help is present in the accounts of Assyrian wars as the annals of Sennacherib and Esarhaddon illustrate (*ANET*, 287–290).

[99] W. Richter, "Die *nāgīd*-Formel" (1965) 71–84; compare the evidence Cross puts forward for the identification of *nāgîd* as "military commander" (*Canaanite Myth and Hebrew Epic*, 219–222; "An Interpretation of the Nora Stone" [1972] 16–17). To the comparative evidence cited by Cross (*Canaanite Myth and Hebrew Epic*, 220, note 5) may be added the use of *ngd* in the Adon Letter (B. Porten, "The Identity of King Adon" [1981] 36). A different understanding of *nāgîd* has been defended recently by P. K. McCarter (*I Samuel*, 178–179, 184–188) and B. Halpern (*The Constitution of the Monarchy in Israel* [1981] 1–11) who argue that the term, here in relation to Saul and elsewhere in most cases, refers to

the king-designate or crown prince. Halpern's discussion includes a helpful summary of recent interpretations of *nāgîd*.

[100]Cross, *Canaanite Myth and Hebrew Epic*, 138; see 137–140.

[101]See Chap. 2.

[102]See Chapter 4 for a description of the *Tendenz* of the Septuagint. Cassuto realized that this poem was not a vision but a recitation of God's deeds (9).

[103]See Chap. 1.

[104]See Chap. 1.

[105]The possibility that the tricolon of the introduction might be narration, like the bicolon which precedes it, rather than supplication, was suggested to me by F. M. Cross.

[106]E.g. Eaton, 167–168.

[107]E.g. Rudolph, 240–241; and others which P. Humbert (*Problèmes du livre d'Habacuc* [1944] 71–72) lists. Those who do consider v 17 an original part of the poem do so by linking the poem to an event, like the Autumn New Year festival, when concerns for political security and agricultural fertility might be combined. See, for example, the comments of Mowinckel (20) and Eaton (160–163).

[108]See F. M. Cross, "Studies in the Structure of Hebrew Verse: The Prosody of the Psalm of Jonah" (1983) 159–167.

[109]See Chap. 1.

[110]*CTA* 5.1.1–5; the translation is that of F. M. Cross (*Canaanite Myth and Hebrew Epic*, 150).

[111]Reading *ybwlm* for *gbwlm* in Ps 105:33.

[112]I must admit, however, that the possibility of linking this verse with the convulsion of nature at the appearance of God in a thunderstorm, rather than with drought or the devastation of war, became much more persuasive after experiencing a series of severe thunderstorms in southern Minnesota while working on this text. Some local farms were devastated by the winds, downpour, and hail. Spring crops were heavily damaged and cattle were killed when barns were blown down by high winds.

[113]This imagistic style is discussed by Cross (*Canaanite Myth and Hebrew Epic*, 22–24), and noted by M. Coogan in his discussion of Judges 5 ("A Structural and Literary Analysis of the Song of Deborah" [1978] 165–166).

[114]See Chap. 1. Cf. *ANEP*, nos. 300, 308; *ANET*, 254, 290.

[115]W. L. Moran, "Some Remarks on the Song of Moses" (1962) 327, note 1.

[116]R. Otto, *The Idea of the Holy* (1973) 31; see esp. 12–40.

[117]F. M. Cross "The Epic Traditions of Early Israel," 19.

[118]See F. M. Cross's discussion of this form and its cultic context in his treatment of Exod 15:1–18 (*Canaanite Myth and Hebrew Epic*, 112–144) and Coogan's comments ("Song of Deborah," 160–166). C. Westermann (*The Praise of God in the Psalms* [1965] 90–93) is incorrect, in my opinion, in defining this genre narrowly on the basis of Judges 5 and limiting it to this poem, Judg 16:23f., Ps 118:15f., and Judith 16. This overlooks the underlying similarities between Exodus 15, Deuteronomy 33, Judges 5, Habakkuk 3, and Psalm 68, in particular the fact that all of these poems are structured according to the ancient conflict scheme outlined above.

[119]Victory odes with some similarities to these biblical songs have been identified in the cultures surrounding Israel. See, for example, P. Hanson's discussion of the Song of Heshbon ("The Song of Heshbon and David's *nîr*" [1968] 297–310) and W. F. Albright's comments on the Assyrian hymn celebrating the victory of Tukulti-Ninurta I over Kashtiliash III, and the Egyptian hymn of the Battle of Kadesh commemorating the victory of Rameses II over the Hittites ("The Song of Deborah in the Light of Archaeology" [1936] 30–31).

[120]See H. Gunkel's description of the hymn of praise (*The Psalms* [1967] 10–13, 30–31).

[121]E.g. S. Mowinckel, 7; Eaton, 159, 167.

[122]See Chapter 2 and D. Robertson, *Linguistic Evidence in Dating Early Hebrew Poetry* (1972).

[123]See Chapter 2 and Albright, *Yahweh and the Gods of Canaan*, 1–52; "The Psalm of Habakkuk," 3–8.

[124]See Chapter 2 and Cross and Freedman, *Studies in Ancient Yahwistic Poetry*, 186.

[125]Meshel, *Kuntillet 'Ajrud*; "Did Yahweh Have a Consort?" 31–34. Exactly why Meshel relates this pilgrimmage site to the journeys of Judean kings, given the strong northern influences there, is not clear to me.

[126]These postexilic hymns are described in more detail and differentiated from Habakkuk 3 in Chapter 4.

[127]Cross, *Canaanite Myth and Hebrew Epic*, 169–194.

[128]Cross, *Canaanite Myth and Hebrew Epic*, 170–173.

[129]Cross, *Canaanite Myth and Hebrew Epic*, 59.

[130]On Psalm 68 see W. F. Albright, "A Catalogue of Early Hebrew Lyric Poems (Psalm LVIII)" (1950–51) 1–39; S. Mowinckel, *Der achtundsechzigste Psalm* (1953) 1–78; M. Dahood, *Psalms*, 2.130–152; Miller, *The Divine Warrior*, 102–113.

[131]May, "Cosmic Connotations of *Mayim Rabbîm*," 11–12.

[132]See Cross, *Canaanite Myth and Hebrew Epic*, 147–194.

[133]Jeremias, *Theophanie*, 43–44.

[134]Together with such scholars as C. Westermann (93–101), G. von Rad ("The Origin of the Day of Yahweh") and F. M. Cross (*Canaanite Myth and Hebrew Epic*, 99–105); and against such scholars as S. Mowinckel (*The Psalms in Israel's Worship* [1967] 1.142–143) and A. Weiser (*The Psalms* [1962] 23–35).

[135]J. Wellhausen, *Prolegomena to the History of Ancient Israel* (1957) 434.

[136]Miller, *The Divine Warrior*, 170–173.

Notes to Chapter 4

[1]Those who now accept the unity of Habakkuk include P. Humbert (*Problèmes du livre d'Habacuc* [1944]), W. F. Albright ("The Psalm of Habakkuk" [1950]), S. Mowinckel ("Zum Psalm des Habakuk" [1953]), J. H. Eaton ("The Origin and Meaning of Habakkuk 3" [1964]), B. Margulis ("The Psalm of Habakkuk: A Reconstruction and Interpretation" [1970]), and W. Rudolph (*Micha, Nahum, Habakuk, Zephanja* [1975]). Those who once questioned Habakkuk's authorship of Chapter 3 include J. Wellhausen (*Die Kleinen Propheten* [1898]), A. B. Davidson (*The Books of Nahum, Habakkuk, and Zephaniah* [1899]), K. Marti, *Dodekapropheten* [1903]), W. Nowack (*Die Kleinen Propheten* [1903]), S. R. Driver (*The Minor Prophets II* [1906]), and G. G. V. Stonehouse (*The Book of Habakkuk* [1911]).

[2]Eaton, 166.

[3]See the arguments and examples advanced by A. Weiser (*The Psalms* [1962] 94–99), S. Mowinckel (*The Psalms in Israel's Worship* [1967] 2.95–99), J. J. Glueck ("Some Remarks on the Introductory Notes of the Psalms" [1963] 30), and B. S. Childs ("Psalm Titles and Midrashic Exegesis" [1971] 137–150). The LXX contains more titles than the MT and the Syriac Psalms have none of the MT or LXX headings but entirely different ones (W. Bloe-

mendaal, *The Headings of the Psalms in the East Syrian Church* [1960]).

[4]Childs, 137. See also the studies by H. M. I. Gevaryahu ("Biblical Colophons: A Source for the 'Biography' of Authors, Texts, and Books" [1975]) and Elieser Slomovic ("Toward an Understanding of the Formation of Historical Titles in the Book of Psalms" [1979]).

[5]F. M. Cross, *Canaanite Myth and Hebrew Epic* (1973) 125.

[6]On Isaiah 13, see O. Kaiser (*Isaiah 13–39* [1974] 1–23). Additional author titles like the ones in Isaiah 13 and Habakkuk 3 may have been added to certain compositions within a prophetic corpus specifically because there was some question about the authenticity of these works. On Jeremiah 46 and the chapters that follow, see J. Bright (*Jeremiah* [1965] 307). Though the opinion is popular again that the Psalm of Jonah comes from the hand of the author of the book (see J. S. Ackerman's recent article "Satire and Symbolism in the Song of Jonah" [1981] and the works he cites in n. 1 on p. 214), there is evidence that the poem contains archaic material (see F. M. Cross, "Studies in the Structure of Hebrew Verse: The Prosody of the Psalm of Jonah" [1983]).

[7]Those who believe the cultic character of Chapter 3 reflects the work of a cult prophet responsible for the entire book of Habakkuk include Humbert, Mowinckel, Eaton, and Margulis. Cf. Albright.

[8]The suffix on *bingînôt* is unreliable. It varies in the versions—1cs in MT, 3ms in LXX, OL, and Syriac, and absent in Vg—and is found in none of the seven occurrences of this term in the psalm titles (Psalms 4, 6, 54, 55, 61, 67, 76). It should be omitted.

[9]C. A. Briggs, *The Book of Psalms* (1914) 1., lxxii f.; Glueck, 31–32; Driver, 91; H.-J. Kraus, *Psalmen* (1972) 1.xxvii. Given this evidence, there is no reason for adopting Mowinckel's alternate proposal "to make shine," i.e. to make Yahweh's face shine, to dispose him to mercy (*The Psalms*, 2.212–213).

[10]Weiser, 22; Mowinckel, *The Psalms*, 2.211; Briggs, 1. lxxxiv f.; F. Delitzsch, *The Psalms* (1873) 1.3. R. Sorg's attempt to make sense of *selâ* in Habakkuk 3 seems completely unconvincing to me (*Habaquq 3 and Selah* [1969]).

[11]Humbert, 204–245.

[12]Humbert, 28–29.

[13]See W. L. Moran, "New Evidence from Mari on the History of Prophecy" (1969); H. B. Huffmon, "The Origins of Prophecy" (1976); and A. R. Johnson, *The Cultic Prophet in Ancient Israel* (1962).

[14]Humbert's analysis of the vocabulary of Habakkuk is found on pp. 80–289. Pp. 204–245 contain his analysis of Chapter 3 in particular. His conclusions for Chapter 3 are pulled together on pp. 240–245.

[15]See Chap. 3; Cross, *Canaanite Myth and Hebrew Epic*, 147–194; P. Hanson, *The Dawn of Apocalyptic* (1975) 300–316.

[16]Wellhausen, 170; Nowack, 269–270; Marti, 327, 348f.; Driver, 99; Davidson, 60; Stonehouse, 125.

[17]Vv 14 and 17 are not to be understood as descriptions of devastations of Israel by the enemy. V 14 is too corrupt to understand clearly. It probably has to do with the scattering of God's enemy (the dragon's carcass) rather than Israel. And v 17 is to be related to nature's blanching at Yahweh's theophany, not to the results of a Babylonian invasion. See Chapter 3 for further treatment of these verses.

[18]Driver, 59–60.

[19]Hanson, *The Dawn of Apocalyptic*. See also his essays on the subject: "Jewish Apocalyptic Against its Near Eastern Environment" (1971); "Zechariah 9 and the Recapitulation of an Ancient Ritual Pattern" (1973); "Apocalypse" and "Apocalypticism" in *IDBSup* (1976) 27–34.

[20]Hanson, *The Dawn of Apocalyptic*, 124.

[21]Cf. Isaiah 34–35 and 24:1–25:8.

[22]The suggestion that the early apocalyptic era should be the place to look for the redactional activity that brought Habakkuk 3 together with the rest of the Habakkuk corpus was first made to me by F. M. Cross.

[23]U. Cassuto, "Chapter iii of Habakkuk and the Ras Shamra Texts" (1975) 5–7. Psalm 74:12–15 (past) and Isa 27:1 (future) are examples Cassuto cites.

[24]H. Gunkel, *Schöpfung und Chaos in Urzeit und Endzeit* (1895).

[25]Cross, *Canaanite Myth and Hebrew Epic*, 343–346, 91–111, and 147–194.

[26]J. Jeremias, "Theophany in the O. T." (1976) 896–898. Compare the comments of G. Henton Davies ("Theophany" [1962] 619–620).

[27]G. von Rad, "The Origin of the Concept of the Day of Yahweh" (1959) 97–108.

[28]See Chap. 2.

[29]Cross, *Canaanite Myth and Hebrew Epic*, 170.

[30]Hanson, *The Dawn of Apocalyptic*, 129, 316–320; "Zechariah 9."

[31]B. S. Childs, *Introduction to the Old Testament as Scripture* (1979) 517; see 515–518.

[32]See Chap. 3.

[33]See the discussions of Mowinckel (*The Psalms*, 2.79–81, 207–211) and Glueck.

[34]B. Bayer, "The Finds That Could Not Be" (1982); cf. W. F. Albright, *Archaeology and the Religion of Israel* (1942) 125–129; and O. R. Sellers, "Musical Instruments of Israel" (1941) 33–47.

[35]Gevaryahu, 42–59. Cf. Lienhard Delekat, "Probleme der Psalmenüberschriften" (1964) 288.

[36]H. Wolff, *Hosea* (1974) 3–4.

[37]The single occurrence of *maśśā'* in Ezekiel (12:10, not a superscription) is dubious (cf. LXX). The use of *maśśā'* in Jeremiah (only 23:33–38, not a superscription) is part of a late expansionistic section. Only the use in v 33 may be original (Bright, 153–155; G. P. Couturier, "Jeremiah" (1968) 322). I follow P. Hanson in identifying Malachi as a block of tradition, like Zechariah 9–11 and 12–14, originally considered part of the book of Zechariah (*The Dawn of Apocalyptic*, 292–293).

[38]*ḥāzâ* is used in Amos 1:1 as well. It is, however, part of an overloaded superscription there and may have been one of several later additions to the title of the book (H. W. Wolff, *Joel and Amos* (1977) 117–118).

[39]Wellhausen, Marti, Nowack, Driver.

[40]Gevaryahu, 42–59. Cf. Childs, "Biblical Titles," and Slomovic.

[41]The concluding element in the title, *'al šigyōnôt*, is obscure. In the first place, the reading is in doubt. The term is omitted in the Syriac (and consequently by the editors of the *NEB*). The LXX has *meta ǭdēs*, employing the same term here as the one

used for *nĕgînôt* at the conclusion of the poem (v 19). Was *nĕgînôt* in both places in the *Vorlage* of the LXX? Even if one accepts the reading of the MT as original, the problem is hardly resolved, since the term occurs only once elsewhere (Ps 7:1, singular and without *ʿal*). Thus both the actual reading and the meaning of the MT are uncertain. None of the alternate readings or interpretations of *šigyōnôt* which have been suggested would be incompatible with the thesis that the title was added by the postexilic editors of Habakkuk. If *šigyōnôt* (or *nĕgînôt*) represents some kind of musical notation (Briggs. 1.lxvii: Driver. 86), it could have originated when Habakkuk 3 was part of a collection of psalms. The rest of the title then would have been added by the postexilic editors. If *šigyōnôt* is to be related to the Akk. *šegû*, "lament" (Humbert, 25; Mowinckel, "Psalm des Habakuk," 7), it would not be incompatible with the intention of *tĕpillâ*. If *šigyōnôt* is to be derived from *šāgâ* to mean "the ignorant, wicked" (Tg, Vg, Aq, Sym), as I think less likely, the phrase "concerning the ignorant, wicked" could refer to the postexilic adversaries of the editors. Given the scanty evidence to go on, the origin of the term and the period of its inclusion in the title of Habakkuk 3 is best left undecided.

[42]See Chap. 1: cf. the Targum at Hab 3:16a.

[43]See Chap. 1.

[44]See S. Levey's suggestion about the specific setting reflected in the translation of this verse (*The Messiah: An Aramaic Interpretation* 1974 95–96).

[45]M. L Margolis. "The Character of the Anonymous Greek Version of Habakkuk, Chapter 3" (1907) 135.

BIBLIOGRAPHY

Abel, F. M. *Géographie de la Palestine*, II. Paris: Librairie Lecoffre, J. Gabalda, 1938.

Ackerman, James S. "Satire and Symbolism in the Song of Jonah." In *Traditions in Transformation*, edited by Baruch Halpern and Jon D. Levenson, pp. 213–246. Winona Lake, Ind.: Eisenbrauns, 1981.

Aharoni, Y. "Arad." In *The Encyclopedia of Archaeological Excavations in the Holy Land*, edited by Michael Avi-Yonah, vol. 1. Englewood Cliffs, N.J.: Prentice-Hall, 1975.

————. "Arad: Its Inscriptions and Temple." *BA* 31 (1968) 2–32.

————. *The Archaeology of the Land of Israel*. Philadelphia: Westminster, 1978.

————. *The Land of the Bible: A Historical Geography*. Philadelphia: Westminster, 1967.

Albright, W. F. *Archaeology and the Religion of Israel*. Baltimore: Johns Hopkins, 1942.

————. "A Catalogue of Early Hebrew Lyric Poems (Psalm LXVIII)." *HUCA* 23 (1950–51) 1–39.

————. "The Egypto-Canaanite Deity Ḥaurôn." *BASOR* 84 (1941) 7–12.

————. "The Furniture of El in Canaanite Mythology." *BASOR* 91 (1943) 39–44.

————. "The Historical Background of Genesis XIV." *Journal of the Society of Oriental Research* 10 (1926) 231–269.

———. "The Land of Damascus between 1850 and 1750 B.C." *BASOR* 83 (1941) 30–36.

———. "Midianite Donkey Caravans." In *Translating and Understanding the Old Testament*, edited by Harry Frank and Wm. Reed, pp. 197–205. Nashville: Abingdon, 1970.

———. "More Light on the Canaanite Epic of Aleyân Baal and Môt." *BASOR* 50 (1933) 13–20.

———. "The Oldest Forms of Hebrew Verse." *JPOS* 2 (1922) 69–86.

———. "The Old Testament and Canaanite Language and Literature." *CBQ* 7 (1945) 5–31.

———. "The Psalm of Habakkuk." In *Studies in Old Testament Prophecy*, edited by H. H. Rowley, pp. 1–18. Edinburgh: T. & T. Clark, 1950.

———. "The Song of Deborah in the Light of Archaeology." *BASOR* 62 (1936) 26–31.

———. "Two Letters from Ugarit (Ras Shamrah)." *BASOR* 82 (1941) 43–49.

———. *Yahweh and the Gods of Canaan*. Garden City, N.Y.: Doubleday, 1968.

Anderson, Bernhard W. *Creation versus Chaos: The Reinterpretation of Mythical Symbolism in the Bible*. New York: Association, 1967.

Arnold, William R. "The Interpretation of *qrnym mydw lw*, Hab 3:4." *AJSL* 21 (1905) 167–172.

Astour, M. C. "Yahwe." In *IDBSup*, p. 971.

———. "Yahwe in Egyptian Topographic Lists." In *Festschrift Elmar Edel* (Band 1, in *Agypten und Altes Testament*), edited by Manfred Gorg, pp. 17–33. Bamberg: Kurt Urlaub, 1979.

Baars, W. "A New Witness to the Text of the Barberini Greek Version of Habakkuk III." *VT* 15 (1965) 381–382.

Bar-Deroma, H. "Kadesh-Barne'a." *PEQ* 96 (1964) 101–134.

Barrick, W. Boyd. "The Meaning and Usage of RKB in Biblical Hebrew." *JBL* 101 (1982) 481–503.

Barthélemy, Dominique. *Les Devanciers d'Aquila.* VTSup, vol. 10. Leiden: E. J. Brill, 1963.

Bartlett, J. R. "The Rise and Fall of the Kingdom of Edom." *PEQ* 104 (1972) 26–37.

Bayer, Bathja. "The Finds That Could Not Be." *BAR* 8 (1982) 20–33.

Beit-Arieh, Itzhaq. "Sinai Survey 1978–9." *IEJ* 29 (1979) 256–257.

Bennett, C.-M. "Edom." In *IDBSup*, pp. 251–252

————. "Ṭawilân (Jordanie)." *RB* 76 (1969) 389–390.

————. "Ṭawilân (Jordanie)." *RB* 77 (1970) 371–374.

Benoit, P; Milik, J. T.; and Vaux, R. de. eds. *Discoveries in the Judean Desert II: (Les Grottes de Murabba'ât).* Oxford: Clarendon, 1961.

Bernhardt, K.-H. "Pharan." In *BHH*, p. 1445.

Bévenot, D. H. "Le Cantique d'Habacuc." *RB* 42 (1933) 499–525.

Blackman, A. M., and Fairman, H. W. "The Myth of Horus at Edfu-II." *JEA* 30 (1944) 5–22.

Blenkinsopp, Joseph. "Ballad Style and Psalm Style in the Song of Deborah: A Discussion." *Bib* 42 (1961) 64–75.

Bloemendaal, W. *The Headings of the Psalms in the East Syrian Church*. Leiden: E. J. Brill, 1960.

Boadt, Lawrence. *Ezekiel's Oracles against Egypt: A Literary and Philological Study of Ezekiel 29–32*. Rome: Biblical Institute, 1980.

Boling, Robert G. *Judges*. AB. Garden City, N.Y.: Doubleday, 1975.

Briggs, C. A., and Briggs, E. G. *The Book of Psalms*. ICC. New York: Scribner's, 1914.

Bright, John. *Jeremiah*. AB. Garden City, N.Y.: Doubleday, 1965.

Brockington, L. H., ed. *The Hebrew Text of the Old Testament: The Readings adopted by the translators of the New English Bible*. Oxford: Oxford University, 1973.

Brownlee, William H. *The Midrash Pesher of Habakkuk*. Missoula, Mont.: Scholars, 1979.

Burney, C. F. *The Book of Judges*. 1918. Reprint. New York: Ktav, 1970.

Caquot, A. "Sur quelques démons de l'Ancien Testament: Reshep, Qeṭeb, Deber." *Sem* 6 (1956) 53–68.

Cassuto, U. "Chapter iii of Habakkuk and the Ras Shamra Texts." 1935–37. Reprint in *Biblical and Oriental Studies*, translated by Israel Abrahams, pp. 3–15. Jerusalem: Magnes, 1975.

Cheyne, T. K. "An appeal for a more complete criticism of the book of Habakkuk." *JQR* (NS) 16 (1908) 3–30.

Childs, Brevard S. *Introduction to the Old Testament as Scripture*. Philadelphia: Fortress, 1979.

———. "Psalm Titles and Midrashic Exegesis." *JSS* 16 (1971) 137–150.

Christiansen, D. L. *Transformation of the War Oracle in Old Testament Prophecy*. Missoula, Mont.: Scholars, 1975.

Churgin, Pinkhos. *Targum Jonathan to the Prophets*. New Haven: Yale University, 1928.

Clifford, Richard J. *The Cosmic Mountain in Canaan and the Old Testament*. Cambridge: Harvard University, 1972.

Cohen, Rudolph. "Did I Excavate Kadesh-Barnea?" *BAR* 7 (1981) 20–33.

Cohen, S. "Edom." In *IDB*, vol. 2, pp. 24–26.

Condamin, Albert. "La forme chorale du ch. III d'Habacuc." *RB* 8 (1898) 133–140.

———. *Poèmes de la Bible*. Paris: Gabriel Beauchesne, 1933.

Coogan, Michael David. Review of *The Canaanite God Rešep*, by William J. Fulco. *JBL* 97 (1978) 111.

———. "A Structural and Literary Analysis of the Song of Deborah." *CBQ* 40 (1978) 143–166.

Couturier, Guy P. "Jeremiah." In *JBC*, pp. 300–336.

Craigie, P. C. "Some Further Notes on the Song of Deborah." *VT* 22 (1972) 349–353.

———. "The Song of Deborah and the Epic of Tukulti-Ninurta." *JBL* 88 (1969) 253–265.

Croatto, José S., and Soggin, J. Alberto. "Die Bedeutung von *šdmwt* im Alten Testament." *ZAW* 74 (1962) 44–50.

Cross, Frank Moore. *Canaanite Myth and Hebrew Epic*. Cambridge: Harvard University, 1973.

———. "The Epic Traditions of Early Israel: Epic Narrative and the Reconstruction of Early Israelite Institutions." In *The Poet and the Historian*, edited by Richard Elliott Friedman, pp. 13–39. Chico, Calif.: Scholars, 1983.

———. "An Interpretation of the Nora Stone." *BASOR* 208 (1972) 13–19.

———. "Notes on a Canaanite Psalm in the Old Testament." *BASOR* 117 (1950) 19–21.

———. "Prose and Poetry in the Mythic and Epic Texts from Ugarit." *HTR* 67 (1974) 1–15.

———. "Studies in the Structure of Hebrew Verse: The Prosody of the Psalm of Jonah." In *The Quest for the Kingdom of God*, edited by H. B. Huffmon, F. A. Spina, and A. R. W. Green, pp. 159–167. Winona Lake, Ind.: Eisenbrauns. 1983.

Cross, Frank Moore, and Freedman, David Noel. *Early Hebrew Orthography*. New Haven: American Oriental Society, 1952.

———. *Studies in Ancient Yahwistic Poetry*. 1950. Reprint. Missoula, Mont.: Scholars, 1975.

Cully, R. C. "Metrical Analysis of Classical Hebrew Poetry." In *Essays on the Ancient Semitic World*, edited by J. W. Wevers and D. B. Redford, pp. 12–28. Toronto: University of Toronto, 1970.

Dahood, Mitchell. "Afterward" to *The Archives of Ebla*, by Giovanni Pettinato. Garden City, N.Y.: Doubleday, 1981.

———. "Ancient Semitic Deities in Syria and Palestine." In *Le Antiche Divintà Semitiche*, edited by Sabatino Moscati, pp. 65–94. Rome: Centro de Studi Semitici, Universita di Roma, 1958.

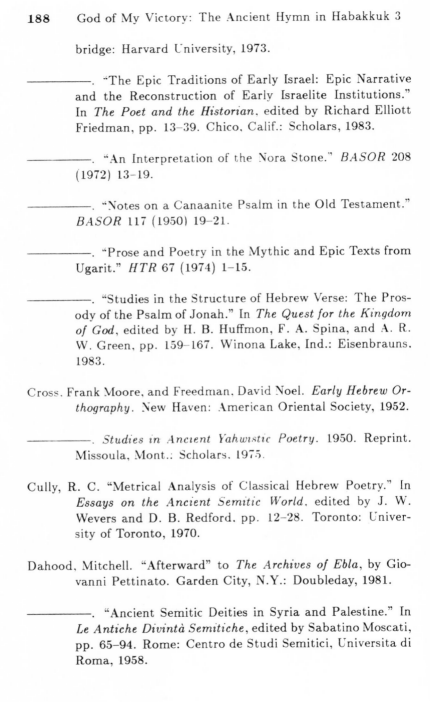

———. "MIŠMĀR, 'Muzzle' in Job 7:12." *JBL* 80 (1961) 270–271.

———. "Poetry, Hebrew." In *IDBSup*, pp. 669–672.

———. *Psalms*. AB. 3 vols. Garden City, N.Y.: Doubleday, 1966–1970.

———. *Ugaritic-Hebrew Philology*. Rome: Pontifical Biblical Institute,1965.

———. "Ugaritic Lexicography." In *Mélanges Eugène Tisserant I*, pp. 81–104. 1964.

Dahood, Mitchell, with the collaboration of Tadeusz Penar. "Ugaritic-Hebrew Parallel Pairs." In *Ras Shamra Parallels*, edited by Loren R. Fisher, vol. 1, pp. 71–382; vol. 2, pp. 1–39. Rome: Pontifical Biblical Institute, 1972, 1975.

Davidson, A. B. *The Books of Nahum, Habakkuk and Zephaniah with Introduction and Notes*. Cambridge: Cambridge University, 1899.

Davies, G. Henton. "Theophany." In *IDB*, vol. 4, pp. 619–620.

Day, John. "Echoes of Baal's Seven Thunders and Lightnings in Psalm XXIX and Habakkuk III 9 and the Identity of the Seraphim in Isaiah VI." *VT* 29 (1979) 143–151.

———. "New Light on the Mythological Background of the Allusion to Resheph in Habakkuk III 5." *VT* 29 (1979) 353–354.

Delcor, Mathias. "La geste de Yahvé au temps de l'Exode et l'espérance du psalmiste en Habacuc iii." In *Miscellanea Biblica B. Ubach*, edited by Romualdo M. Díaz, pp. 9–16. Barcelona: Casa Provincial de Caridad, Imprenta-Escula, 1954.

Delekat, Lienhard. "Probleme der Psalmenüberschriften." *ZAW*

76 (1964) 280–297.

———. "Zum Hebräischen Wörterbuch." *VT* 14 (1964) 7–66.

Delitzsch, Franz. *Der Prophet Habakuk*. Leipzig: Karl Tauchnitz, 1843.

———. *The Psalms*. 3 vols. Edinburgh: T. & T. Clark, 1873.

Driver, G. R. *Canaanite Myths and Legends*. 2d ed., rev. by J. C. L. Gibson. Edinburgh: T. & T. Clark, 1978.

———. "Critical Note on Habakkuk 3.7." *JBL* 62 (1943) 121.

———. "Hebrew Notes." *ZAW* 52 (1934) 51–56.

———. "Hebrew Notes." *VT* 1 (1951) 241–250.

———. "Linguistic and Textual Problems: Minor Prophets. III." *JTS* 39 (1938) 393–405.

———. "Studies in the Vocabulary of the Old Testament VI." *JTS* 34 (1933) 375–385.

Driver, S. R. *Introduction to the Literature of the Old Testament*. New York: Scribner's, 1914.

———. *The Minor Prophets, II. Nahum, Habakkuk, Zephaniah, Haggai, Zechariah, Malachi*. Edinburgh: T. C. & E. C. Jack, 1906.

Duhm, Bernhard. *Das Buch Habakuk*. Tübingen: J. C. B. Mohr (Paul Siebeck), 1906.

Dumbrell, William J. "Midian—A Land or a League." *VT* 25 (1975) 323–337.

———. "The Midianites and Their Transjordanian Successors." Th.D. dissertation, Harvard University, 1970.

Eaton, J. H. *Obadiah, Nahum, Habakkuk and Zephaniah*. London: SCM, 1961.

————. "The Origin and Meaning of Habakkuk 3." *ZAW* 76 (1964) 144–171.

Eissfeldt, Otto. *The Old Testament: An Introduction*. New York: Harper & Row, 1965.

————. "Protektorat der Midianiter über ihrer Nachbarn im lezten Viertel des 2. Jahrtausends v. Chr." *JBL* 87 (1968) 383–393.

Emerton, J.A. "New Light on Israelite Religion: The Implications of the Inscriptions from Kuntillet 'Ajrud." *ZAW* 94 (1982) 2–21.

Erman, Adolf. *Die Religion der Ägypter*. Berlin: Walter de Gruyter, 1934.

Faulkner, R. O. "The Bremner-Rhind Papyrus: The Book of Overthrowing 'APEP." *JEA* 23 (1937) 166–185; 24 (1938) 41–53.

Fisher, L. R., and Knutson, F. B. "An Enthronement Ritual at Ugarit." *JNES* 28 (1969) 157–167.

Fitzgerald, Aloysius. "Hebrew Poetry." In *JBC*, pp. 238–244.

Freedman, David Noel. "Divine Names and Titles in Early Hebrew Poetry." In *Magnalia Dei: The Mighty Acts of God*, edited by Frank Moore Cross, Werner E. Lemke, and Patrick D. Miller, pp. 55–105. Garden City, N.Y.: Doubleday, 1976.

————. "The Name of the God of Moses." *JBL* 79 (1960) 151–156.

————. *Pottery, Poetry, and Prophecy: studies in early Hebrew poetry*. Winona Lake, Ind.: Eisenbrauns, 1980.

———. Prolegomenon to *The Forms of Hebrew Poetry*, by G. B. Gray. New York: Ktav, 1972.

Fulco, William J. *The Canaanite God Rešep*. New Haven: American Oriental Society, 1976.

Gaster, Theodor H. "An Ancient Eulogy on Israel: Deuteronomy 33:3–5, 26–29." *JBL* 66 (1947) 53–62.

———. "The Battle of the Rain and the Sea." *Iraq* 4 (1937) 21–32.

———. "On Habakkuk 3.4." *JBL* 62 (1943) 345–346.

Geller, Stephen A. *Parallelism in Early Biblical Poetry*. Missoula, Mont.: Scholars, 1979.

Gevaryahu, H. M. I. "Biblical Colophons: A Source for the 'Biography' of Authors, Texts, and Books." VTSup 28 (1975) 42–59.

Ginsberg, H. L. "Lexicographical Notes." *ZAW* 51 (1933) 308.

———. "The Rebellion and Death of Ba'lu." *Or* 5 (1936) 161–198.

Giveon, Raphael. *Les Bedoins Shosou des documents égyptiens*. Leiden: E. J. Brill. 1971.

———. "The Cities of Our God (2 Samuel 10:12)." *JBL* 83 (1964) 415–416.

———. "Toponymes ouest-asiatiques à Soleb." *VT* 14 (1964) 239–255.

Glueck, J. J. "Some Remarks on the Introductory Notes of the Psalms." In *Studies on the Psalms*, Papers read at the 6th Meeting of Die O. T. Werkgemeenskap in Suid-Afrika. Potchefstroom, South Africa: Pro Rege-Pers Beperk. 1963.

Glueck, Nelson. *Explorations in Eastern Palestine, II*. AASOR, vol. 15. New Haven: American Schools of Oriental Research, 1935.

Gold, V. R. "Seir." In *IDB*, vol. 4, p. 262.

———. "Teman." In *IDB*, vol. 4, pp. 533–534.

Good, Edwin M. "The Barberini Greek Version of Habakkuk III." *VT* 9 (1959) 11–30.

———. "The Text and Versions of Habakkuk 3: a study in textual history." Ph.D. dissertation, Columbia University, 1958.

Gordon, Cyrus H. *Ugaritic Textbook*. Rome: Pontifical Biblical Institute, 1965.

Gressmann, Hugo. *Altorientalische Bilder zum Alten Testament*. Berlin: Walter de Gruyter, 1927.

———. "Bemerkungen des Herausgebers: Wichtige Zeitschriftenaufsätze." *ZAW* 1 (1924) 353–365.

Gunkel, Hermann. *The Psalms: A Form-Critical Introduction*. 1930. Reprint. Philadelphia: Fortress, 1967.

———. *Schöpfung und Chaos in Urzeit und Endzeit*. Gottingen: Vandenhoeck & Ruprecht, 1895.

Hackett, Jo Ann. *The Balaam Text from Deir 'Allā*. Chico, California: Scholars, 1984.

Halpern, Baruch. *The Constitution of the Monarchy in Israel*. Chico, California: Scholars, 1981.

Hanson, Paul D. "Apocalypse, Genre." In *IDBSup*, pp. 27–28.

———. "Apocalypticism." In *IDBSup*, pp. 28–34.

————. *The Dawn of Apocalyptic*. Philadelphia: Fortress, 1975.

————. "Jewish Apocalyptic Against its Near Eastern Environment." *RB* 78 (1971) 31–58.

————. "The Song of Heshbon and David's *nîr*." *HTR* 61 (1968) 297–320.

————. "Zechariah 9 and the Recapitulation of an Ancient Ritual Pattern." *JBL* 92 (1973) 37–59.

Hehn, Johannes. *Hymnen und Gebete an Marduk*. Leipzig: J. C. Hinrichesche Buchhandlung, 1905.

Held, Moshe. "*mḫṣ/*mḫš* in Ugaritic and other Semitic Languages." *JAOS* 79 (1959) 169–176.

Herdner, Andrée. *Corpus des tablettes en cunéiformes alphabétiques*. Paris: Imprimerie Nationale, 1963.

Holladay, John S., Jr. "The Day(s) the Moon Stood Still." *JBL* 87 (1968) 166–178.

Horst, Friedrich. "Nahum bis Malachi." In *Die Zwölf Kleinen Propheten*, by T. H. Robinson. 1938. Reprint. Tübingen: Mohr, 1954.

Housman, A.E. *Selected Prose*. Cambridge: Cambridge University, 1962.

Huffmon, H. B. "The Origins of Prophecy." In *Magnalia Dei: The Mighty Acts of God*, edited by Frank Moore Cross, Werner E. Lemke, and Patrick D. Miller, pp. 171–186. Garden City, N.Y.: Doubleday, 1976.

Humbert, Paul. *Problèmes du livre d'Habacuc*. Neuchâtel: Secrétariat de l'Université, 1944.

Irwin, William A. "The Mythological Background of Habakkuk.

Chapter 3." *JNES* 15 (1956) 47–50.

————. "The Psalm of Habakkuk." *JNES* 1 (1942) 10–40.

Jacobsen, Thorkild. *The Treasures of Darkness*. New Haven: Yale University, 1976.

Jefferson, Helen Genevieve. "Is Psalm 110 Canaanite?" *JBL* 73 (1954) 152–156.

Jenni, E. "'Komen' in theologischen Sprachgebrauch des Alten Testaments." In *Wort-Gebot-Glaube*, edited by J. J. Stamm and E. Jenni, pp. 251–261. Zurich: Zwingli, 1970.

Jeremias, Jörg. *Theophanie*. Neukirchen-Vluyn: Neukirchener, 1965.

————. "Theophany in the OT." In *IDBSup*, pp. 896–898.

Jöcken, Peter. *Das Buch Habakuk*. Koln-Bonn: Peter Hanstein, 1977.

Johnson, Aubrey R. *The Cultic Prophet in Ancient Israel*. 2nd ed. Cardiff: University of Wales, 1962.

Kaiser, Otto. *Isaiah 13–39*. Philadelphia: Westminster, 1974.

Keller, Carl-A. *Nahoum. Habacuc. Sophonie*. CAT XI B. Neuchâtel, Switzerland: Delachaux & Niestlé, 1971.

Kelley, Fred T. "The Strophic Structure of Habakkuk." *AJSL* 18 (1901–2) 94–119.

Knauf, Ernst A. "Midianities and Ishmaelites." In *Midian, Moab, and Edom*, edited by John F. A. Sawyer and David J. A. Clines, pp. 147–162. Sheffield: Journal for the Study of the Old Testament, 1983.

Kundtzon, J. A., ed. *Die El-Amarna-Tafeln*. Leipzig: J. C. Hinrichs, 1915. Reprint. Aalen: Otto Zeller, 1964.

Kraeling, Emil G. *Rand McNally Bible Atlas*. New York: Rand McNally, 1956.

Kraft, C. F. "Some Further Observations Concerning the Strophic Structure of Hebrew Poetry." In *A Stubborn Faith*, edited by E. C. Hobbs. Dallas: Southern Methodist University, 1956.

———. *The Strophic Structure of Hebrew Poetry*. Chicago: University of Chicago, 1938.

Kraus, Hans-Joachim. *Psalmen*. BKAT. 2 vols. Neukirchen-Vluyn: Neukirchener, 1972.

Kuenen, Abraham. *The Prophets and Prophecy in Israel*. London: Longmans, Green, 1877.

Kugel, James L. *The Idea of Biblical Poetry: Parallelism and its History*. New Haven: Yale University, 1981.

Lachmann, Johann. *Das Buch Habbakuk*. Aussig: Selbstverlag des Verfassers, 1932.

Landes, G. M. "Midian." In *IDB*, vol. 3 pp. 375–376.

Landsberger, F. "Poetic Units within the Song of Songs." *JBL* 73 (1954) 203–216.

Larôche, E. "Notes sur le panthéon hourrite de Ras Shamra." *JAOS* 88 (1969) 150.

Lehmann, Manfred R. "A New Interpretation of the term *šdmwt*." *VT* 3 (1954) 361–371.

Levey, Samson H. *The Messiah: An Aramaic Interpretation*. Cincinnati: Hebrew Union College, 1974.

Lewy, J. "The Late Assyro-Babylonian Cult of the Moon and its Culmination at the Time of Nabonidus." *HUCA* 19 (1945–46) 405–489.

Liebreich, L. J. "The Compilation of the Book of Isaiah." *JQR* 46 (1956) 259–277; 47 (1956) 114–138.

———. "Psalms 34 and 145 in Light of Their Key Words." *HUCA* 27 (1956) 181–192.

Lind, Millard C. *Yahweh is a Warrior*. Scottdale, Penn.: Herald, 1980.

Loewenstamm, Samuel E. "The Killing of Mot in Ugaritic Myth." *Or* 41 (1972) 378–382.

———. "The Muzzling of Tannin in Ugaritic Myth." *IEJ* 9 (1959) 260–261.

Lohfink, N. *Lectures in Deuteronomy*. Rome: Pontifical Biblical Institute, 1968.

Lundbom, J. R. *Jeremiah: A Study in Ancient Hebrew Rhetoric*. Missoula, Mont.: Scholars, 1975.

McCarter, P. Kyle. *I Samuel*. AB. Garden City, N.Y.: Doubleday, 1980.

Margolis, Max L. "The Character of the Anonymous Greek Version of Habakkuk, Chapter 3." 1907. Reprint in *Old Testament and Semitic Studies*, edited by R. F. Harper, F. Brown, and G. F. Moore, pp. 133–142. Chicago: University of Chicago, 1908.

Margulis, Baruch. "The Psalm of Habakkuk: A Reconstruction and Interpretation." *ZAW* 82 (1970) 409–441.

Marti, Karl. *Dodekapropheton*. Tübingen: J. C. B. Mohr, 1903.

May, Herbert G., ed. *Oxford Bible Atlas*. London: Oxford University, 1962.

———. "Some Cosmic Connotations of *Mayim Rabbîm* 'Many Waters.'" *JBL* 74 (1955) 9–21.

Mazar, Benjamin. "The Sanctuary of Arad and the Family of Hobab the Kenite." *JNES* 24 (1965) 297–303.

————. "Yahweh came out from Sinai." In *Temples and High Places in Biblical Times*, edited by Avraham Biran, pp. 5–9. Jerusalem: The Nelson Glueck School of Biblical Archaeology of Hebrew Union College—Jewish Institute of Religion, 1981.

Meshel, Ze'ev. "Did Yahweh Have a Consort?" *BAR* 5 (1979) 24–35.

————. *Kuntillet 'Ajrud: A Religious Centre from the Time of the Judaean Monarchy on the Border of Sinai*. Israel Museum Catalog no. 175. Jerusalem: Spertus Hall, 1978.

————. "A Religious Center at Kuntillet-Ajrud, Sinai." In *Temples and High Places in Biblical Times*, edited by Avraham Biran, p. 161. Jerusalem: The Nelson Glueck School of Biblical Archaeology of Hebrew Union College—Jewish Institute of Religion, 1981.

Meshel, Ze'ev, and Meyers, Carol. "The Name of God in the Wilderness of Zin." *BA* 39 (1976) 6–10.

Mihelic, J. L. "Paran." In *IDB*, vol. 3, p. 657.

Milik, J. T. "'Prière de Nabonide' et autres écrits d'un cycle de Daniel, fragments de Qumran 4." *RB* 63 (1956) 407–15.

Miller, Patrick D., Jr. *The Divine Warrior in Early Israel*. Cambridge: Harvard University, 1973.

————. "El the Warrior." *HTR* 60 (1967) 411–431.

————. "Two Critical Notes on Psalm 68 and Deuteronomy 33." *HTR* 57 (1964) 240–243.

Möller, H. "Strophenbau der Psalmen." *ZAW* 50 (1932) 240–256.

Montgomery, J. A. *The Books of Kings*. ICC. New York: Scribner's, 1951.

————. "Stanza-Formation in Hebrew Poetry." *JBL* 64 (1945) 379–384.

Moor, J. C. de. Review of *The Violent Goddess*, by Arvid S. Kapelrud. *UF* 1 (1969) 223–227.

Moran, W. L. "Deuteronomy." In *A New Catholic Commentary on Holy Scripture*, edited by R. C. Fuller, pp. 256–276. London: Nelson, 1969.

————. "New Evidence from Mari on the History of Prophecy." *Bib* 50 (1969) 15–56.

————. "Some Remarks on the Song of Moses." *Bib* 43 (1962) 317–327.

Moulton, R. G. *The Literary Study of the Bible*. Boston: Heath, 1899.

Mowinckel, Sigmund. *Der achtundsechzigste Psalm*. Oslo: I Kommisjon Jacob Dybwad, 1953.

————. "Drive and or Ride in the OT." *VT* 12 (1962) 278–299.

————. *The Psalms in Israel's Worship*. 2 vols. New York: Abingdon, 1967.

————. *Real and Apparent Tricola in Hebrew Psalm Poetry*. Oslo: I Kommisjon Hos H. Aschehoug (W. Nygaard), 1957.

————. "Zum Psalm des Habakuk." *TZ* 9 (1953) 1–23.

Muilenburg, James. "Form Criticism and Beyond." *JBL* 88 (1969) 1–18.

———. "A Study in Hebrew Rhetoric: Repetition and Style." *VT* 1 (1953) 97–111.

Musil, Alois. *The Northern Hedjaz*. New York: Czech academy of sciences and arts & Charles R. Crane, 1926.

North, Christopher. *The Second Isaiah*. Oxford: Oxford University, 1964.

Noth, Martin. *Numbers*. Philadelphia: Westminster, 1968.

Nowack, W. *Die Kleinen Propheten*. Göttingen: Vandenhoeck & Ruprecht, 1903.

O'Connor, M. *Hebrew Verse Structure*. Winona Lake, Ind.: Eisenbrauns, 1980.

Otto, Rudolph. *The Idea of the Holy*. 1923. Reprint. London: Oxford University, 1973.

Parr, P. "Contacts between North West Arabia and Jordan in the Late Bronze Ages." In *Studies in the History and Archaeology of Jordon*, edited by Adnan Hadidi, pp. 127–133. Amman, Jordan: Department of Antiquities.

Parr, P. J.; Harding, G. L.; and Dayton, J. E. "Preliminary Survey in N. W. Arabia, 1968." *Bulletin of the Institute of Archaeology*, University of London 8–9 (1968–69) 193–241.

Patton, John H. *Canaanite Parallels in the Book of Psalms*. Baltimore: Johns Hopkins, 1944.

Pettinato, Giovanni. *The Archives of Ebla*. Garden City, N.Y.: Doubleday, 1981.

Pfeiffer, Robert H. *Introduction to the Old Testament*. Rev. ed. New York: Harper & Row, 1949.

Pope, Marvin H. *Job*. AB. Garden City, N.Y.: Doubleday, 1973.

Porten, Bezalel. "The Identity of King Adon." *BA* 44 (1981) 36–52.

Posener, G. *Princes et pays d'Asie et de Nubie*. Brussels: Fondation égyptologique reine Elisabeth, 1940

———. "Syria and Palestine, c. 2160–1780 B.C." CAH_3 vol. I, pt. 2, pp. 532–594.

Propp, William H. "The Skin of Moses' Face." Unpublished paper.

Rad, Gerhard von. *Der Heilig Krieg im alten Israel*. Göttingen: Vandenhoeck & Ruprecht, 1958.

———. "The Origin of the Concept of the Day of Yahweh." *JSS* 4 (1959) 97–108.

Radday, Yehuda T. "AND in Isaiah." *Revue de l'Organisation Internationale pour l'Etude des Langues Anciennes par l'Ordinateur* 2 (1974) 25–41.

Radday, Yehuda T., and Shore, H. "The Definite Article: A Type- and/or Author-Specifying Discriminant in the Hebrew Bible." *Bulletin of the Association for Literary and Linguistic Computing* 3 (1976) 23–31.

Richter, W. "Die *nāgīd*-Formel." *BZ* 9 (1965) 71–84.

Robertson, David A. *Linguistic Evidence in Dating Early Hebrew Poetry*. Missoula, Mont.: Society of Biblical Literature, 1972.

Robinson, Theodore H. "Basic Principles of Hebrew Poetic Form." In *Festschrift für Alfred Bertholet*, edited by W. Baumgartner, 0. Eissfeldt, K. Elliger, and L. Rost. Tübingen: J. C. B. Mohr (Paul Siebeck), 1950.

Rothenberg, Benno, and Glass, Jonathan. "Midianite Pottery." Hebrew. *Eretz Israel* 15 (1981) 85–114.

Rudolph, Wilhelm. *Micha, Nahum, Habakuk, Zephanja.* KAT XIII$_3$. Gütersloh: Gutersloher Verlagshaus Gerd Mohn, 1975.

Sabourin, Leopold. *The Psalms: Their Origin and Meaning.* 2 vols. Staten Island: Alba House, 1969.

Sasson, Jack M. "Bovine Symbolism in the Exodus Narrative." *VT* 18 (1968) 380–387.

Sawyer, John F. A., and Clines, David J. A., eds. *Midian, Moab and Edom: The History and Archaeology of Late Bronze and Iron Age Jordan and North-west Arabia.* Sheffield: JSOT, 1983.

Schmid, Herbert. "Jahwe und die Kulttraditionen von Jerusalem." *ZAW* 26 (1955) 168–197.

Schnutenhaus, F. "Das Kommen und Erscheinen Gottes im Alten Testament." *ZAW* 76 (1964) 1–22.

Schökel, Luis Alonso. *Doce Profetas Menores.* Madrid: Ediciones Christiandad, 1966.

Seeligmann, I. L. "A Psalm from Pre-Regal Times (Dt. 33:2–5, 26–29)." *VT* 14 (1964) 75–92.

Sellers, Ovid R. "Musical Instruments of Israel." *BA* 4 (1941) 33–47.

Simons, J. *The Geographical and Topographical Texts of the Old Testament: A Concise Commentary in XXXII Chapters.* Leiden: E. J. Brill, 1959.

Sinker, Robert. *The Psalm of Habakkuk.* Cambridge: Deighton, Bell, 1890.

Skehan, P. "Texts and Versions." In *JBC*, pp. 561–589.

Slomovic, Elieser. "Toward an Understanding of the Formation of

Historical Titles in the Book of Psalms." *ZAW* 91 (1979) 350–380.

Smend, Rudolf. *Yahweh War and Tribal Confederation.* Nashville: Abingdon, 1970.

Smith, George Adam. *The Book of the Twelve Prophets*, II. London: Hodder and Stoughton, 1928.

Sorg, R. *Habaquq 3 and Selah.* Fifield, Wisc.: King of Martyrs Priory, 1969.

Speiser, E. A. *Genesis.* AB. Garden City, N.Y.: Doubleday, 1964.

———. "'People' and 'Nation' of Israel." *JBL* 79 (1960) 157–163.

Stager, Lawrence E. "The Archaeology of the East Slope of Jerusalem and the Terraces of the Kidron." *JNES* 41 (1982) 111–121.

Stephens, Ferris J. "The Babylonian Dragon Myth in Habakkuk 3." *JBL* 43 (1924) 290–293.

Stonehouse, G. G. V. *The Book of Habakkuk.* London: Rivingtons, 1911.

Stummer, F. *Sumerisch-akkadische Parallelen zum Aufbau alttestamentlicher Psalmen.* Paderborn: Ferdinand Schöningh, 1922.

Thackeray, Henry St. John. *A Grammar of the Old Testament in Greek*, vol. 1. Cambridge: Cambridge University, 1909.

———. "Primitive Lectionary Notes in the Psalm of Habakkuk." *JTS* 12 (1911) 191–213.

Torrey, C. C. "The Prophecy of Habakkuk." In *Jewish Studies in Memory of George A. Kohut*, edited by S. W. Baron & A. Marx, pp. 565–582. New York: Alexander Kohut

Memorial Foundation, 1935.

Vaux, Roland de. "Téman, Ville ou région d'Edom?" *RB* 76 (1969) 379–385.

Vischer, Wilhelm. *Der Prophet Habakuk*. Neukirchen: Buchhandlung des Erziehungsvereins, 1958.

Vollers, K. A. *Das Dodekapropheton der Alexandriner*. Berlin: Mayer & Mueller, 1880.

Wakeman, Mary K. *God's Battle with the Monster*. Leiden: E. J. Brill, 1973.

Walker, H. H., and Lund, N. W. "The Literary Structure of the Book of Habakkuk." *JBL* 53 (1934) 355–370.

Watson, Paul L. "The Death of 'Death' in the Ugaritic Texts." *JAOS* 92 (1972) 60–64.

Weiser, Artur. *The Psalms*. Philadelphia: Westminster, 1962.

Wellhausen, Julius. *Die Kleinen Propheten*. Berlin: Georg Reimer, 1898.

————. *Prolegomena to the History of Ancient Israel*. 1878. Reprint. New York: Meridian Books, 1957.

Westermann, Claus. *The Praise of God in the Psalms*. Richmond, Virginia: John Knox, 1965.

Wharton, J. A. "People of God." In *IDB*, vol. 3, pp. 727–728.

Whitaker, Richard E. "A formulaic analysis of Ugaritic Poetry." Ph.D. dissertation, Harvard University, 1970.

Wolf, C. Umhau. "Terminology of Israel's Tribal Organization." *JBL* 65 (1946) 45–49.

Wolff, Hans Walter. *Hosea*. Philadelphia: Fortress, 1974.

———. *Joel and Amos*. Philadelphia: Fortress, 1977.

Wright, G. Ernest, and Filson, Floyd V., eds. *The Westminster Historical Atlas to the Bible*. Philadelphia: Westminster, 1945.

Yadin, Yigael. *The Art of Warfare in Biblical Lands*. 2 vols. New York: McGraw-Hill, 1963.

Ziegler, Joseph, ed. *Duodecim Prophetae*. Göttingen: Vandenhoeck & Ruprecht, 1943.